Cocos2d Game Development Blueprints

Design, develop, and create your own successful
iOS games using the Cocos2d game engine

Jorge Jordán

BIRMINGHAM - MUMBAI

Cocos2d Game Development Blueprints

First published: January 2015

Production reference: 1230115

Published by Packt Publishing Ltd.
Livery Place
35 Livery Street
Birmingham B3 2PB, UK.

ISBN 978-1-78398-788-7

www.packtpub.com

Cover image by Vanesa Domingo (vanesadomingo@insaneplatypusgames.com)

Credits

Author
Jorge Jordán

Reviewers
Saeed Afshari
Nader Eloshaiker
Mohsin Mahmood

Commissioning Editor
Ashwin Nair

Acquisition Editor
Richard Brookes-Bland

Content Development Editor
Sumeet Sawant

Technical Editor
Siddhi Rane

Copy Editors
Safis Editing
Ameesha Green

Project Coordinator
Judie Jose

Proofreaders
Ameesha Green
Steve Maguire
Jonathan Todd

Indexer
Mariammal Chettiyar

Graphics
Vanesa Domingo

Production Coordinator
Aparna Bhagat

Cover Work
Aparna Bhagat

About the Author

Jorge Jordán is an iOS indie developer who has been passionate about how things work since his childhood. This is the reason why he graduated in Computer Science and became a Java developer. After buying his first iPhone, he became deeply interested in its technology and spent his spare time learning how to develop apps for Apple smartphones.

Over time, he founded Insane Platypus Games (`http://insaneplatypusgames.com/`) where he tries to make his dreams and games come true. He is also a member of the tutorial team at `http://www.raywenderlich.com/`.

In his free time, he loves to play video games and bass guitar, and to watch TV series.

You can follow him on Twitter `@jjordanarenas`.

I would like to thank my girlfriend, Angélica, for being so patient and for her support while I was spending almost all of my spare time writing this book. Also, I would like to thank my family, especially my mom and my brother, for always believing in me; it is thanks to them that I am the person I am.

Thanks to Vane (`vanesadomingo@insaneplatypusgames.com`) for creating all the art for this book and designing those charismatic characters.

Also, thanks to all my friends: the canupis, Javi Sáez, the jiervos, Kike, Pedro, Guille, Carmelo, and more, for all the laughs and the good times we spent together.

Finally, I want to thank the reviewers of this book for making it better and the rest of the people at Packt Publishing for making it real.

About the Reviewers

Saeed Afshari is an independent game developer based in Luxembourg. He has published more than twenty titles on the iOS App Store and Google Play under the brand Neat Games, and is focused on developing mobile games for iOS and Android.

He is a member of the Games, Interaction and Novel Interface Technologies (IGNITE) research collective at the University of Luxembourg, working on natural and novel user interfaces and understanding how people interact with games, and how games should interact with people. His current research projects deal with interaction with mobile games, virtual reality head mounted displays, and behavior change through serious gaming. He is the game developer for the European Commission project "LiveCity" which deals with long distance multiplayer gaming on multi-touch tables.

With over fifteen years of experience in game development and interactive media, he has built up skills in platforms including OpenGL, DirectX, Unity, Cocos2d-x, and also interaction design for natural user interfaces and virtual reality. He has invented an algorithm to track permanent magnets for use in mobile games, in particular in the form of a magnetic joystick. He is willing to consult and collaborate on creating games and interactive software targeted for education, entertainment, and social networks.

For more information about Saeed and Neat Games, you can contact `pr@neat-games.com`.

Nader Eloshaiker is an Electrical Engineer in Computer Systems. His first involvement with technology started during his secondary school years when he built and sold 8-bit audio digitizers connected to the parallel port of a Commodore Amiga 500.

He became deeply involved in the home upgrade consumer market, always finding employment relating to computers and electronics.

At the birth of web-hosted databases for retail websites, he worked with Mark Cavallo of AEON Graphics developing high-end e-commerce web applications. Since then, he has been involved in a number of creative and advanced web projects with Mark.

For most of his professional career, he has worked at one of the largest automotive manufacturers in the world, based in Australia, managing global engineering design data.

He was also employed at Swinburne University of Technology as an adjunct teaching fellow while working full time as an engineer. His subjects included: object-oriented software design, Java development, web development, server-side web development, and user interface design. He also taught and was the convener for a Masters subject in internet networking infrastructure.

He has an open source application hosted by GitHub entitled Teamcenter Engineering Admin View, used to manage system security and workflow configuration for Siemens data management software. He has also developed BigZip, a free Java-based Winzip equivalent with an intuitive user interface that is ahead of its time.

His current project is developing an original iPhone game with Mark Cavallo. The last 5 years have seen him develop a vast wealth of knowledge with Cocos2d and iOS. This is an exciting direction for Nader and one he will continue to expand upon with his new company, Rotate Gears (http://www.rotategears.com/).

I would like to personally thank my loving and incredibly smart wife, Hanaa, as well as my adorable 1-year old son, Zain, both of whom have been very patient with me while I spent a lot of time researching Cocos2d and Apple's API so that I could develop my game. I would like to also acknowledge Mark Cavallo, who is my partner at Rotate Gears. His expertise as an artist and intuitive knowledge of game design has injected some amazing creativity into the game. Finally, I would like to thank my beautiful 5-year old daughter, Raya, who has been the source of my inspiration to develop a game. I hope that when this game is released, I will be able to spend more time at home and watch her grow into a woman.

Mohsin Mahmood is an active programmer and passionate developer of iOS Cocos2d-based games. He participated in development of various game projects and some of them are highly successful. Apart from this, he also worked in iOS large-scale business applications. As a technology junkie, he loves to develop with top-notch technologies.

With several years of experience in game and business application development, he has build up skills in cross-platform technologies. Currently, he is performing his duties as a senior software engineer.

For more information about him, contact cocosjunkie@gmail.com.

I would like to express my special gratitude to Packt Publishing, as well as to Indrani Mitra who believed in me. Also, I would like to thank Judie Jose for her kind guidance and coordination.

I would also like to thank my wife, Samra, and my sister, who helped me a lot in finalizing this project within the time frame.

www.PacktPub.com

Support files, eBooks, discount offers, and more

For support files and downloads related to your book, please visit www.PacktPub.com.

Did you know that Packt offers eBook versions of every book published, with PDF and ePub files available? You can upgrade to the eBook version at www.PacktPub.com and as a print book customer, you are entitled to a discount on the eBook copy. Get in touch with us at service@packtpub.com for more details.

At www.PacktPub.com, you can also read a collection of free technical articles, sign up for a range of free newsletters and receive exclusive discounts and offers on Packt books and eBooks.

https://www2.packtpub.com/books/subscription/packtlib

Do you need instant solutions to your IT questions? PacktLib is Packt's online digital book library. Here, you can search, access, and read Packt's entire library of books.

Why subscribe?

- Fully searchable across every book published by Packt
- Copy and paste, print, and bookmark content
- On demand and accessible via a web browser

Free access for Packt account holders

If you have an account with Packt at www.PacktPub.com, you can use this to access PacktLib today and view 9 entirely free books. Simply use your login credentials for immediate access.

Table of Contents

Preface

I grew up playing video games; I remember my Amstrad CPC 128K as one amazing computer that brought to my home several of the games I played in the arcades and I feel lucky for being born at that time. Thanks to that, I've known titles that have passed into history and I've been a witness to the evolution of the video game industry; from the first handheld games to the iPhone 6 and iPad Air 2, passing through the first computers and video consoles to the current next-gen.

This hobby became a passion and I realized very early that I would like to learn to develop video games so I could understand how my preferred titles were built, and this is one of the things I want you to learn through this book. In fact, there are three important things that I would like you to have learned by the end of the book:

- Love for games: I think that playing any kind of game is one of the most important things in this life. Playing games in a balanced way can make your brain faster; you can learn culture, make friends, laugh, or even live a different life; that's why we should not stop playing.

- Love for development: When I was a child, I realized that I wanted to be a developer because I wanted to know how to build the things I used to play. Once I became a developer, I realized how many things you can build by yourself with just a keyboard, and I think that making your own game or your own app can be compared to writing a book or recording a film. At the end, it is the same thing; you are creating something from nothing. So that's why I think that there are three things people should do before dying: have a child, plant a tree, and develop a game.

- Autonomy: I would like you to have learned all the tools you will need to develop whatever is in your mind and to understand how to solve the problems you will find during this process.

From time to time, we hear news about a new game that is breaking the market and turning people crazy in a few weeks, achieving thousands and thousands of downloads, hundreds of thousands of profits from its in-app purchases, or millions of dollars in revenue. What makes this game so addictive? This is the question that most of us mobile game developers ask ourselves and the answer is always similar: a good idea. That's why most of us keep trying daily to think of good ideas to be the pillars of our next game, but this idea never comes to mind.

If you think about it, these addictive games are based on simple things and most of them are based on previous games, but their developers have included some features that make us want to play over and over. That's why it's important to learn which techniques were used to develop successful games from the past and the present.

But to achieve this, it's important to be equipped with the most appropriate tools in order to focus on playability rather than squeezing our brains trying to figure out how to do what we want. Hence, we have developed the games included in this book using Cocos2d because it's based on Objective-C, a language that I'm sure most of you are familiar with.

Cocos2d v3.0

Cocos2d for iOS (`http://www.cocos2d-iphone.org`) is one of the most powerful and popular frameworks to develop 2D games with. Its popularity is due to its features: it's open source and 2D; has a wide and collaborative community; supports sprites, collisions, scenes, transitions, audio effects, actions, physics, and animations; and has a lot more features.

At the time of writing this book, the current version is Cocos2d v3.0, released a few months ago, so if you have previous experience with this framework, it is possible that you will find some differences and new features.

Pure Objective-C

The syntax has been improved so method names conform to conventions and the code is now better structured. Also, the C libraries have been removed so now we will use just the Core Foundation classes.

ARC

Previously, the new projects created in Cocos2d didn't use Automatic Reference Counting (ARC) by default, but you could enable ARC with a little refactoring process. Now you can forget all these headaches of retaining, releasing, and autoreleasing memory as v3 is ARC-only.

CCDirector

The former [CCDirector sharedDirector].winSize feature has been replaced by the new [CCDirector sharedDirector].viewSize feature.

CCLayer

CCNode has replaced CCLayer. Previously, CCLayer was used mainly to support for touch and accelerometer events but since every node inherits from CCResponder and has this ability, it's no longer needed. Now CCLayer can't be inherited to create new classes to represent scenes; instead of this class, you should use CCScene from now onward.

CCArray

In the first versions of Cocos2d, CCArray was used thanks to the speed it provided. However, this advantage is no longer the case and during Cocos2d v2, a lot of developers were recommending not to use this class to manage arrays. That's why it has been deprecated in this new version and is no longer available.

OALSimpleAudio

CocosDenshion's SimpleAudioEngine, an external class, previously supported sound and audio effects. From now, ObjectAL's OALSimpleAudio class has replaced SimpleAudioEngine. This new class is focused on doing what we need in a simple way, converting complex actions into easy tasks.

CCAction

Almost all the action classes have been renamed to something like CCActionNameAction; despite this, its syntax remains unaltered.

CCActionCallBlock

Good-bye CCCallBlock, hello CCActionCallBlock. Something similar to what happened to CCAction also happens to CCCallBlock; it has been renamed but its syntax remains unaltered.

Sequences

The former CCSequence class is now named CCActionSequence and the most important change in this case is that when passing the array of actions to the sequences, you don't have to pass a nil object as the last element.

Schedule update

In the previous version, you should execute scheduleUpdate in order to schedule the update method to be called every frame. This is not needed anymore; now you just need to implement the update method in the way you want to work.

Enabling touches

Touch handling is now performed by CCNode and therefore by its descendants. To enable it now, you will need to set userInteractionEnabled to TRUE and implement either touchBegan, touchMoved, touchEnded, or touchCancelled.

Accelerometer events

As with touches, to enable accelerometer events handling, you need to set userInteractionEnabled to TRUE and you will also need to add the Core Motion framework.

Physics

Unlike what happened in Cocos2d v2, physics are now based on Chipmunk. Previously, we had both Box2D and Chipmunk to implement physics, but now the only library will be Chipmunk.

What this book covers

In this book, you will find eight chapters, each covering a different genre of video games. The aim of the book is that you learn the features of Cocos2d at the same time as you discover the singularities of several games that have been or are currently successful in the video game industry.

Chapter 1, Sprites, Sounds, and Collisions, covers the first steps of developing with Cocos2d v3.0. This chapter will guide you through how to create a horizontal-scroll game in which you will create sprites from an image. You will also learn how to move sprites across the screen thanks to executing actions, and in case it's needed, how to manage collisions. Also, you will learn how to show score labels and how to play background music and sound effects. The best of all, this game will be available on both iPhone and iPad devices.

Chapter 2, Explosions and UFOs, shows the process of developing a classic shoot 'em up in which the accelerometer takes control of the movement. In this game, you will learn to load and set up particle systems such as explosions and fire and draw primitives (lines, circles, and squares) on a CCNode instance. In addition, you will be introduced to the parallax effect and you will implement it in the game.

Chapter 3, Your First Online Game, teaches you the development of a turn-based game with the particularity that it will allow you to play against another player thanks to the configuration of Game Center in your game. Also, you will learn how to drag, scale, and rotate sprites and how to include labels using bitmap fonts. As this is a turn-based game, you will learn to include timers to control each player's turn.

Chapter 4, Beat All Your Enemies Up, takes you back to the 80s and 90s as you learn to develop one of the classic arcade genres: the beat 'em up. In this chapter, you will learn to create an iPad-only game in which players will move thanks to a track pad you will develop. As this kind of game demands that the characters perform different movements, you will learn to animate the sprites using several image files to optimize sprites' management. You will also will learn how to use sprite sheets.

Chapter 5, Scenes at the Highest Level, covers the development of a brain game in which you will create a tutorial so players can learn the basics of the game. You will learn how to load data from external files to configure the different scenes and how to create transitions between these scenes. In order to keep the user's data, you will learn how to save this information.

Chapter 6, Physics Behavior, introduces you to the physics world but the high-level one because you will learn to take advantage of Chipmunk, a physics engine available in Cocos2d. You will learn to set up and run a Chipmunk simulation and to create and reuse bodies. Collisions are managed by this library too, so you will learn how to use collision filters and listeners to create a sports game.

Chapter 7, Jump and Run, creates a platform game that will handle specific collision logic and manage multiple touches. Also, you will learn how to use multiple sprites to texture varied terrain and you will learn how to add a menu to the game so players can configure some setups.

Chapter 8, Defend the Tower, teaches you how to create a tower defense game and you will learn how to provide Artificial Intelligence to non-playable characters. In addition, you will develop a pathfinder algorithm so these NPCs know which path is best for them. Through this chapter, you will also learn to include notifications and in-app purchases.

What you need for this book

To develop this book's games, you will need the following hardware and software:

- An Intel-based Mac running Mac OS X 10.8.4 or later
- The latest Xcode version (5.1.1 at the time of writing this book)
- To be enrolled in the iOS Developer Program if you want to test the games on a device and to use in-app purchases
- An iOS device to test games on

You don't need wide development experience in either Objective-C or Cocos2d as these chapters guide you step by step so you understand what is happening. However, you do need to have an intermediate knowledge level of Cocos2d and an understanding of Objective-C.

Who this book is for

If you are a passionate gamer, you like developing, or you're just curious, this book is for you. It has been written to teach 2D game development to app creators and also to teach Objective-C to game developers. In both cases, you will find a common point: games. If you have developed several apps and now you want them to include gamification, or if you have been developing games using other frameworks and you want to take advantage of what Cocos2d offers, this book is for you.

Conventions

In this book, you will find a number of text styles that distinguish between different kinds of information. Here are some examples of these styles and an explanation of their meaning.

Code words in text, database table names, folder names, filenames, file extensions, pathnames, dummy URLs, user input, and Twitter handles are shown as follows: "A CCScene class is a class that inherits from CCNode and whose main purpose is to contain the behavior of a single scene in the game."

A block of code is set as follows:

```
// Create a colored background (Dark Grey)
CCNodeColor *background = [CCNodeColor nodeWithColor:[CCColor
colorWithRed:0.2f green:0.2f blue:0.2f alpha:1.0f]];
[self addChild:background];
```

New terms and **important words** are shown in bold. Words that you see on the screen, for example, in menus or dialog boxes, appear in the text like this: "In the project navigator, select the **Resources** group, right-click and select **Add Files to "RunYetiRun"**...."

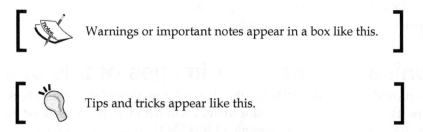

Warnings or important notes appear in a box like this.

Tips and tricks appear like this.

Sometimes, you are going to be challenged by me requesting you to try to solve a particular situation. These challenges will be labeled as 1-star, 2-star, or 3-star challenges depending on the difficulty of the task, but they can be solved with the knowledge acquired throughout the book. They will look like this:

1-star challenge – accurate collision detection

Reader feedback

Feedback from our readers is always welcome. Let us know what you think about this book—what you liked or disliked. Reader feedback is important for us as it helps us develop titles that you will really get the most out of.

To send us general feedback, simply e-mail feedback@packtpub.com, and mention the book's title in the subject of your message.

If there is a topic that you have expertise in and you are interested in either writing or contributing to a book, see our author guide at www.packtpub.com/authors.

Customer support

Now that you are the proud owner of a Packt book, we have a number of things to help you to get the most from your purchase.

Downloading the example code

You can download the example code files from your account at http://www.packtpub.com for all the Packt Publishing books you have purchased. If you purchased this book elsewhere, you can visit http://www.packtpub.com/support and register to have the files e-mailed directly to you.

Downloading the color images of this book

We also provide you with a PDF file that has color images of the screenshots/diagrams used in this book. The color images will help you better understand the changes in the output. You can download this file from: https://www.packtpub.com/sites/default/files/downloads/7887OS_ColoredImages.pdf.

Errata

Although we have taken every care to ensure the accuracy of our content, mistakes do happen. If you find a mistake in one of our books—maybe a mistake in the text or the code—we would be grateful if you could report this to us. By doing so, you can save other readers from frustration and help us improve subsequent versions of this book. If you find any errata, please report them by visiting http://www.packtpub.com/submit-errata, selecting your book, clicking on the **Errata Submission Form** link, and entering the details of your errata. Once your errata are verified, your submission will be accepted and the errata will be uploaded to our website or added to any list of existing errata under the Errata section of that title.

To view the previously submitted errata, go to https://www.packtpub.com/books/content/support and enter the name of the book in the search field. The required information will appear under the **Errata** section.

Piracy

Piracy of copyrighted material on the Internet is an ongoing problem across all media. At Packt, we take the protection of our copyright and licenses very seriously. If you come across any illegal copies of our works in any form on the Internet, please provide us with the location address or website name immediately so that we can pursue a remedy.

Please contact us at copyright@packtpub.com with a link to the suspected pirated material.

We appreciate your help in protecting our authors and our ability to bring you valuable content.

Questions

If you have a problem with any aspect of this book, you can contact us at questions@packtpub.com, and we will do our best to address the problem.

1
Sprites, Sounds, and Collisions

In the first chapter of this book, I will introduce you to the basics of developing games, specifically how to do it with Cocos2d. I'm sure that most of you have heard technical terms such as sprites and collisions before but how many of you know how to create and work with them? Throughout this chapter, I will teach you enough to answer this question and I will guide you through building a horizontal scrolling game similar to *Jetpack Joyride* and *Flappy Bird* that will run on both iPhone and iPad.

In this chapter, we will look at the following:

- How to create a Cocos2d game that will run on iPhone and iPad
- How to enable touch detection
- How to manage collisions
- How to load images and sounds
- How to play sound effects
- How to create score labels and update them

Creating a new Cocos2d project

In this book, we work with the latest Xcode version (5.1.1 at the time of writing), Cocos2d v3.0.0, and iOS7.

If you are familiar with Xcode, creating a new project should be easy enough to do alone but I would like to explain what the project creation process looks like in Cocos2d v3.

First of all:

1. Create a new Cocos2d project in Xcode by selecting **File | New | Project…**.

2. Click on the **cocos2d v3.x** template under **iOS** and you should see the two icons shown in the following screenshot:

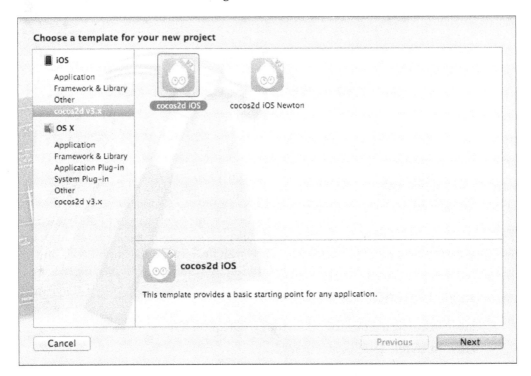

3. Choose the **cocos2d iOS** template and click on **Next**.

4. Call it RunYetiRun and make sure **Universal** is chosen on the **Device Family** menu before clicking on **Next**.

5. Select the place where you want your project to be saved and click on **Create**.

I would like you to focus on the project navigator, the section on the left that contains the folders and files that will give life to our game:

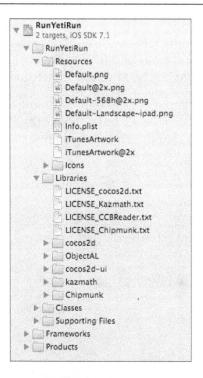

This pane contains a hierarchy of files and folders in your Cocos2d project that does not reflect the real location of the files on your hard drive. In other words, the pane shows the files in your Xcode project and lets you organize these files in a way that is unique to Xcode.

Folders in the navigator are called **groups** and are used to organize the classes, images, and the rest of the files, but moving them will not affect their real location on your hard drive. In fact, moving files in Finder will mean Xcode won't be able to find them anymore, so we must pay attention when reorganizing our project's files.

At this point, you only need to know about the existence of the **Resources** and **Classes** groups. The first of them is where you will place your images, properties, and audio files, and the second, as its name suggests, contains the classes of the project. Let's take a look at the latter:

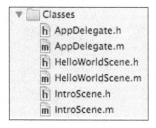

If you have experience working with the previous version of Cocos2d, you should notice that the former `HelloWorldLayer` class has been replaced by `HelloWorldScene` and `IntroScene`, and if you take a look at these classes, you will discover that they inherit from `CCScene` instead of `CCLayer`.

Just a quick note: the use of `CCScene` is mainly grouping nodes in a scene, which was the purpose of `CCLayer` in Cocos2d v2, but don't worry about it as we will discuss this new feature later in this chapter. For now you just need to know how a new Cocos2d v3 project looks.

In Xcode, look at the project window in the center, where you will see the default properties of the new project:

As you can see, there are three sections on this screen: **Identity**, **Deployment Info**, and **App Icons**, but we will just pay attention to the second one. In this section, you can configure:

- **Deployment Target**: The earlier iOS version that will be able to install and run the game, which is **5.0**.

- **Devices**: The family of devices that will be able to install and run the game. It will show the property we chose during the project creation process.

- **Main Interface**: Allows you to select the main XIB file.

- **Device Orientation**: The orientations supported by your game. We want it to be landscape as we are going to develop a horizontal game.

- **Status Bar Style**: The way the status bar will be shown.

We don't need to modify these properties because they meet our requirements, so let's run the project.

Run Xcode Run

Now that we have our newly created project, let's see how it looks. Click on **Run** at the top-left of the Xcode window and it will run the project in the iOS Simulator, which defaults to an iOS 6.1 iPhone:

Voilà! You've just built your first **Hello World** example with Cocos2d v3, but before going further, let's take a look at the code to understand how it works.

  We will be using iOS Simulator to run the game unless otherwise specified.

Understanding the default project

We are going to take an overview of the classes available in a new project, but don't worry if you don't understand everything; the objective of this section is just to get familiar with the look of a Cocos2d game.

If you open the `main.m` class under the **Supporting Files** group, you will see:

```
int main(int argc, char *argv[]) {

    @autoreleasepool {
        int retVal = UIApplicationMain(argc, argv, nil,
        @"AppDelegate");
        return retVal;
    }
}
```

As you can see, the `@autorelease` block means that ARC is enabled by default on new Cocos2d projects so we don't have to worry about releasing objects or enabling ARC.

ARC is the acronym for **Automatic Reference Counting** and it's a compiler iOS feature to provide automatic memory management of objects. It works by adding code at compile time, ensuring every object lives as long as necessary, but not longer.

On the other hand, the block calls `AppDelegate`, a class that inherits from `CCAppDelegate` which implements the `UIApplicationDelegate` protocol. In other words, the starting point of our game and the place to set up our app is located in `AppDelegate`, like a typical iOS application.

If you open `AppDelegate.m`, you will see the following method, which is called when the game has been launched:

```
- (BOOL)application:(UIApplication *)application
didFinishLaunchingWithOptions:(NSDictionary *)launchOptions
{
    [self setupCocos2dWithOptions:@{
        CCSetupShowDebugStats: @(YES),
    }];

    return YES;
}
```

Here, the only initial configuration specified is to enable the debug stats, specifying the option `CCSetupShowDebugStats: @(YES)`, that you can see in the previous block of code.

The number on the top indicates the amount of draw calls and the two labels below are the time needed to update the frame and the frame rate respectively.

 The maximum frame rate an iOS device can have is 60 and it's a measure of the smoothness a game can attain: the higher the frame rate, the smoother the game.

You will need to have the top and the bottom values in mind as the number of draw calls and the frame rate will let you know how efficient your game will be.

The next thing to take care of is the `startScene` method:

```
- (CCScene *) startScene
{
    // The initial scene will be GameScene
    return [IntroScene scene];
}
```

This method should be overriden to indicate the first scene we want to display in our game. In this case, it points to `IntroScene` where the `init` method looks like the following code:

```
- (id) init
{
    // Apple recommends assigning self with super's return value
    self = [super init];
    if (!self) {
        return(nil);
    }

    // Create a colored background (Dark Gray)
    CCNodeColor *background = [CCNodeColor nodeWithColor:[CCColor
    colorWithRed:0.2f green:0.2f blue:0.2f alpha:1.0f]];
    [self addChild:background];

    // Hello world
    CCLabelTTF *label = [CCLabelTTF labelWithString:@"Hello World"
    fontName:@"Chalkduster" fontSize:36.0f];
    label.positionType = CCPositionTypeNormalized;
    label.color = [CCColor redColor];
```

```
        label.position = ccp(0.5f, 0.5f); // Middle of screen
        [self addChild:label];

        // Helloworld scene button
        CCButton *helloWorldButton = [CCButton buttonWithTitle:@"[
        Start ]" fontName:@"Verdana-Bold" fontSize:18.0f];
        helloWorldButton.positionType = CCPositionTypeNormalized;
        helloWorldButton.position = ccp(0.5f, 0.35f);
        [helloWorldButton setTarget:self
        selector:@selector(onSpinningClicked:)];
        [self addChild:helloWorldButton];

        // done
        return self;
    }
```

This code first calls the initialization method for the superclass IntroScene by
sending the [super init] message. Then it creates a gray-colored background
with a CCNodeColor class, which is basically a solid color node, but this background
won't be shown until it's added to the scene, which is exactly what [self
addChild:background] does. The red "Hello World" label you can see in the
previous screenshot is an instance of the CCLabelTTF class, whose position will be
centered on the screen thanks to label.position = ccp(0.5f, 0.5f).

 Cocos2d provides the cpp(coord_x, coord_y) method, which
is a precompiler macro for CGPointMake and both can be used
interchangeably.

The last code block creates CCButton that will call onSpinningClicked once we
click on it.

Don't worry about all these new classes we have been talking about up to now as we
will discuss them further in later sections. This source code isn't hard at all, but what
will happen when we click on the **Start** button? Don't be shy, go back to the iOS
Simulator and find out!

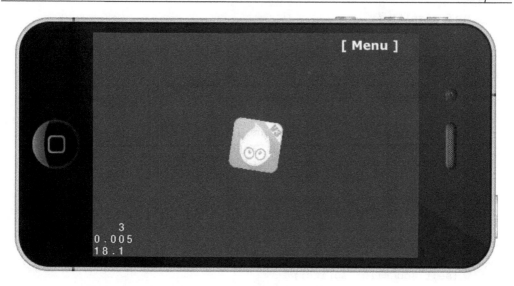

If you take a look at the onSpinningClicked method in IntroScene.m, you will understand what happened:

```
- (void)onSpinningClicked:(id)sender
{
    // start spinning scene with transition
    [[CCDirector sharedDirector] replaceScene:[HelloWorldScene
    scene]
        withTransition:[CCTransition
        transitionPushWithDirection:CCTransitionDirectionLeft
        duration:1.0f]];
}
```

This code presents the HelloWorldScene scene replacing the current one (InitScene) and it's being done by pushing HelloWorldScene to the top of the scene stack and using a horizontal scroll transition that will last for 1.0 second. Let's take a look at the HelloWorldScene.m to understand the behavior we just experienced:

```
@implementation HelloWorldScene
{
    CCSprite *_sprite;
}

- (id)init
{
    // Apple recommends assigning self with super's return value
    self = [super init];
```

```
    if (!self) {
        return(nil);
    }

    // Enable touch handling on scene node
    self.userInteractionEnabled = YES;

    // Create a colored background (Dark Gray)
    CCNodeColor *background = [CCNodeColor nodeWithColor:[CCColor
    colorWithRed:0.2f green:0.2f blue:0.2f alpha:1.0f]];
    [self addChild:background];

    // Add a sprite
    _sprite = [CCSprite spriteWithImageNamed:@"Icon-72.png"];
    _sprite.position =
    ccp(self.contentSize.width/2,self.contentSize.height/2);
    [self addChild:_sprite];

    // Animate sprite with action
    CCActionRotateBy* actionSpin = [CCActionRotateBy
    actionWithDuration:1.5f angle:360];
    [_sprite runAction:[CCActionRepeatForever
    actionWithAction:actionSpin]];

    // Create a back button
    CCButton *backButton = [CCButton buttonWithTitle:@"[ Menu ]"
    fontName:@"Verdana-Bold" fontSize:18.0f];
    backButton.positionType = CCPositionTypeNormalized;
    backButton.position = ccp(0.85f, 0.95f); // Top Right of
    screen
    [backButton setTarget:self
    selector:@selector(onBackClicked:)];
    [self addChild:backButton];

    // done
    return self;
}
```

This piece of code is very similar to the one we saw in IntroScene.m, which is why
we just need to focus on the differences. If you look at the top of the class, you can
see how we are declaring a private instance for a CCSprite class, which is also a
subclass of CCNode, and its main role is to render 2D images on the screen.

The CCSprite class is one of the most-used classes in Cocos2d game development, as it provides a visual representation and a physical shape to the objects in view.

Then, in the `init` method, you will see the instruction `self.userInteractionEnabled = YES`, which is used to enable the current scene to detect and manage touches by implementing the `touchBegan` method, which will be covered in detail later in this book.

The next thing to highlight is how we initialize a `CCSprite` class using an image, positioning it in the center of the screen. If you read a couple more lines, you will understand why the icon rotates as soon as the scene is loaded. We create a `360`-degree rotation action thanks to `CCRotateBy` that will last for `1.5` seconds. But why is this rotation repeated over and over? This happens thanks to `CCActionRepeatForever`, which will execute the rotate action as long as the scene is running.

The last piece of code in the `init` method doesn't need explanation as it creates a `CCButton` that will execute `onBackClicked` once clicked. This method replaces the scene `HelloWorldScene` with `IntroScene` in a similar way as we saw before, with only one difference: the transition happens from left to right.

Did you try to touch the screen? Try it and you will understand why `touchBegan` has the following code:

```
-(void) touchBegan:(UITouch *)touch withEvent:(UIEvent *)event {
    CGPoint touchLoc = [touch locationInNode:self];

    // Move our sprite to touch location
    CCActionMoveTo *actionMove = [CCActionMoveTo
    actionWithDuration:1.0f position:touchLoc];
    [_sprite runAction:actionMove];
}
```

This is one of the methods you need to implement to manage touch. The others are `touchMoved`, `touchEnded`, and `touchCancelled`. When the user begins touching the screen, the sprite will move to the registered coordinates thanks to a commonly used action: `CCActionMoveto`. This action just needs to know the position that we want to move our sprite to and the duration of the movement.

Now that we have had an overview of the initial project code, it is time to go deeper into some of the classes we have shown. Did you realize that `CCNode` is the parent class of several classes we have seen? You will understand why if you keep reading.

CCNode

Sometimes called a scene hierarchy, the **scene graph** is a hierarchy of every Cocos2d node that's currently active.

We call them nodes because they inherit from the class CCNode (http://www.cocos2d-swift.org/docs/api/Classes/CCNode.html), the base class to display objects in Cocos2d.

The usual picture of a scene graph is a root CCScene node with several node children such as CCButton, CCSprite, and CCLabelTTF. For example, the graph of an initial Cocos2d project looks like the following:

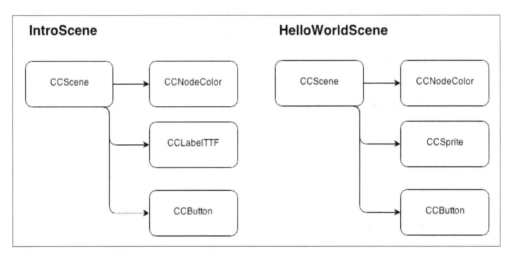

One important feature of CCNode in the current Cocos2d version is that it inherits from CCResponder, which allows all the objects derived from CCNode to handle user touches and mouse events.

I said that CCNode is the base class to display objects, but what are the classes that inherit from it? You can see the CCNode class hierarchy in the following graph:

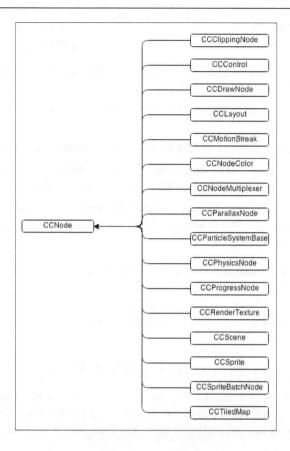

As I mentioned in the previous section, scenes will no longer derive from CCLayer (as has been the case in previous Cocos2d versions) and if you look closely at the CCNode class hierarchy in the preceding graph, you will realize that this class doesn't appear in it. It means that CCLayer has been deprecated and doesn't exist anymore, due to the fact that CCNode now supports user interaction, which was basically the purpose of CCLayer besides grouping nodes, a task perfectly accomplished by CCScene.

One important CCNode property is positionType. This property makes reference to how a node's position will be interpreted and can take three different values:

- CCPositionUnitPoints: The node's position will be set in points. This is the default value.

- CCPositionUnitScaled: The node's position will be scaled, for example, to be supported by iPhone and iPad.

- CCPositionUnitNormalized: The node's position will be relative to its parent node.

Another important property is `contentSizeType`, which means that the size of the node's content will be interpreted in different ways depending on its value:

- `CCSizeUnitPoints`: This is the default value and means that the size will be set in points

- `CCSizeUnitScaled`: The node's content size will be scaled by the factor indicated

- `CCSizeUnitNormalized`: The size will be relative to its parent container size

- `CCSizeUnitInset`: The size of the node's content will be the same as its parent node, but it will be inset by the indicated value

- `CCSizeUnitInsetScaled`: The size of the node's content will be the same as its parent node, but it will be inset by the indicated value that will be multiplied by a scale factor

This class is one of the most important because our games will have plenty of classes that derive from it, such as `CCButton` (inherits from `CCControl`), `CCParallaxNode`, `CCParticleSystemBase`, `CCSprite`, `CCLabelTTF` (inherits from `CCSprite`), `CCLabelBMFont` (inherits from `CCSpriteBatchNode`), or `CCScene`.

Your first game – RunYetiRun

The purpose of this game is the following: a monster avalanche has begun while our yeti friend was trying to scare some trekkers (not to be confused with *Star Trek* fans) and he has to escape on a sledge from the dangerous snowballs rolling down the mountain.

Maybe you won't believe me but the instructions we have seen during the previous section are almost enough on their own to develop this game. We will need only one scene, where we will place a mountain background image, the snowballs, and the yeti. The snowballs' movement will be controlled by actions, the yeti will move thanks to touches on the screen, and we will place a score label at the top to track how many snowballs we have avoided successfully. Only two new things will be necessary to develop this game: managing collisions and playing sounds.

Creating the CCScene class

A `CCScene` (http://www.cocos2d-swift.org/docs/api/Classes/CCScene.html) is a class that inherits from `CCNode` and whose main purpose is to contain the behavior and the nodes of a single scene of the game. Commonly, you will split your games into different scenes, so, for instance, you will have a scene for the main menu, a scene for the game itself, and another scene for the pause menu. As our first game won't have a main screen or pause menu, all the logic will be in `GameScene`.

We don't need the scenes included in our project by default, so feel free to delete them. We create our scene as a new class, so in Xcode, be sure the group **Classes** is selected in the project navigator before selecting **File | New | File...** and you will see the dialog shown in the following screenshot:

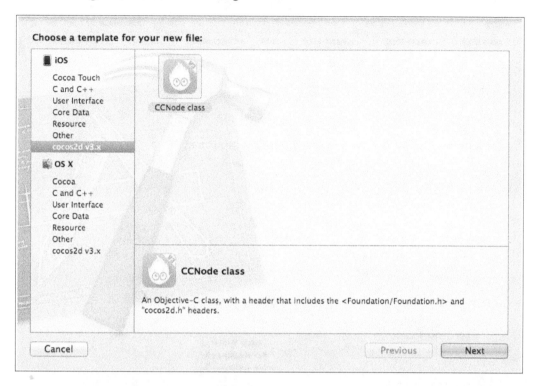

Cocos2d provides a template to create new classes inherited from CCNode, but as we have discussed in the previous section, we will derive our scene from CCScene:

1. Click on **Next** and replace the default CCNode with CCScene as the parent class.

2. Click on **Next** again, call it GameScene, and be sure that the **RunYetiRun** target is selected before clicking on **Create**.

At this point, our newly created GameScene is empty and will do nothing, but we just need to add the + (GameScene *) scene method and implement - (id) init to give it the characteristics of a common scene.

Go ahead and replace `GameScene.h` with the following code:

```objc
#import <Foundation/Foundation.h>
#import "cocos2d.h"

@interface GameScene : CCScene {

}

+(GameScene *) scene;

@end
```

Do the same with `GameScene.m` with the following lines:

```objc
#import "GameScene.h"

@implementation GameScene

+(GameScene *) scene {
    return [[self alloc] init];
}

-(id) init {
    self = [super init];
    if (!self) {
        return(nil);
    }
    return self;
}

@end
```

The last thing we need to do is to update `AppDelegate` to start `GameScene` in spite of `IntroScene`. To achieve it, replace the contents of `AppDelegate.m`:

```objc
#import "AppDelegate.h"
#import "GameScene.h"

@implementation AppDelegate

-(BOOL)application:(UIApplication *)application
didFinishLaunchingWithOptions:(NSDictionary *)launchOptions
{
```

```
  [self setupCocos2dWithOptions:@{
    CCSetupShowDebugStats: @(YES),
  }];

  return YES;
}

-(CCScene *)startScene
{
  // The initial scene will be GameScene
  return [GameScene scene];
}

@end
```

Now that `HelloWorldScene` and `IntroScene` are no longer needed, you can delete them if you haven't already done so. If you run the project now, you will only see the debug stats on a black screen, but don't worry, we are going to fix this with a few lines, so just keep reading!

Adding the first CCSprite class

It would be true to say that the `CCSprite` (http://www.cocos2d-swift.org/docs/api/Classes/CCSprite.html) class is one of the most commonly used when developing games, as this is what games are: a bunch of sprites moving and interacting on a screen.

Basically, a `CCSprite` class is a class derived from `CCNode` and its purpose is to represent and manage sprites, which are objects made up of a 2D image or a subrectangle of an image. To create a sprite, you first need to add the image you want to use to the **Resources** group, so complete the following steps:

1. Unzip the code files of this chapter from the code bundle and go back to Xcode.
2. Right-click on the **Resources** group and select **Add Files to "RunYetiRun"**....
3. It will open a dialog where you will select the `yeti.png` image from the RunYetiRun folder.
4. Be sure that **Copy items into destination group's folder (if needed)** is selected and click on **Add**.

Downloading the example code

You can download the example code files from your account at http://www.packtpub.com for all the Packt Publishing books you have purchased. If you purchased this book elsewhere, you can visit http://www.packtpub.com/support and register to have the files e-mailed directly to you.

The next step is to declare the `private` sprite variable we will use to manage our yeti friend, so in GameScene.m replace `@implementation GameScene` with the following lines of code:

```
@implementation GameScene
{
    // Declaring a private CCSprite instance
    CCSprite *_yeti;
}
```

Add the following lines before `return self;` in the `init` method:

```
// Creating the yeti sprite using an image file and adding it to
the scene
_yeti = [CCSprite spriteWithImageNamed:@"yeti.png"];
[self addChild:_yeti];
```

When specifying filenames, you need to take care, as they are case-sensitive. In addition, the desired image format is .png as it's more efficient than .jpg and .jpeg.

The `addChild` method adds a new child to the specified container (GameScene in this case) and this is how we add new nodes to the scene.

Ok, now it is time to run the game and see what we've just done:

The sprite has been placed in the bottom-left of the screen that corresponds to the coordinate (0,0), and due to the fact that the sprite texture is centered on the sprite's position, we can only see the top-right part of the yeti:

Anchor points

This center point of a sprite is known as the **anchor point**, an attribute used by nodes to perform all the transformations and position changes around it. By default, the anchor point in a CCNode class (don't forget our GameScene derives from it) is placed in the bottom-left corner, that is, (0,0); but with a CCSprite, the anchor point is placed at the very center of their texture (0.5, 0.5), which is why the majority of the yeti is not displayed on the screen.

For our game, we want our yeti to be placed at the same distance from the top and the bottom of the screen and near the right side, so add the following lines of code just before the `return self;` instruction:

```
// Positioning the yeti centered
CGSize screenSize = [CCDirector sharedDirector].viewSize;
_yeti.position = CGPointMake(screenSize.width * 3 / 4,
screenSize.height / 2);
```

At this point, I would like to highlight two important things. For those who have been working with Cocos2d v2, you should note that the former `[CCDirector sharedDirector].winSize` has been deprecated and we should use `[CCDirector sharedDirector].viewSize` instead.

This method returns the size of the view in points, so we will use this line to retrieve the width and height of the device screen. This way we can place nodes using relative positions in the future.

 When developing games for all devices (iPhone and iPad) it is recommended to work with relative positions. This way the location of nodes in the viewing window will be the same across all devices.

The `CCDirector` class is a singleton class: a globally accessible class that can only be instantiated once at any time that handles the main screen, and is responsible for executing the different scenes. Due to its nature, to access it you have to call the static method `sharedDirector` as we just saw in the previous code lines.

We place the yeti sprite with `CGPointMake (coord_x, coord_y)`.

Note that we are indicating the sprite position after adding it to the scene, which means that we can modify it whenever we want; it's not necessary to do it before `[self addChild:_yeti]`. Run the game again and you will see the yeti in the correct position:

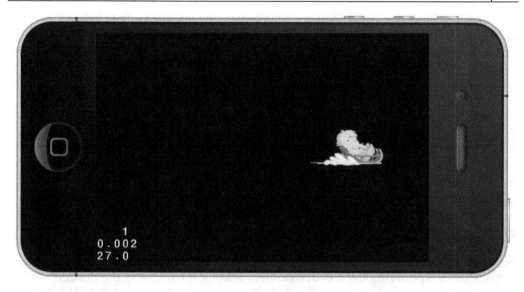

Ok, I must admit that it looks more like a space yeti than a mountain one, but it's just a matter of background.

Placing things in context

Yetis can't live in space; they need mountains, wind, and snow to be happy, and that's why we will put him in the environment he likes. In this case, we will follow almost the same steps that we did to add the yeti but with a few differences.

Let's add the background image to the project so we can use it in the future:

1. In the project navigator, select the **Resources** group.
2. Right-click and select **Add Files to "RunYetiRun"…**.
3. Look for the `background.png` file in the `RunYetiRun` folder, select it, and click on **Add**.

Then add the following lines to `GameScene.m` after the `_yeti.position = CGPointMake(screenSize.width * 3 / 4, screenSize.height / 2)` instruction:

```
// Adding the background image
CCSprite *background = [CCSprite
spriteWithImageNamed:@"background.png"];
background.position = CGPointMake(screenSize.width / 2,
screenSize.height / 2);
[self addChild:background z:-1];
```

The first two lines are already known to you: we are creating a sprite using the background image we have just added to the project and positioning it in the middle of the screen. However, there is an intriguing z argument when sending the message addChild to the current scene. It's the **z-order** and it represents the depth of the node; in other words it indicates the order in which the node will be drawn.

You can think of it as the layer organization in image processing software, where you can specify which layer is shown over the rest. The default value for z-order is 0, which is why we specified the -1 value because we want our background to be placed behind other layers. Can you see what would happen if you change -1 to 0? In this case, the background should be called foreground because it is now placed over our yeti. As we have specified the default value, the node will be drawn in the order we add it to the scene, so the poor yeti will be buried under snow even before breaking free from the avalanche!

So, once you know this, you can decide the most convenient way of adding sprites to your scene: specifying the z-order value or adding the nodes in the desired order. As this game is pretty simple, we just need to add the sprites in order of appearance, although in complex scenes you will want to keep them in a specific order (for example, when loading enemies that you want to be covered by some objects on the scene), but that is another matter.

The following image represents the resultant layers depending on the z-order value: background (*z-order = -1*), sprites (*z-order = 0*), and score label (*z-order > 0*):

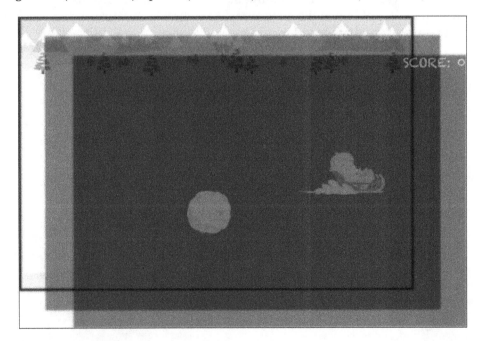

Ok, enough talking. Time to run and see the yeti chilling out on his sledge without being conscious of what is going to happen.

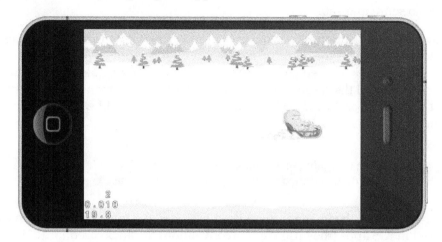

Now that we have a background and a sprite, we should talk about the different resolutions of a universal game (runnable on both iPhone and iPad). As you already know, there are several iOS devices on the market with different screen sizes and resolutions, so we need to adapt our visual sources to each of them. Take a look at the following table as a reference of the different specifications:

	iPhone	iPhone Retina	iPhone 5	iPad	iPad Retina
Devices	iPhone 1G-3GS	iPhone 4, 4S	iPhone 5, 5C, 5S	iPad	iPad Air
	iPod Touch 1G-3G	iPod Touch 4G	iPod Touch 5G	iPad 2	iPad Mini Retina
Resolution	480 x 320	960 x 640	1136 x 640	1024 x 768	2048 x 1536
Cocos2d file suffix	`file.png`	`file-hd.png`	`file-iphone5hd.png`	`file-ipad.png`	`file-ipadhd.png`

At the time of writing this book, there are five different resolution families with five different filenames; not bad considering they support more than 15 devices. It means that if you want your game to be displayed in the native resolution of all these devices, you will need to provide five images with the particular suffix. So, for example, if you want your game to be played properly on the first iPhone and iPod Touch generation, you will need `file.png`, but if you want it to be also displayed with the expected resolution on all the iPhone family, you will need `file-hd.png` and `file-iphone5hd.png`.

One important thing included in the current Cocos2d version is that support for Retina displays is enabled by default, as Apple began to make it mandatory; it makes no sense to disable it.

The aim of this convention is to avoid programmatically downscaling the image, which adversely affects the game's performance. You should never upscale an image because it won't look very engaging, but you can try to downscale a high-resolution image to support all the resolutions. However, it's not recommended due to the amount of memory and CPU cycles a non-Retina device would waste performing this action.

 When designing image files, it is recommended to do it to the highest resolution and then downscale it for the lower ones.

As you may realize, the image suffixes used in Cocos2d games aren't the same as those used in iOS apps (they use the @2x convention). It can be used for Retina files, but Cocos2d doesn't recommend that.

For all of these reasons, and as we don't want to reposition nodes or lose image quality, each time we add an image in this chapter, we should add five different images. At the moment, we lack four images for the yeti sprite and four more images for the background:

1. Right-click on **Resources** and select **Add Files to "RunYetiRun"**....

2. You'll find `yeti-hd.png`, `yeti-iphone5hd.png`, `yeti-ipad.png`, `yeti-ipadhd.png`, `background-hd.png`, `background-iphone5hd.png`, `background-ipad.png`, and `background-ipadhd.png` in the `RunYetiRun` folder, so select these eight files and click on **Add**.

If you want to see how the yeti looks on other devices, go ahead and run it now.

Time for CCAction

We don't want our yeti to slide down the mountain in just one direction; what will happen if there is an obstacle? We will enable touch detection to move him up and down to dodge all the snowballs rolling down the mountain.

First of all, we need our game to manage touches, so add the following line in the `init` method, just before `return self`:

```
// Enabling user interaction
self.userInteractionEnabled = TRUE;
```

Implement `touchBegan` by adding the following code lines:

```
-(void)touchBegan:(UITouch *)touch withEvent:(UIEvent *)event
{
    // Moving the yeti to the touched position
    CGPoint touchLocation = [touch locationInNode:self];
    [self moveYetiToPosition:touchLocation];
}
```

Before going further, in `GameScene.h`, declare `moveYetiToPosition` by adding the following lines just after the `+(GameScene *) scene;` instruction:

```
-(void) moveYetiToPosition:(CGPoint)nextPosition;
```

Implement it on `GameScene.m`:

```
-(void) moveYetiToPosition:(CGPoint)nextPosition{

    // Preventing the yeti going out of the landscape
    CGSize screenSize = [CCDirector sharedDirector].viewSize;

    float yetiHeight = _yeti.texture.contentSize.height;

    if (nextPosition.y > screenSize.height - 3 * yetiHeight/2) {
        nextPosition.y = screenSize.height - 3 * yetiHeight/2;
    } else if (nextPosition.y < yetiHeight) {
        nextPosition.y = yetiHeight;
    }

    // We don't want to worry about the x coordinates
    nextPosition.x = _yeti.position.x;

    // The constant yeti speed
    float yetiSpeed = 360.0;

    // We want the yeti to move on a constant speed
    float duration = ccpDistance(nextPosition, _yeti.position) /
    yetiSpeed;

    // Move the yeti to the touched position
    CCActionMoveTo *actionMove = [CCActionMoveTo
    actionWithDuration:duration
    position:CGPointMake(_yeti.position.x, nextPosition.y)];

    [_yeti runAction:actionMove];
}
```

Ok, it's a big piece of code, but don't worry, you will understand it in no time at all. The first thing we are doing is enabling the scene to manage touches thanks to the `userInteractionEnabled` property.

We were discussing a few pages ago why `CCLayers` are not used any more, because now all the nodes inherit from `CCResponder` and can handle touch events, so we just need to enable this feature and implement `touchBegan` to respond to any interaction as soon as it happens.

In `touchBegan`, we just get the location of the touch event and pass it to the `moveYetiPosition` method, where all the magic is going to happen. We are moving the yeti up and down but we don't want him to go off the background and look odd, so if we detect a new touch in positions close to the upper or lower edges of the background (the trees and the gray layer on the bottom), we will replace it with the maximum and minimum y coordinates the yeti can move to. These maximum and minimum coordinates will be three times the half height of the yeti on the upper screen edges, and the yeti height on the lower screen edge, as the sprite anchor is placed at the center of the image. Then we update the x coordinate of `nextPosition` to the yeti's x coordinate because we want to focus only on vertical displacement. That way it doesn't matter where on the screen we touch, as the movement will only take into account the vertical distance.

So, once we know the next position, we just need to focus on the movement itself. In Cocos2d there are a large number of methods to perform all the actions we will need in a game. At this moment, we will just focus on movement actions, specifically on `CCMoveTo`. This action moves the sprite to the next position in a specified duration and can be concurrently called, resulting in a movement that will be the sum of the different movements. There is a similar action called `CCMoveBy` that generates a movement by the next position using relative coordinates, but we want to move to an absolute position to be sure we are avoiding the snowballs. As we want our yeti to always move at the same speed (360), we will need to update the duration of the action using basic physics. Do you remember the formula used to calculate the speed?

$$speed = distance/time$$

We already know the speed and distance values, but we need to calculate how much time (`duration`) it will take to move the sprite to the next position at a speed that equals 360. The `ccpDistance` method calculates the distance between the yeti and the next position and that's how we know the distance to be covered.

The last line [_yeti runAction:actionMove]; triggers the action and without it there won't be movement at all, as it sends the message runAction with the action we just created to the node we want to move.

Just one thing before testing these new changes: to make our code fancier we should follow the healthy habit of declaring constant variables whenever we use constant values, so delete the line float yetiSpeed = 360.0; and add the following code to GameScene.m after the GameScene.h import:

```
// The constant yeti speed
#define yetiSpeed 360.0;
```

Also, declare two private float variables to keep the top and bottom limits of the available screen stored. In GameScene.m, add the following lines after CCSprite *_yeti;:

```
// Available screen limits
float _topLimit;
float _bottomLimit;
```

Initialize these values in the init method, just after enabling user interaction:

```
// Initializing playable limits
_topLimit = screenSize.height - 3 * _yeti.texture.contentSize.
height/2;
_bottomLimit = _yeti.texture.contentSize.height;
```

On the moveYetiToPosition method, modify the following lines:

```
    if (nextPosition.y > screenSize.height - 3 * yetiHeight/2) {
        nextPosition.y = screenSize.height - 3 * yetiHeight/2;
    } else if (nextPosition.y < yetiHeight) {
        nextPosition.y = yetiHeight;
    }
```

Add these new code lines:

```
    if (nextPosition.y > _topLimit) {
        nextPosition.y = _topLimit;
    } else if (nextPosition.y < _bottomLimit) {
        nextPosition.y = _bottomLimit;
    }
```

Delete the following no longer needed lines from moveYetiToPosition:

```
// Preventing the yeti going out of the landscape
CGSize screenSize = [CCDirector sharedDirector].viewSize;
float yetiHeight = _yeti.texture.contentSize.height;
```

Ok, enough code for now. Run the project and see how our yeti moves happily up and down!

However, if you touch the screen several times, you will see strange movement behavior: the yeti moves further than expected. Don't worry, it's due to the nature of the CCMoveTo class itself. When I introduced this action, I specified that it could be concurrently called resulting in a movement that will be the sum of the individual movements, but in our case it makes our yeti look crazy. To take control of the movement, we will take advantage of one important method when calling actions: stopActionByTag.

Actions under control

In Cocos2d, we can trigger and stop actions whenever we want, so we can control what is happening all the time. After running the movement action on the yeti, we realize that it's not behaving as we wanted: it's chaining movements and the sprite is not placed on the desired position. We can solve it thanks to the action-canceling methods available in CCNode (don't forget CCSprite inherits from this class):

- stopAction:(CCAction * action)
- stopActionByTag:(NSInteger)
- stopAllActions

The first removes a specified action, the second removes the action specifying a tag number, and the last cancels every action running on the node. In our case, we don't want to stop all actions because we may want to execute another action in the future, so we should stop the action with the `stopActionByTag:(NSInteger)` tag.

We just need to make two changes in our code. In `moveYetiToPosition`, add the following lines before running `actionMove`:

```
// Controlling actions
[actionMove setTag:0];
```

At the very beginning of `touchBegan`, add:

```
// Controlling actions
[_yeti stopActionByTag:0];
```

Great, the yeti is now moving smoothly on the snow, but it's time to make some noise and begin a big avalanche, isn't it?

Throwing some snowballs

As soon as an avalanche begins, a lot of snowballs roll down the mountain. We will represent the snowballs with an array filled with sprites that will vertically cover the entire available screen: there will be as many snowballs as can fit within the height of the background. Also, as we are developing this game for any kind of iOS device, the size of the snowball array will depend on the height of the device, so it will be indicated during the initialization of the scene.

Let's do these changes step by step. First, in `GameScene.m`, declare the variables for both the array of snowballs and number of snowballs by adding the following lines after `float _bottomLimit`:

```
// Declare snowballs array
NSMutableArray *_snowBalls;

// Declare number of snowballs
int _numSnowBalls;
```

We are using `NSMutableArray`, the iOS class used to create modifiable arrays of objects, and not `CCArray` as it has been deprecated. During the lifetime of the previous Cocos2d version, many people suggested stopping using `CCArray` because its benefits were limited, but it had many restrictions, which is why it's not available anymore.

For the moment we are declaring all the global variables as private as we don't need to share them with other scenes, and we will keep this approach until we need to publish some variables.

The next step is to initialize the variables we just declared, but first we will need an image to create the snowball sprites:

1. In Xcode, right-click on the **Resources** group in the project navigator.

2. Select **Add Files to "RunYetiRun"...**.

3. Look for `snowball0.png`, `snowball1.png`, and `snowball2.png` (and the corresponding `-hd.png`, `-iphone5hd.png`, `-ipad.png`, and `-ipadhd.png`) included in the `RunYetiRun` folder and click on **Add**.

Now let's calculate how many snowballs fit on the screen. In the `init` method, add the following lines just after enabling user interaction:

```
// Creating a temporal sprite to get its height
CCSprite *tempSnowBall = [CCSprite
spriteWithImageNamed:@"snowball0.png"];
float snowBallHeight =
tempSnowBall.texture.contentSize.height;

// Calculate number of snowballs that fits in the screen
_numSnowBalls = (screenSize.height - 3 *
_yeti.texture.contentSize.height/2) / snowBallHeight;
```

We are creating a temporal sprite with the snowball texture and then we are getting its height by accessing the texture content size. Once we know the image height, we can divide the available screen size by the image height, and we will get a number that will correspond to the number of items the snowball array will have.

Note that when calculating the available screen size, we are taking into account the whole screen that will be filled with snowballs; in other words, we don't calculate it as `_topLimit - _bottomLimit` as this variables refers to the anchor point of the yeti sprite and we want to take into account the top of its texture for the top limit and the bottom of its texture for the bottom limit when calculating the available screen. That's why the available screen is (`screenSize.height - 3 * _yeti.texture.contentSize.height/2`).

We can now initialize the snowball array. Add the following lines just before
`return self;`:

```
// Initialize array with capacity
_snowBalls = [NSMutableArray arrayWithCapacity:_numSnowBalls];

for (int i = 0; i < _numSnowBalls;i++) {
      CCSprite *snowBall = [CCSprite
      spriteWithImageNamed:[NSString
      stringWithFormat:@"snowball%i.png", i % 3]];
      // Add the snowball to the scene
      [self addChild:snowBall];

      // Add the snowball to the array
      [_snowBalls addObject:snowBall];
}
[self initSnowBalls];
```

First we use the `arrayWithCapacity` method to specify the number of items our
array will have and, using a `for` loop, we create a snowball sprite that we add to the
scene and the array. If you look closely, we are formatting the filename to initialize
each ball with one of the three images we have available. Also pay attention to the
`addChild` line we need to add each sprite to the scene, because if we don't do it the
sprites won't appear. The final line in the loop is simple: we are just adding another
node to the array.

At this point, there is no visual update and you may be getting a compilation
error. Don't worry, we're going to fix it right now, so let's begin by initializing
the snowball positions.

Rolling down the hill

In this step, we will initialize the snowballs and make them roll down, trying to
hit the yeti. Perhaps this task looks easy — and it is — but it will be a good chance
to explain some new concepts.

First of all, we will wrap this initialization in an instance method, which is
why you should include the following line in `GameScene.h` just after declaring
`moveYetiToPosition`:

```
-(void) initSnowBalls;
```

Going back to GameScene.m, you need to implement it by adding:

```
-(void) initSnowBalls {

    CCSprite *tempSnowBall = [_snowBalls objectAtIndex:0];

    // Position y for the first snowball
    int positionY = _bottomLimit;

    // Calculate the gaps between snowballs to be positioned
    proportionally
    CGSize screenSize = [CCDirector sharedDirector].viewSize;
    float blankScreenSize = (screenSize.height - 3 *
    _yeti.texture.contentSize.height/2) - _numSnowBalls *
    tempSnowBall.contentSize.height;
    float gap = blankScreenSize / (_numSnowBalls - 1);

    for (int i = 0; i < _snowBalls.count; i++){

        CCSprite *snowBall = [_snowBalls objectAtIndex:i];

        // Put the snow ball out of the screen
        CGPoint snowBallPosition = CGPointMake(-
        snowBall.texture.contentSize.width / 2, positionY);
        positionY += snowBall.contentSize.height + gap;
        snowBall.position = snowBallPosition;

        [snowBall stopAllActions];
    }

    [self schedule:@selector(throwSnowBall:) interval:1.5f];
}
```

At the beginning of the method, we are retrieving one snowball as a temporal variable to get its height, because we want to place each snowball in a different y position but always inside the playable screen. That's why the initial positionY variable is equal to _bottomLimit as it's the lowest point the yeti will reach (remember anchor points?) and we will use it to know where to place the next snowball.

As we want to position each snowball proportionally to the available screen, we first calculate how much space will be kept blank when all the snowballs are drawn. It is the available screen height minus the height of the number of snowballs on the screen.

Then we divide this blank space by one snowball less than the total, because we don't want to leave a gap when placing the first snowball. This gap variable will be used later to calculate the next snowball position.

Then, with a for loop we iterate over the array, retrieving each sprite and performing the following actions:

1. Initialize a new CGPoint, placing it half the width of the snowball out of the screen (on the left) and in the y position calculated.

2. Update the positionY variable by increasing it by a snowball height plus the gap.

3. Assign the new position to the snowball.

4. Stop every running action on the snowball, as we want it to lie still.

The following image represents the resultant screen after performing the preceding steps:

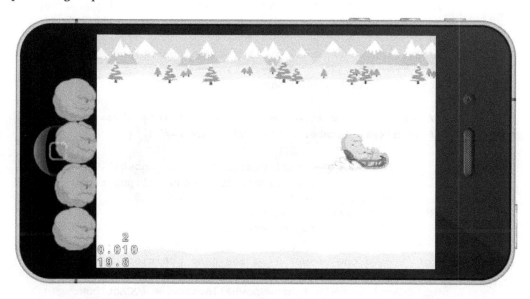

Now that we have initialized the snowballs and they are waiting to attack, it is time to throw them at the yeti! We will do it thanks to the last line:

```
[self schedule:@selector(throwSnowBall:) interval:1.5f];
```

It means that we are scheduling the method throwSnowBall to execute once every 1.5 seconds. If you pay attention to the syntax of the previous instruction, you can see that we specify the method we want to schedule through selector, which is the name of the method including colons and parameter names.

There are several ways of scheduling selectors. These include specifying a delay or a set number of repetitions:

- `schedule:interval`: Schedules a method that will be triggered after the number of seconds specified as the interval

- `schedule:interval:repeat:delay`: Similar to the previous method but it also allows us to specify the number of repetitions and a desired initial delay in seconds

In this chapter, we will use the first version.

Now you need to implement `throwSnowBall`, so paste the following piece of code into `GameScene.m`:

```
-(void) throwSnowBall:(CCTime) delta {
    for (int i = 0; i < _numSnowBalls; i++){

        // Get a random number between 0 and the size of the array
        int randomSnowBall = arc4random_uniform(_numSnowBalls);

        // Select the snowball at the random index
        CCSprite *snowBall = [_snowBalls
        objectAtIndex:randomSnowBall];

        // Don't want to stop the snow ball if it's already moving
        if ([snowBall numberOfRunningActions] == 0) {

            // Specify the final position of the snowball
            CGPoint nextSnowBallPosition = snowBall.position;
            nextSnowBallPosition.x = [CCDirector
            sharedDirector].viewSize.width +
            snowBall.texture.contentSize.width / 2;

            // Move the snowball to its next position out of the
            screen
            CCActionMoveTo *throwSnowBallAction = [CCActionMoveTo
            actionWithDuration:1 position:nextSnowBallPosition];

            // Reset the position of the snowball to reuse it
            CCActionCallBlock *callDidThrown = [CCActionCallBlock
            actionWithBlock:^{

                CGPoint position = snowBall.position;
                position.x = -snowBall.texture.contentSize.
                width / 2;
```

```
                    snowBall.position = position;
        }];

        // Execute the movement and the reset in a sequence
        CCActionSequence *sequence = [CCActionSequence
        actionWithArray:@[throwSnowBallAction,
        callDidThrown]];
        [snowBall runAction:sequence];

        // To avoid moving more than one snowball at the same
        time
        break;
    }
  }
}
```

Don't be scared of this block of harmless code; at least you are not the yeti who is about to be buried by tons of snow! This method covers the snowball's movement and the recovery of its initial position. Let's look at it line by line.

As with every time we perform an action on the snowballs array, we loop into it thanks to the global variable _numSnowBalls. We want to throw one snowball at a time but we don't want to do it sequentially because it would be too easy for the yeti to learn the sequence. To make things harder, we will randomly decide what snowball to throw, and it is as easy as using the arc4random_uniform(_numSnowBalls) mathematical function included in the stdlib.h library (after iOS 4.3) to obtain a random number between 0 and _numSnowballs. You can also use two more approaches:

```
int randomSnowBall = arc4random() % _numSnowballs;
int randomSnowBall = CCRANDOM_0_1() * _numSnowballs;
```

Both of them calculate a random number within our array size but arc4random_uniform gives a more uniform distribution of the random results.

With the random number calculated, we take the snowball sprite corresponding to this array index, and before doing anything else, we check if it has a running action. This check is done by sending the message numberOfRunningActions to the node and it will help us to avoid stopping snowballs in the middle of their movement, in case we get the same sprite in the next interval. The numberOfRunningActions message returns the number of actions running plus the actions scheduled to run, that way we know what is happening.

In the next two lines, we are going to calculate the final position we want the snowball moved to using its initial position. We just need to modify the x coordinate because we want it to stop as soon as it goes off the screen on the right-hand side, and it corresponds to the screen plus half of the sprite's width.

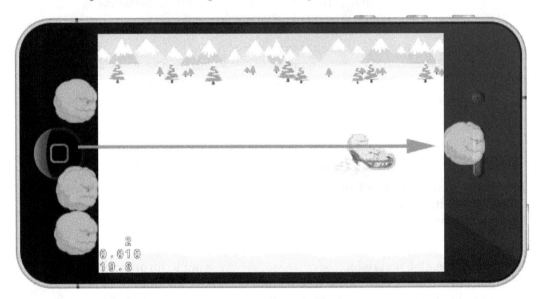

Once we know the snowball's final position, we just need to decide the duration of the movement to set up the throwSnowBallAction action. As we don't want to make it too hard, the snowballs will take 1 second to cover the entire screen width, enough for the yeti to avoid them. Note that this time we don't need to calculate the duration dynamically because the displacement always has the same distance.

In this case, we are not executing the action right now because we need to perform some updates after this action finishes. We will solve it by concatenating one action after throwSnowBallAction, but in this case it won't be CCActionMoveTo but CCActionCallBlock. The CCActionCallBlock class (called CCCallBlock in Cocos2d v2) allows you to set up an action with a typical Objective-C block and we are going to take advantage of this feature to update the snowballs' positions as soon as they fade from view.

```
CCActionCallBlock *callDidThrown = [CCActionCallBlock
actionWithBlock:^{

    CGPoint position = snowBall.position;
    position.x = -snowBall.texture.contentSize.width / 2;
    snowBall.position = position;
}];
```

The block of code gets the current snowball position (off the right-hand side of the screen) and sets its x coordinate back to the left, off the screen too, because we want to reset its position. Then we just need to concatenate `throwSnowBallAction` and `callDidThrown` to make the snowball cross the screen from left to right and vice versa. We will do it thanks to `CCActionSequence` (called `CCSequence` in Cocos2d v2).

```
CCActionSequence *sequence = [CCActionSequence
actionWithArray:@[throwSnowBallAction, callDidThrown]];
[snowBall runAction:sequence];

break;
```

The sequence allows us to execute an array of actions (even an array of just one action) that will take place one after the other. That's why we include our `CCActionMoveTo` and `CCActionCallBlock` classes, but nothing will happen until we ask the sprite to run the sequence action. If you have been working with arrays in either Objective-C or previous Cocos2d versions, you will notice that the array we've sent to the sequences has not a `nil` value in the last position; in Cocos2d v3, this technique is not needed anymore.

If you are asking yourself why I put a `break` instruction at the end, it's just to prevent throwing more than one snowball each time `throwSnowBall` is called.

Ok, that's a lot of writing this time but it was necessary to explain this behavior. Let's amuse ourselves a little by running the game and looking at the snowballs passing over and over. Relaxing, isn't it?

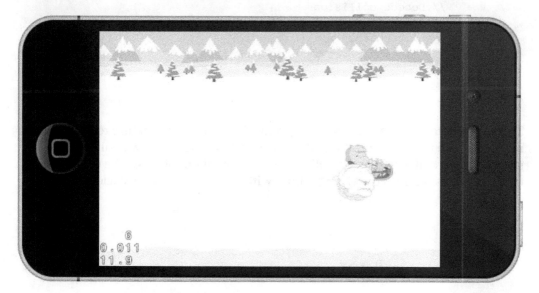

If you need to know why we can't see the snowball returning to its initial position although we didn't set it to be invisible, the reason is inside `CCActionCallBlock`: we set `snowBall.position = position;` and it moves the sprite to this position instantly without intermediate updates.

Managing collisions

At the moment, our yeti is beginning to think that something is going wrong and he is right, but lucky him that the snowballs can't hit him…yet.

We just need to introduce collisions to the logic of our game to make him fear for his life. So come on, let's make the snowballs collide with the yeti.

First, before writing more code, it's important to know that Cocos2d allows you to schedule a method that will be called in every frame. This method is `(void) update:(CCTime)delta` and we can take advantage of it to make common checks for collision detection.

Previous versions of Cocos2d required a call to `[self scheduleUpdate]` to activate this feature, but in Cocos2d v3 it's not needed any more, you just need to implement the `update` method with your desired logic and it will be called automatically.

In our case, implement it in `GameScene.m` by adding the following block of code:

```
-(void) update:(CCTime)delta {
    for (CCSprite *snowBall in _snowBalls){
        // Detect collision
        if (CGRectIntersectsRect(snowBall.boundingBox,
        _yeti.boundingBox)) {
            [snowBall setVisible:FALSE];
        }
    }
}
```

This method iterates the snowball array and tries to find if its texture rectangle intersects with the yeti's rectangle. When a collision is detected, we will set the snowball to invisible and let it continue its movement out of view. We could use other solutions but for now we are happy with just making the obstacle invisible.

Come on, run the project and check this behavior!

This image is a mock-up, because when a snowball collides with the yeti, it disappears and it's impossible to distinguish this situation from the initial one when no snowball is visible. Don't worry, let's do some things to make it more credible.

First, declare the following method in `GameScene.h`:

```
-(void) manageCollision;
```

Call it by adding the following in `GameScene.m`, when the collision has been detected, after `[snowBall setVisible:FALSE];`:

```
// Managing collisions
[self manageCollision];
```

As a final step, implement it by adding the following lines to `GameScene.m`:

```
-(void) manageCollision {

    _yeti.color = [CCColor redColor];
    CCAction *actionBlink = [CCActionBlink actionWithDuration:0.9
    blinks:3];
    CCActionCallBlock *callDidBlink = [CCActionCallBlock
    actionWithBlock:^{
      // Recover the visibility of the snowball and its tint
      [_yeti setVisible:TRUE];
      _yeti.color = [CCColor whiteColor];
    }];
```

```
CCActionSequence *sequence = [CCActionSequence
actionWithArray:@[actionBlink, callDidBlink]];
[_yeti runAction:sequence];

}
```

From the preceding code, you will understand it quickly. We are tinting the yeti with a predefined red color in the CCColor class (if you take a look at the CCColor class reference, you will see that there are several predefined colors we can use). After that, we are creating a CCActionBlink class that consists of making the sprite blink a fixed number of times during the specified interval. However, we need to set the yeti's visibility to TRUE at the end of the blink action as otherwise it finishes with the disappearance of the yeti, and we don't want that… at least not at this very moment! To achieve it, we concatenate CCActionCallBlock, where we update the visibility after the blink action and set its tint color to white again. Easy, right? I decided to execute the red tint plus blink action as it's commonly used in video games to represent when a character has been hit.

There is only one thing left, we need to recover the visibility of the snowballs once they arrive at the end of their movement! Can you guess where we are going to do it? Do you remember the CCActionCallBlock instance named callDidThrown inside the throwSnowBall method? You just need to add the following line at the end of the block:

```
// Recovering the visibility of the snowball
[snowBall setVisible:TRUE];
```

If you run the game now, you will feel that a collision is happening.

But what happens if the yeti avoids a snowball — nothing? Not even a banana or whatever yetis eat? Let's at least give him a bunch of points!

Adding labels

How can a game exist without a score? Gamers need an incentive to keep playing again and again and usually it consists of beating their own score record, so we will learn in this section how to display a label on the screen and update it dynamically.

Cocos2d provides two classes that inherit from CCSprite to visualize labels:

- CCCLabelTTF
- CCLabelBMFont

We are going to focus on the first one along this chapter.

CCLabelTTF

The CCLabelTTF class displays labels using a rendered TrueType font texture.

> The TrueType font is a vector-based font format that was designed to represent all the style variants of a letter. If you want to know which of these fonts are available in iOS, visit http://iosfonts.com.

They are simple but they have a performance handicap if you need to update a label frequently, because every time you modify its text you are creating a new CCLabelTTF instance. In this game, we are going to update the score label each time the yeti avoids a snowball, but that doesn't matter as I will teach you how to display this kind of label so you will be able to use them whenever it's convenient.

In this step, we will need an integer variable to track the score, a label, and a Boolean variable, which we will use as a flag to know when to increase the score. So first of all, let's declare the following variables in GameScene.m:

```
// Label to show the score
CCLabelTTF *_scoreLabel;

// Score count
int _gameScore;

// Collisions flag
BOOL _collisionDetected;
```

Now we should initialize them, so add the following code to the `init` method:

```
// Initialize score count
_gameScore = 0;

// Initialize score label
_scoreLabel = [CCLabelTTF labelWithString:[NSString
stringWithFormat:@"SCORE: %i", _gameScore]
fontName:@"Chalkduster" fontSize:15];
_scoreLabel.color = [CCColor orangeColor];
_scoreLabel.position = CGPointMake(screenSize.width,
screenSize.height);
[self addChild:_scoreLabel];

// Initialize the collision flag to false
_collisionDetected = FALSE;
```

Initializing an integer and a Boolean variable is easy enough, so I will not waste your time explaining it. Let's focus on how we are initializing the score label. We are creating a new `CCLabelTTF` specifying its font name, its size, and its text. For the font, I chose `Chalkduster` because of its childish look, but you can use any of the available fonts in iOS, which you can find at `http://iosfonts.com`. Note that `labelWithString` accepts `NSString` so we can include both numbers and text in the label. Also, I set its color to orange so we can differentiate the label from the background.

Run the game and you will see the brand-new label in the top-right corner:

Wait, don't throw this book into a fire! I set the score offscreen deliberately because I wanted to introduce one important feature of anchor points. The anchor point attribute is useful to align textures, as in this particular case, so we will take advantage of it to right-align the score label. To achieve that, we just need to modify the position of its anchor point. So, going back to the `init` method, you just need to add:

```
// Right-aligning the label
_scoreLabel.anchorPoint = CGPointMake(1.0, 1.0);
```

Then execute:

```
[self addChild:scoreLabel];
```

This way, when the label size increases due to scores of three or four digits, the label will grow to the left, keeping all digits visible.

Updating labels

In this section, you will learn how to implement the logic to update labels. For this purpose, we will take into account the Boolean flag we declared previously, which we will use to identify whether to increase the score or not.

It will take a couple of changes and a new method. In `GameScene.h`, add the following line to declare a method we will use to update the score:

```
-(void) increaseScore;
```

Going back to `GameScene.m`, as we want to identify when a collision happens, there is nothing better than using the methods we have created previously. In the `manageCollision` method, add the following line at the very beginning:

```
_collisionDetected = TRUE;
```

That way we will be able to identify moment-by-moment whether the yeti has been hit.

In the `throwSnowBall` method, you may remember we created a `CCActionCallBlock` to update the snowball's position when its movement has finished. Find this line of code:

```
[snowBall setVisible:TRUE];
```

Before the preceding code, add the following lines of code:

```
// Evaluating if a collision happened
if (!_collisionDetected){
    [self increaseScore];
}
```

Then we will implement the `increaseScore` method. You just need to add:

```
-(void) increaseScore{
    _gameScore += 10;
    [_scoreLabel setString:[NSString stringWithFormat:
    @"SCORE: %i", _gameScore]];
}
```

As a final step, we will need to reset the Boolean flag to false and we will make this change after the whole snowball sequence is done. Add the following line just before `break;`:

```
_collisionDetected = FALSE;
```

Ok, let's see what we have done so far. As soon as we detect a collision, we update the Boolean flag to TRUE and we will use it at the end of the snowball movement to know if we have to increase the label. If the flag's value is FALSE, it means that the yeti has survived the attack of one snowball and we will execute `increaseScore`, rewarding the yeti with some points to make him happy.

With this method, we increase the score by 10 points and update the label using the `setString` method, keeping the same format as when we created it.

Now that we have a flag to control when a collision happens, we will use it to minimize the times the method `manageCollision` is called. It's been happening repeatedly, because when a snowball collides with the yeti, although we are making it invisible, it's complying with the conditions of the collision. And this is happening every frame until the snowball passes the yeti completely, with the consequent number of calls to `manageCollision`. To avoid this behavior, go to the `update` method and replace the following condition:

```
if (CGRectIntersectsRect(snowBall.boundingBox, _yeti.boundingBox)) {
```

with a new one:

```
if (CGRectIntersectsRect(snowBall.boundingBox, _yeti.boundingBox)
&& !_collisionDetected) {
```

Let's go! Run the game and you will see how our yeti earns points when he survives!

Making some noise

Video games are like movies: they need music and sound effects to transmit the emotions they want the players to feel. Good movies usually come with amazing soundtracks that make you remember a particular scene, and this also applies to good video games. But you may be thinking, "I'm not a musician, nor a producer!" Don't worry, the Internet has plenty of sites where you can find free and paid resources you can use in your games, but first let's introduce a new class for playing audio in Cocos2d.

OALSimpleAudio

The `OALSimpleAudio` class is the new class included in Cocos2d v3 to play audio files. If you have developed games using previous versions, you will need to forget `SimpleAudio` as it's not used any more, but don't worry, the new class is easier to use and more powerful. One feature to highlight is that it plays all formats supported by iOS, and this is important when thinking about creating audio resources. For this chapter, I created one background song and two sound effects, and I will show you how I made them and what tools I used.

Voice memos

I used this app, included in iOS by default, to record a growl made by myself, because the format in which the audio file is exported, `.m4a`, is supported by iOS and is as easy to use as touching one button and sending the file to your computer. If you have a different mobile device, I'm sure it includes an audio recorder that you can use too. This way in a few minutes I got `growl.m4a`, which the yeti will play whenever a snowball hits it. I know it's not the best audio quality, but I wanted to use it just to show you this possibility.

Audacity

Next I thought that the snowballs needed a sound too, because they are not quiet when they are rolling down a mountain. I went to `http://soundbible.com/` and looked for a realistic avalanche sound, then downloaded a public domain 8-second file, but it was too long for the movement of the snowballs, whose duration is only one second, so I used the audio-editing tool Audacity (`http://audacity.sourceforge.net`) to cut a piece of the desired duration. This is a very useful and easy-to-use tool for audio production. It allows you to record from the internal microphone or from an external sound card, cut and paste, adding and deleting tracks. In this case, I used Audacity just to create a new audio file from the original, selecting a 1-second piece and exporting it as a `.mp3` file (`avalanche.mp3`).

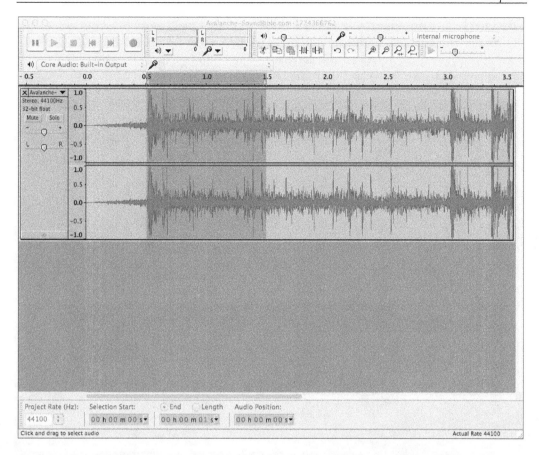

GarageBand

This software is integrated in OS X by default and is a professional tool for music production, so it's perfect for our game's background music. However, it requires a little more experience to take advantage of its whole potential. I created a track using some preset banjo loops, making sure that the beginning and the end match because this file will be played in a loop until the end of the game.

I decided to add another track with a wind sound so it feels more like being on a mountain, and I found a sound made by Mark DiAngelo (`http://soundbible.com/1810-Wind.html`) that I think is perfect. I just had to export the song (`background_music.mp3`) and that's it!

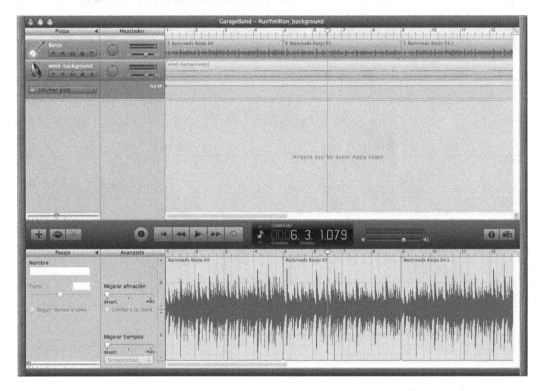

This is how a GarageBand project looks. As you can see there are two tracks: one is for the banjo and the other one contains the wind effect.

Audio resources

I said at the beginning of this section that the Internet is full of places where you can find resources to use in your games, and here are some examples of websites where you can download them:

- `http://soundbible.com`: You can find free sound clips and effects under different licenses.

- `http://www.partnersinrhyme.com`: It has plenty of free and paid sources. It has a very interesting database.

- `http://www.pacdv.com/sounds`: It does not have a very extensive database, but all its resources are free and high quality.
- `http://www.freesound.org`: It contains different license resources as well as a forum where you will find help on creating new resources and attribution help.

Playing audio files

Now that we know how to create and get audio files, it's time to play them in our own game.

First you will need to add the audio resources to the project:

1. Right-click on the **Resources** group in the project navigator on the left.
2. Select **Add Files to "RunYetiRun"…**.
3. In the `RunYetiRun` folder, you will find `background_music.mp3`, `avalanche.mp3`, and `growl.m4a`. Select them and click on **Add**.

Then, in the `init` method, just before `return self;`, add the following line:

```
// Playing background music
[[OALSimpleAudio sharedInstance] playBg:@"background_music.mp3"
loop:YES];
```

In this way, we are specifying that we want to play background music that will loop infinitely.

The next step is playing a sound when a snowball starts moving, so go to the `throwSnowBall` method and add the following code just before creating `CCActionSequence`:

```
// Playing sound effects
[[OALSimpleAudio sharedInstance] playEffect:@"avalanche.mp3"];
```

It will play an audio effect, in this case the sound of the snowball rolling down and trying to hit the yeti.

Finally, we want to make the yeti growl when it's hit and it's as easy as adding the following line of code at the very beginning of `manageCollision`:

```
// Playing sound effects
[[OALSimpleAudio sharedInstance] playEffect:@"growl.m4a"];
```

In this case, we will play an audio effect in the same way we just did with the snowball sound.

It's possible that you want to preload sound effects to avoid the little lag happening when you play a sound for the first time. To achieve this you can add the following lines to the `init` method:

```
[[OALSimpleAudio sharedInstance] preloadEffect:@"avalanche.mp3"];
[[OALSimpleAudio sharedInstance] preloadEffect:@"growl.m4a"];
```

Now you can run the game and enjoy the new sounds!

Game over

Now that our yeti is in a rush avoiding snowballs and trying to win as many points as it can, it's time to set a game over condition. The game will finish as soon as the score reaches a specified value, and when it happens we will trigger the actions needed to stop the game.

As we are going to compare the current score with a score target, we need to declare it. In GameScene.m, add the following line after `BOOL _collisionDetected;`:

```
// Score target
int _gameOverScore;
```

Initialize its value before `[self initSnowBalls];`:

```
// Initialize the score target
_gameOverScore = 150;
```

There is nothing new here, we are just declaring an integer and initializing its value to 150. You can set the value that you want: the higher the score, the more chances the snowballs will get to hit the yeti!

Now we must detect when the score target has been reached, and this task is best performed as soon as the score increases, in other words, in the `increaseScore` method. Go there and add the following lines after `_gameScore += 10;`:

```
// If we reach the score target, the game is over
if (_gameScore >= _gameOverScore){
    [self gameOver];
    return;
}
```

If the condition is true, the score has been reached, then we call the `gameOver` method and exit from `increaseScore`.

We just need to declare and implement the new method. In `GameScene.h`, add the following line:

```
- (void) gameOver;
```

Back in `GameScene.m`, implement it by adding the following lines:

```
- (void) gameOver{

    CGSize screenSize = [CCDirector sharedDirector].viewSize;

    // Initializing and positioning the game over label
    CCLabelTTF *gameOverLabel = [CCLabelTTF
    labelWithString:@"LEVEL COMPLETE!" fontName:@"Chalkduster"
    fontSize:40];

    gameOverLabel.color = [CCColor greenColor];
    gameOverLabel.position = CGPointMake(screenSize.width/2,
    screenSize.height/2);

    [self addChild:gameOverLabel];

    // Removing score label
    [self removeChild:_scoreLabel];

    // Stop throwing snowballs
    [self unscheduleAllSelectors];

    // Disable touches
    self.userInteractionEnabled = FALSE;

    // Stop background music and sound effects
    [[OALSimpleAudio sharedInstance] stopEverything];
}
```

This method just needs to highlight the `removeChild` call. It removes the label from the scene and forces the cleanup of all running and scheduled actions.

Run the code and try to achieve 150 points without being touched!

1-star challenge – accurate collision detection

The collision detection we implemented is a little inaccurate due to the yeti's texture. The CGRectIntersectsRect class is working properly but the collision is being triggered as soon as the snowball enters into contact with the snow under the sledge. Now that you know how to calculate the distance between two points, try to detect the collisions when the distance between the snowball and the anchor point of the yeti is small enough.

The solution

To achieve this new collision detection, we just need to modify one line. Go to the update method and modify the condition:

```
if (CGRectIntersectsRect(snowBall.boundingBox, _yeti.boundingBox)
&& !_collisionDetected) {
```

By the new one using ccpDistance:

```
if(ccpDistance(snowBall.position, _yeti.position) <=
_yeti.contentSize.width/2) {
```

As we want to know the distance between the snowball and the yeti, we check it in the `for` loop and we just calculate the distance between their positions. I decided that if this distance is lower than half the yeti, it's close enough to be a collision.

2-star challenge – having three lives

We have developed a way to end the game using a top score to reach, but you know most of the time games end because you've lost all your lives. I want you to take what you learned when creating the score label on the screen and put a lives label in the top-left corner of the screen that will represent the lives left. This label will show the number of lives as a countdown starting from 3, and this counter will decrease when a snowball hits the yeti. Then, as soon as the counter arrives at 0, you will stop the game and show a red **GAME OVER** label in the center of the screen, similar to the previous **LEVEL COMPLETED** label.

The solution

This is very similar to what we did to make the score count and game over labels. To achieve this, you will need an integer variable for the lives counter and a label to show its value. So in `GameScene.m`, add the following lines after `int _gameOverScore;`:

```
int _numLives;
CCLabelTTF *_livesLabel;
```

Initialize their values by adding the following code lines to the `init` method, just before `return self;`:

```
_numLives = 3;

_livesLabel = [CCLabelTTF labelWithString:[NSString
stringWithFormat:@"Lives: %i", _numLives]
fontName:@"Chalkduster" fontSize:15];

_livesLabel.color = [CCColor orangeColor];
_livesLabel.anchorPoint = CGPointMake(0.0, 1.0);
_livesLabel.position = CGPointMake(0, screenSize.height);

[self addChild:_livesLabel];
```

We are setting the number of lives counter to 3 and initializing the label with the appropriate text formatted to show this counter. Then we configure the label to be orange colored and we set its anchor point to the top-left because we want it left and top-aligned. Once we have set the anchor point, we can set its position to the top-left corner of the screen, and don't forget to add it to the scene.

Until now we've just initialized the variables, so let's make them work! As we want the counter to decrease when a snowball hits the yeti, we will perform this update on the `manageCollision` method. Go there and add the following lines at the very beginning of the method:

```
_numLives--;
[_livesLabel setString:[NSString stringWithFormat:@"Lives: %i",
_numLives]];
if (_numLives == 0) {
    [self gameOverLives];
    return;
}
```

The first thing to do is decrease the counter and update the label. Then, if the counter arrives at 0, we need to finish the game and exit from the method. We just need to declare the `gameOverLives` method by adding the following line to `GameScene.h`:

```
-(void) gameOverLives;
```

Implement the method in `GameScene.m`:

```
-(void) gameOverLives{

    CGSize screenSize = [CCDirector sharedDirector].viewSize;
    // Initializing and positioning the game over label
    CCLabelTTF *gameOverLabel = [CCLabelTTF labelWithString:@"GAME
OVER" fontName:@"Chalkduster" fontSize:50];

    gameOverLabel.color = [CCColor redColor];
    gameOverLabel.position = CGPointMake(screenSize.width/2,
    screenSize.height/2);

    [self addChild:gameOverLabel];

    [self removeChild:_livesLabel];

    // Removing score label
    [self removeChild:_scoreLabel];
```

```
    // Stop throwing snowballs
    [self unscheduleAllSelectors];

    // Disable touches
    self.userInteractionEnabled = FALSE;

    // Stop background music and sound effects
    [[OALSimpleAudio sharedInstance] stopEverything];
}
```

This method is very similar to the one we implement to finish the game due to the achievement of the score target, which is why I will just focus on the differences. In this case, we create a red label with the text GAME OVER and put it in the center of the screen. Then we remove both score and lives labels and stop scheduled selectors and sounds. That's it!

Summary

At the beginning of this chapter, we had our first contact with a Cocos2d project. We created a new project and took an overview of it, understanding some of the classes that are part of this framework.

Then we were introduced to CCNode, one of the main classes, as it's the class parent for some of the most important objects we will use when developing games. Also, we showed how the scene graph should look, with a parent CCScene node as root and the different children nodes hanging from it.

You learned how to create a scene and add sprites to it, taking into account their anchor point to position them in the desired place. You also learned to add a background image with a customized z-order to be sure it lies behind the rest of the nodes.

I explained to you the characteristics to bear in mind when developing a game for both iPhone and iPad devices, such as screen resolution and relative positions.

Then you enabled user interaction to handle touches, which you used to know where to move the yeti using the CCActionMoveTo action. At the same time, you learned how to keep a sprite within the screen limits.

You learned how to set up a bunch of enemies, snowballs in this case, in an array, initializing their positions to keep them out of view waiting to attack. At this point, you learned how to get one snowball randomly and to apply a horizontal movement until it reached the right-hand edge of the screen.

Also, you handled the collisions between the snowballs and the yeti and took advantage of it to create a tint and blink action to execute when a collision happens.

To give some playability to the game, you learned how to place labels using their anchor points and how to initialize and update their text.

Toward the end of the chapter, you learned where you can get some audio sources and how you can create your own. Once you had the background music and the sound effects, you learned how to use them in your game.

In the last section of the chapter, you learned how to declare a condition to finish the game and which actions are needed to illustrate the game is over.

Now that we know how to load and move sprites, let's take them further to create complex objects and realistic effects.

2
Explosions and UFOs

One of the most interesting characteristics in iOS devices is the **accelerometer**, thanks to which you can, among other functionalities, control the movement of the main character of a game without needing to touch the screen. In this chapter, you will learn how to take advantage of this feature and mix it with particles such as explosions and fire to develop a classic shoot 'em up game like 1942, but in this case, the enemies will be UFOs. As you will need some spaceships, you will learn how to create them by extending the CCSprite class and I will also teach you how to implement the **parallax effect** to create an illusion of depth in a 2D game. To conclude, I will introduce you to geometric primitives such as lines, squares, and circles and how to draw them.

Things you will learn in this chapter include:

- How to use the accelerometer
- How to load and set up a particle system
- How to create sprites that extend CCSprite
- How to implement the parallax effect in a 2D game
- How to draw geometric primitives on a CCNode class

Handling the accelerometer input

Since the apparition of the first iPhone generation, mobile devices are equipped with a 3-axis accelerometer (x, y, and z) to detect orientation changes and it has modified the course of handheld games. It allows players to interact with games without the need to touch the screen, and it allows developers to create new subgenres of games too.

Throughout this chapter, you will mix this hardware feature with a classic arcades genre to develop the following game: the planet Earth has been attacked by an army of UFOs whose sole purpose is to wipe out all of mankind, but fortunately, a mad scientist equipped with some of his inventions is brave enough to defend us.

To control the movements of Dr. Nicholas Fringe, our mad scientist, you will take advantage of the accelerometer, but first of all you need a clean Xcode project. As you learned in the previous chapter how to create a new project and how to get it ready to start developing, we will skip this step, so open the code files of this chapter from the code bundle, where you'll find `ExplosionsAndUFOs_init.zip`, which contains the initial project.

Linking the CoreMotion framework

The first thing we will need to do to enable accelerometer management is link the CoreMotion framework:

1. Open the `ExplosionsAndUFOs` project you just unzipped and go to the **General** properties screen where you will see the already linked frameworks at the bottom.

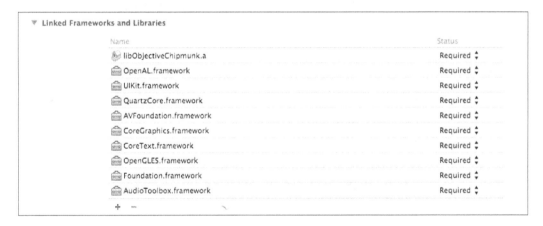

2. Click on **+** and a dialog will appear where you will see the available frameworks to be linked.

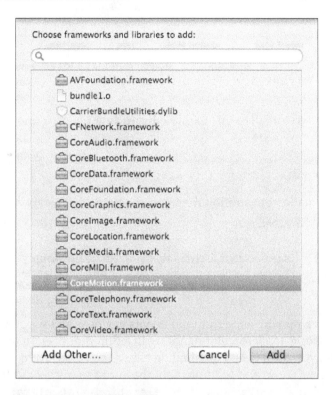

3. Look for **CoreMotion.framework** and click on **Add**.

This framework allows our game to receive gyroscope and accelerometer data, which we can process and work with. It includes a set of classes to get, manage, and measure motion data such as attitude, rotation rate, acceleration, or number of steps taken by the user. In our case, we are going to use `CMMotionManager`, the class in charge of the management of four types of motion: raw accelerometer data, raw gyroscope data, raw magnetometer data, and processed device-motion data; in other words, what Dr. Nicholas Fringe needs to fly over the clouds.

The next thing we need to do is include the `CoreMotion` classes; to achieve this, add the following line to `GameScene.h` after `import "cocos2d.h"`:

```
#import <CoreMotion/CoreMotion.h>
```

Then you will need to declare a private instance variable of CMMotionManager, so go to GameScene.m and replace @implementation GameScene with the following block of code:

```
@implementation GameScene
{
    // Declaring a private CMMotionManager instance variable
    CMMotionManager *_accManager;
}
```

Now you just need to initialize this variable by adding the next line in the init method before return self;:

```
    // Initialize motion manager
    _accManager = [[CMMotionManager alloc] init];
```

This way, you've made your motion manager ready to start receiving data from the accelerometer and gyroscope.

 It's important to stress that you should create only one CMMotionManager instance as multiple instances can adversely impact the rate of the data received.

If you've been working with accelerometer events in Cocos2d 2.x, you will realize that we are initializing accelerometer handling in a different way. In fact, in the previous version, you didn't need to initialize CMMotionManager but to enable isAccelerometerEnabled and to implement the accelerometer:(UIAccelerometer *)accelerometer didAccelerate:(UiAcceleration *)acceleration method. This method in a class is derived from CCLayer, which is currently deprecated in Cocos2d 3.x.

Once you have initialized the CMMotionManager instance, there is one thing left to do to start and finish receiving motion data and that is manually starting and stopping it. An effective strategy to carry it out is to take advantage of the onEnter and onExit methods available in every class that inherits CCNode, and remember CCScene is one of them.

onEnter and onExit

These two methods are very useful to control what is happening when a node enters or leaves the main screen, as they are called as soon as a node comes into action or leaves. In total, there are four methods to cover the application behavior when a node enters or leaves with a transition:

- onEnter: This is called when the transition starts
- onEnterTransitionDidFinish: This is called when the transition finishes

- onExit: This is called when the transition finishes

- onExitTransitionDidStart: This is called when the transition starts

We need to activate accelerometer management as soon as the scene appears and deactivate it when the scene disappears; that's why we're going to focus just on the common versions of onEnter and onExit.

Go ahead and include the following method implementations in GameScene.m:

```
// Start receiving accelerometer events
- (void)onEnter {
    [super onEnter];
    [_accManager startAccelerometerUpdates];
}

// Stop receiving accelerometer events
- (void)onExit {
    [super onExit];
    [_accManager stopAccelerometerUpdates];
}
```

One thing to emphasize is the call to the super implementations [super onEnter] and [super onExit]. This means that we are not overriding these methods but extending their behavior because we want to keep their parent functionality.

Converting accelerometer input into movements

Now that our game is waiting for moving data, we need something to realize what is happening when you move your device.

 Remember that this time you will need a physical iOS device as iOS Simulator isn't capable of simulating this data.

Let's create a sprite for our crazy scientist so we can move him along the screen. In Xcode, follow these steps:

1. Right-click on the **Resources** group and select **Add Files to "ExplosionsAndUFOs"**....

2. Select the scientist.png image you will find in the Resources folder.

3. Be sure that **Copy items into destination group's folder (if needed)** is selected and click on **Add**.

In this chapter, we are not covering `Universal` apps, so when specifying an image name, you will find its `-hd.png` version too, which will cover all iPhone devices but you won't find the versions related to iPads.

First, we will declare private instance variables for both accelerometer data and acceleration by adding the next lines after `CMMotionManager *_accManager;`:

```
// Declare accelerometer data variable
CMAccelerometerData *_accData;

// Declare acceleration variable
CMAcceleration _acceleration;
```

Then declare the `CCSprite` private instance variable for our scientist by adding the following line:

```
// Declaring a private CCSprite instance variable
CCSprite *_scientist;
```

Initialize it by adding the following lines to the `init` method just before `return self;`:

```
// Initialize the scientist
_scientist = [CCSprite spriteWithImageNamed:@"scientist.png"];

CGSize screenSize = [CCDirector sharedDirector].viewSize;

_scientist.position = CGPointMake(screenSize.width/2,
_scientist.contentSize.height);
[self addChild:_scientist];
```

This block of code is pretty simple: you're initializing a sprite using the scientist's image you just added to the project and then you're placing it in a relative position before adding it to the scene.

Nothing new so far. Now it's time to make the scientist move on the palm of our hand. First add the following block of code to `GameScene.m`:

```
-(void) update:(CCTime)delta{

    // Getting accelerometer data
    _accData = _accManager.accelerometerData;

    // Getting acceleration
```

```
_acceleration = _accData.acceleration;

// Calculating next position on 'x' axis
CGFloat nextXPosition = _scientist.position.x +
_acceleration.x * 1500 * delta;

// Calculating next position on 'y' axis
CGFloat nextYPosition = _scientist.position.y +
_acceleration.y * 1500 * delta;

// Avoiding positions out of bounds
nextXPosition = clampf(nextXPosition,
_scientist.contentSize.width / 2, self.contentSize.width -
_scientist.contentSize.width / 2);
nextYPosition = clampf(nextYPosition,
_scientist.contentSize.height / 2, self.contentSize.height -
_scientist.contentSize.height / 2);

_scientist.position = CGPointMake(nextXPosition,
nextYPosition);
}
```

We are using the update method to retrieve data from the accelerometer, from which we take the acceleration information. Then we calculate the next position on the *x* and *y* axes as the sum of the current scientist position plus the multiplication of the acceleration on the corresponding axis, delta, and a constant that I decided to be 1500.

By default, the delta variable's value is *1/60* as the update method is called every frame and the default frame rate is 60 fps. The act of multiplying the velocity of a node by delta is what developers call **framerate independent movement** and it's a very sensitive issue. It means that if the framerate drops below 60 fps, the movement of the node won't be affected. However, it will affect a framerate-dependent node (the node's velocity isn't multiplied by delta), decreasing its performance by slowing it down and being overloaded.

But what causes a framerate drop? System events, loading textures, or large sprites may cause your game's framerate to drop, so you will need to keep in mind the debug stats while developing the game. Applying the delta solution can have side effects too, such as bad collision detection on low framerates. But for now and for convenience, we will keep our node's framerate independent, that is, we will multiply its velocity by delta.

Going back to the preceding code, once we've calculated the next positions, we seek to ensure that these positions are inside the screen. Do you remember how we solved this issue in the previous chapter? The `clampf` function is a fancier way of dealing with nodes going out of bounds, you just need to provide the position you want to check, and the minimum and maximum positions available and it will do the rest for you.

Okay, time to run the game for the very first time!

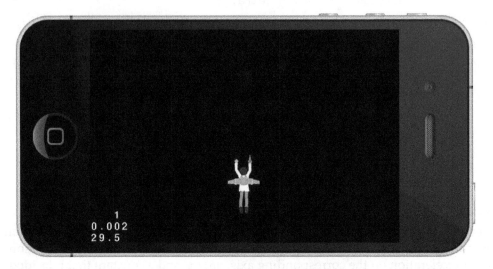

As you can see, there are two unwanted things: the movement of our sprite is opposite to what we expected and the display orientation is landscape, but we are developing a shoot 'em up so it should be portrait.

In fact, the unexpected movement is due to the display orientation but wait and breathe, as we're going to solve both problems with just one line of code; if you don't believe me, keep reading.

Go to the `didFinishLaunchingWithOptions` method on `AppDelegate.m` and add the following setup option to `setupCocos2dWithOptions`:

```
CCSetupScreenOrientation: CCScreenOrientationPortrait,
```

Run the game again and this will verify that everything is under control now.

There is another way of managing accelerometer input and that is making use of the `startAccelerometerUpdatesToQueue:withHandler` method available in `CMMotionManager`. It receives a queue of operations and invokes a `CMAccelerometerHandler` block to handle the accelerometer data. For now, we will keep it simple using the `startAccelerometerUpdates` approach.

Calibrating the accelerometer

As one last thing, you may have noticed that you must keep your device flat because if you position it in the usual way, the scientist will move to the bottom of the screen as soon as the game starts. This has a pretty easy solution; we just need to take into account the initial acceleration values so we can compensate for them and stand the device comfortably as we wish.

Declare the next variable just after `CMAcceleration _acceleration;`:

```
// Declare the initial acceleration variable
CMAcceleration _initialAcceleration;
```

Go back to the `update` method, and add these lines after `_acceleration = _accData.acceleration;`:

```
// As soon as we get acceleration store it as the initial
acceleration to compensate
if (_initialAcceleration.x == 0 && _initialAcceleration.y == 0
&& _acceleration.x != 0 && _acceleration.y != 0) {
    _initialAcceleration = _acceleration;
}
```

This block detects when the device starts receiving acceleration data and we store the first piece of information in the `initialAcceleration` variable so we can compensate for the inclination.

Find these two lines:

```
CGFloat nextXPosition = _scientist.position.x + _acceleration.x *
1500 * delta;

CGFloat nextYPosition = _scientist.position.y + _acceleration.y *
1500 * delta;
```

Replace them with these two lines:

```
CGFloat nextXPosition = _scientist.position.x + (_acceleration.x -
_initialAcceleration.x) * 1500 * delta;

CGFloat nextYPosition = _scientist.position.y + (_acceleration.y -
_initialAcceleration.y) * 1500 * delta;
```

We are modifying the original movement strategy; now we subtract the initial acceleration on both axes from the current acceleration so the user is not required to keep the device flat.

If you run the game now, you will notice that you can stand your device as you want!

Before going ahead, let's clean the code a little. I decided to multiply the node's velocity by `1500` as it provided the desired results, but you can modify it at your convenience. Add the following line at the top of `GameScene.m` just after `#import "GameScene.h"`:

```
// Acceleration constant multiplier
#define ACCELERATION_MULTIPLIER 1500.0
```

Modify these lines:

```
CGFloat nextXPosition = _scientist.position.x + (_acceleration.x -
_initialAcceleration.x) * 1500 * delta;

CGFloat nextYPosition = _scientist.position.y + (_acceleration.y -
_initialAcceleration.y) * 1500 * delta;
```

Replace them with the following ones:

```
CGFloat nextXPosition = _scientist.position.x + (_acceleration.x -
_initialAcceleration.x) * ACCELERATION_MULTIPLIER * delta;

CGFloat nextYPosition = _scientist.position.y + (_acceleration.y -
_initialAcceleration.y) * ACCELERATION_MULTIPLIER * delta;
```

We have created a constant and replaced the hardcoded values so we can quickly change the velocity of both axes by just updating a constant. This way, the code looks cleaner.

 Using constants instead of hardcoded values is one of the key points in clean code development.

On the other hand, let's make screenSize a private variable so we can use its value whenever we need. First, add the following line after the line declaring the _scientist sprite:

```
// Declare global variable for screen size
CGSize _screenSize;
```

Then go back to the init method and find the following line:

```
CGSize screenSize = [CCDirector sharedDirector].viewSize;
```

Replace it with the following one:

```
_screenSize = [CCDirector sharedDirector].viewSize;
```

Finally, find this line:

```
_scientist.position = CGPointMake(screenSize.width/2,
_scientist.contentSize.height);
```

Replace it with this line:

```
_scientist.position = CGPointMake(_screenSize.width/2,
_scientist.contentSize.height);
```

Again, this last block of code is a variable replacement so we can use `screenSize` globally in the class.

Now that we've put our scientist on the screen and we can move him, let's give him a sky to fly through!

Implementing the parallax effect in Cocos2d

The parallax effect is a scrolling technique used in 2D games that simulates depth and displacement by moving the foreground layers faster than background layers. This technique was developed initially to be used in traditional animation in the 1930s and was first used in computer games in the early 80s.

This effect consists of making our brain think that we are looking at displacement similar to what happens when we are traveling on a train: we can see the trees near the railway passing fast, but if we look to the houses placed further away, they pass a little slower, and if you look at the mountains in the background, they look almost immobile. If we place our scientist over a ground layer that will displace slowly and above this layer we scroll a clouds layer from the top to the bottom of the screen, our brain will think that Dr. Fringe is flying over the clouds thanks to his amazing backpack-reactor.

CCParallaxNode

As the parallax effect is a very common technique used in 2D games, Cocos2d includes `CCParallaxNode`, a class inherited from `CCNode` that will facilitate our work.

Thanks to this class's method `addChild:z:parallaxRatio:positionOffset` we can specify the nodes (children) that will take part in the parallax scrolling, which will move faster or slower depending on the ratio configured. We can also indicate the z-order and the parallax offset to use. Don't worry if you don't understand how it works right now, it's better when you can see the effect running.

First of all, you will need to add some images to your project as they will be used to create the different layers, so follow these steps:

1. In the project navigator, select the **Resources** group.
2. Right-click and select **Add Files to "ExplosionsAndUFOs"....**

3. Select the `background1.png`, `background2.png`, `background3.png`, `background4.png`, `clouds1.png`, and `clouds2.png` files from the `Resources` folder.

4. Be sure that **Copy items into destination group's folder (if needed)** is selected and click on **Add**.

These are the background images you just added:

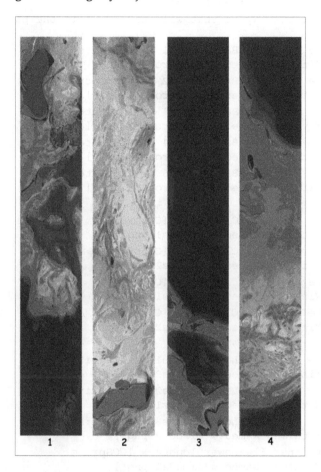

As you can see, the four background images are components of a whole image that will simulate us flying over the Earth. I cut it into four subdivisions because we can't load images bigger than 4096 x 4096 pixels.

The `clouds1.png` and `clouds2.png` images are two different layers that we will combine to achieve the parallax effect.

Now add the following line at the end of the `init` method, just before `return self;`:

```
// Configure parallax effect
[self configureParallaxEffect];
```

We will implement the method by adding the following code in `GameScene.m`:

```objc
-(void) configureParallaxEffect{
    // Create the layers that will take part in the parallax
    effect
    CCSprite *parallaxBackground1 = [CCSprite
    spriteWithImageNamed:@"background1.png"];
    CCSprite *parallaxBackground2 = [CCSprite
    spriteWithImageNamed:@"background2.png"];
    CCSprite *parallaxBackground3 = [CCSprite
    spriteWithImageNamed:@"background3.png"];
    CCSprite *parallaxBackground4 = [CCSprite
    spriteWithImageNamed:@"background4.png"];
    CCSprite *parallaxBackground5 = [CCSprite
    spriteWithImageNamed:@"background1.png"];

    CCSprite *parallaxClouds1 = [CCSprite
    spriteWithImageNamed:@"clouds1.png"];
    CCSprite *parallaxClouds2 = [CCSprite
    spriteWithImageNamed:@"clouds2.png"];
    CCSprite *parallaxClouds3 = [CCSprite
    spriteWithImageNamed:@"clouds1.png"];
    CCSprite *parallaxClouds4 = [CCSprite
    spriteWithImageNamed:@"clouds2.png"];

    CCSprite *parallaxLowerClouds1 = [CCSprite
    spriteWithImageNamed:@"clouds2.png"];
    CCSprite *parallaxLowerClouds2 = [CCSprite
    spriteWithImageNamed:@"clouds1.png"];
    CCSprite *parallaxLowerClouds3 = [CCSprite
    spriteWithImageNamed:@"clouds2.png"];
    CCSprite *parallaxLowerClouds4 = [CCSprite
    spriteWithImageNamed:@"clouds1.png"];

}
```

A parallax effect needs several layers to move at different speeds in order to simulate depth and displacement; that's why we need to create a CCSprite instance for each of them and why we're using the images we just added to the project. As we want to simulate that Dr. Fringe is flying over the whole planet, we need a very large background, but we have to deal with the restriction that we can't load images bigger than 4096 x 4096; that's why we divided the background into four smaller images. We're going to concatenate them one after the other until we fly all around the world. Sometimes, you will need to add an extra parallax sprite (as we're doing with parallaxBackground5) to cover the blank spaces between the first background and the last to achieve endless scrolling.

Before doing anything else, we will modify the sprites' anchor point to the bottom-left corner so we can align the sprites with the screen easily. To achieve this, add the following lines just at the end of configureParallaxEffect:

```
// Modify the sprites anchor point
parallaxBackground1.anchorPoint = CGPointMake(0, 0);
parallaxBackground2.anchorPoint = CGPointMake(0, 0);
parallaxBackground3.anchorPoint = CGPointMake(0, 0);
parallaxBackground4.anchorPoint = CGPointMake(0, 0);
parallaxBackground5.anchorPoint = CGPointMake(0, 0);

parallaxClouds1.anchorPoint = CGPointMake(0, 0);
parallaxClouds2.anchorPoint = CGPointMake(0, 0);
parallaxClouds3.anchorPoint = CGPointMake(0, 0);
parallaxClouds4.anchorPoint = CGPointMake(0, 0);

parallaxLowerClouds1.anchorPoint = CGPointMake(0, 0);
parallaxLowerClouds2.anchorPoint = CGPointMake(0, 0);
parallaxLowerClouds3.anchorPoint = CGPointMake(0, 0);
parallaxLowerClouds4.anchorPoint = CGPointMake(0, 0);
```

For the moment, we're just setting up layers to ease layers movement. Then add these lines in the same method:

```
// Modify opacity
parallaxLowerClouds1.opacity = 0.3;
parallaxLowerClouds2.opacity = 0.3;
parallaxLowerClouds3.opacity = 0.3;
parallaxLowerClouds4.opacity = 0.3;

parallaxClouds1.opacity = 0.8;
parallaxClouds2.opacity = 0.8;
parallaxClouds3.opacity = 0.8;
parallaxClouds4.opacity = 0.8;
```

We're modifying the opacity for the clouds layers. We want to place both cloud layers between the scientist and the ground, each of them with a different opacity as we want to simulate that they're different types of clouds and we want to see what is behind them. The opacity of a node is a value that may vary from 0 to 1, which means that we're setting 80 and 30 percent of the original opacity to `parallaxClouds#` and `parallaxLowerClouds#` respectively.

Then we add the following lines at the end of `configureParallaxEffect`:

```
// Define start positions
CGPoint backgroundOffset1 = CGPointZero;
CGPoint backgroundOffset2 = CGPointMake(0,
parallaxBackground1.contentSize.height);
CGPoint backgroundOffset3 = CGPointMake(0,
parallaxBackground1.contentSize.height +
parallaxBackground2.contentSize.height);
CGPoint backgroundOffset4 = CGPointMake(0,
parallaxBackground1.contentSize.height +
parallaxBackground2.contentSize.height +
parallaxBackground3.contentSize.height);
CGPoint backgroundOffset5 = CGPointMake(0,
parallaxBackground1.contentSize.height +
parallaxBackground2.contentSize.height +
parallaxBackground3.contentSize.height +
parallaxBackground4.contentSize.height);

CGPoint lowerClouds1Offset = CGPointMake(0,
_screenSize.height);
CGPoint lowerClouds2Offset = CGPointMake(0, _screenSize.height
+ 3 * parallaxBackground1.contentSize.height);
CGPoint lowerClouds3Offset = CGPointMake(0, _screenSize.height
+ 6 * parallaxBackground1.contentSize.height);
CGPoint lowerClouds4Offset = CGPointMake(0, _screenSize.height
+ 9 * parallaxBackground1.contentSize.height);

CGPoint clouds1Offset = CGPointMake(0, _screenSize.height);
CGPoint clouds2Offset = CGPointMake(0, _screenSize.height + 3
* parallaxBackground1.contentSize.height);
CGPoint clouds3Offset = CGPointMake(0, _screenSize.height + 6
* parallaxBackground1.contentSize.height);
CGPoint clouds4Offset = CGPointMake(0, _screenSize.height + 9
* parallaxBackground1.contentSize.height);
```

With these lines, we're initializing the different offsets that we will need for each layer of the parallax node; in other words, we are specifying its position on the screen. As the background will cover the screen initially, we give a CGPointZero value to the first background layer's offset that is equivalent to CGPointMake(0, 0). Then, we prepare the rest of parallaxBackground# (parallaxBackground1, parallaxBackground2, parallaxBackground3, and parallaxBackground4) to be placed one after the other and then we set backgroundOffset5 at the end to cover the blank space the backgrounds leave behind as they scroll down.

Cloud's offsets don't need to cover the whole space; that's why we set them at a higher position so they will appear as we fly.

Once we have all we need to create a parallax effect, we can initialize the parallax node and append the children to it. Add the following lines just after the offset's initialization:

```
// Initialize parallax node
CCParallaxNode *parallaxNode = [CCParallaxNode node];

// Add parallax children defining z-order, ratio and offset
[parallaxNode addChild:parallaxBackground1 z:0
parallaxRatio:CGPointMake(0, 1)
positionOffset:backgroundOffset1];
[parallaxNode addChild:parallaxBackground2 z:0
parallaxRatio:CGPointMake(0, 1)
positionOffset:backgroundOffset2];
[parallaxNode addChild:parallaxBackground3 z:0
parallaxRatio:CGPointMake(0, 1)
positionOffset:backgroundOffset3];
[parallaxNode addChild:parallaxBackground4 z:0
parallaxRatio:CGPointMake(0, 1)
positionOffset:backgroundOffset4];
[parallaxNode addChild:parallaxBackground5 z:0
parallaxRatio:CGPointMake(0, 1)
positionOffset:backgroundOffset5];

[parallaxNode addChild:parallaxLowerClouds1 z:1
parallaxRatio:CGPointMake(0, 2)
positionOffset:lowerClouds1Offset];
[parallaxNode addChild:parallaxLowerClouds2 z:1
parallaxRatio:CGPointMake(0, 2)
positionOffset:lowerClouds2Offset];
[parallaxNode addChild:parallaxLowerClouds3 z:1
parallaxRatio:CGPointMake(0, 2)
positionOffset:lowerClouds3Offset];
```

```
[parallaxNode addChild:parallaxLowerClouds4 z:1
parallaxRatio:CGPointMake(0, 2)
positionOffset:lowerClouds4Offset];

[parallaxNode addChild:parallaxClouds1 z:2
parallaxRatio:CGPointMake(0, 3) positionOffset:clouds1Offset];
[parallaxNode addChild:parallaxClouds2 z:2
parallaxRatio:CGPointMake(0, 3) positionOffset:clouds2Offset];
[parallaxNode addChild:parallaxClouds3 z:2
parallaxRatio:CGPointMake(0, 3) positionOffset:clouds3Offset];
[parallaxNode addChild:parallaxClouds4 z:2
parallaxRatio:CGPointMake(0, 3) positionOffset:clouds4Offset];
```

The preceding lines configure the behavior of the different layers by giving them the proper z-order value, ratio, and position offset. With z-order, we will configure which layers will be shown above or below, `positionOffset` receives a `CGPoint` instance that will multiply the speed of the node in the x and y axes, and the position offset sets the clouds' initial position.

We also need to modify the scientist's z-order so go to the line where we added the scientist's sprite to the scene:

```
[self addChild:_scientist];
```

Replace it with:

```
[self addChild:_scientist z:1];
```

Thanks to z-order, we place the ground layer on the lower level (*z-order = 0*), then the lower clouds layer (*z-order = 1*), and the top clouds layer (*z-order = 2*). These z-order values don't concern the scene hierarchy but they do concern parallax node's hierarchy, and will indicate the order in which parallax layers will be placed. We need to update the scientist z-order because we added the parallax node to the scene with its default z-order value, and if we don't change it, the scientist will appear behind the background layer and will be hidden to our eyes.

Once we've decided the order of the layers, we need to specify the ratio of the layer's movement. In our case, we are configuring `parallaxBackground#` to move at the same speed as `CCParallaxNode`, `parallaxLowerClouds#` to move at double the speed of `CCParallaxNode`, and `parallaxClouds#` to move at three times the speed of `CCParallaxNode`. You will realize that we just specified these `parallaxRatio` values for the y axis; that's because we're planning to only scroll vertically.

If you remember the concept the parallax effect is based on, we are going to simulate depth and movement by scrolling layers at different speeds; that's why we set different values, but you can modify the parallax ratio at your convenience to achieve the desired effect.

Now that the parallax node is configured, we can add it to the scene as a common node. Then there is only one thing left to do: create the movement actions. Add these lines at the end of `configureParallaxEffect`:

```
[self addChild:parallaxNode];

// Create a move action
CCActionMoveBy *move1 = [CCActionMoveBy actionWithDuration:24
position:CGPointMake(0, -
(parallaxBackground1.contentSize.height +
parallaxBackground2.contentSize.height +
parallaxBackground3.contentSize.height +
parallaxBackground4.contentSize.height))];

CCActionMoveBy *move2 = [CCActionMoveBy actionWithDuration:0
position:CGPointMake(0, parallaxBackground1.contentSize.height
+ parallaxBackground2.contentSize.height +
parallaxBackground3.contentSize.height +
parallaxBackground4.contentSize.height)];

// Create a sequence with both movements
CCActionSequence *sequence = [CCActionSequence
actionWithArray:@[move1, move2]];

// Create an infinite loop for the movement action
CCActionRepeatForever *loop = [CCActionRepeatForever
actionWithAction:sequence];

// Run the action
[parallaxNode runAction:loop];
```

As we want to move all the layers from the top to the bottom, we will need to configure a movement action that displaces the layers until they reach a desired point. In our case, we set the final point at a negative position equal to the sum of all the background's height; this way it will show all the background layers falling down one after the other, simulating that it's scrolling repeatedly.

As you know from the previous chapter, we can specify the duration of the movement, and the backpack-reactor is powerful enough to fly around the world in just 24 seconds.

We need to recover the original layer's position; that's why we create another movement action that will set the parallax node to the original position instantly. If we concatenate both movements in a sequence, it will look like nothing happened and if we run this sequence indefinitely using `CCActionRepeatForever`, this will achieve the endless parallax scrolling that we need. Then if `parallaxNode` runs the created `loop` action, magic will happen. Run the game on Xcode and enjoy your first parallax effect—don't you feel like Walt Disney?

You can see that Dr. Nicholas Fringe looks like he is falling from the sky because he has nothing to make him fly, that is, his backpack-reactor is shut down. Don't worry, as we're about to give him a hand to save his life.

Particle systems

I always say that video games are comparable to films, differences aside, because they tell stories, have an argument, different scenes, a soundtrack, and special effects. Yes, you read correctly, you can add special effects, or **particle systems** as they're commonly known in computer games, to your games.

In computer graphics, this technique is commonly used because it simulates several natural and meteorological phenomena such as snow, sun, rain, fire, meteors, and smoke. It also simulates other special effects such as spirals, explosions, fireworks, and other lighting effects by using a large amount of small images. If you think about natural phenomena, like rain for example, it is composed of hundreds of water droplets and so that's what we need to replicate if we want to simulate a particle system in Cocos2d.

You might be thinking that this task must be hard and offers little possibilities, but in this section, you will learn to create and customize your own particle effects easily.

CCParticleSystem

The class responsible for creating and managing particle effects is CCParticleSystem, a subclass of CCParticleSystemBase, which inherits from CCNode. It offers some features that its parent class doesn't, such as:

- Floating-point numbers in particle sizes
- Subrectangles
- Batched rendering to improve performance
- Rotation
- Scalation

This class allows you to configure several attributes to achieve the effect you're looking for, but before customizing a particle system, let's create a simple one.

We will need a private CCParticleSystem instance variable, so in GameScene.m, add the following line after CGSize _screenSize;:

```
// Declare a private CCParticleSystem instance variable
CCParticleSystem *_fire;
```

Note how we use the underscore character to identify private variables. On the other hand, instance variables can also be declared as private by specifying the @private modifier.

Then add the following lines to the `init` method, just after `[self configureParallaxEffect];`:

```
// Init the fire particle
_fire = [CCParticleFire node];

// Place the fire
_fire.position = CGPointMake(_scientist.position.x,
_scientist.position.y);

// Add the particle system to the scene
[self addChild:_fire z:1];
```

As you can see, creating a particle system is as easy as creating a common sprite. We declared a `CCParticleSystem` instance and then initialized it by sending the `node` message to `CCParticleFire` so we have a fire particle. Then we place the fire in the middle of the scientist's back and we add it to the scene with a z-order of 1 to be above the parallax node. Pretty short and simple, isn't it? Run the project and let's see what happens.

Where is the fire? Don't worry, I introduced this issue deliberately to expose a particularity of `CCParticleSystem`. If you take a look at **Target Output** at the bottom of the Xcode screen, you will see the following log:

```
2014-05-29 23:12:18.760 ExplosionsAndUFOs[13561:60b] -[CCFileUtils fu
llPathForFilename:contentScale:] : cocos2d: Warning: File not found:
fire.png
2014-05-29 23:12:18.761 ExplosionsAndUFOs[13561:60b] cocos2d: Couldn't
find file:fire.png

2014-05-29 23:14:17.359 ExplosionsAndUFOs[13561:60b] cocos2d:
animation stopped
2014-05-29 23:14:17.385 ExplosionsAndUFOs[13561:60b] cocos2d:
animation started with frame interval: 4.00
2014-05-29 23:14:17.405 ExplosionsAndUFOs[13561:60b] cocos2d:
animation stopped
```

Okay it is important to notice that our particle system is looking for a file named `fire.png` and is not finding it; that's why there is no visual representation. This means that we must provide the texture to be used to represent the particles.

You can solve this issue by following these steps:

1. In the project navigator, select the **Resources** group.
2. Right-click and select **Add Files to "ExplosionsAndUFOs"...**.

3. Select the `fire.png` file (which I downloaded from `http://misteraibo.
deviantart.com/art/Fire-311421529`) in the `Resources` folder you
unzipped and click on **Add**.

Run your game and you will see something like the following screenshot:

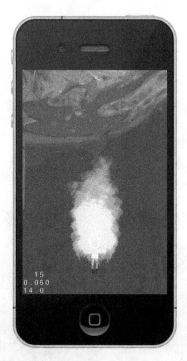

You just created your first particle system by adding the `fire.png` file into your
project. It's the default file the particle system will look for, but you can choose a
different file to create the effect. The next line shows how to apply a texture created
with a custom file to our fire particle system:

```
_fire.texture = [CCTexture textureWithFile:@"flame.png"];
```

If you think about it, this feature allows you to create a large variety of particle
systems. What should happen if you use the image of a bubble as a particle?
Let's check it.

Again in the project navigator:

1. Right-click on the **Resources** group and select **Add Files to
"ExplosionsAndUFOs"**....

2. Select `bubble.png` in the `Resources` folder and click on **Add**.

Then go back to `GameScene.m` and add the following line in the `init` method, before `[self addChild:_fire z:1];`:

```
// Create particle from a texture
_fire.texture = [CCTexture textureWithFile:@"bubble.png"];
```

Run the project and you will see what happens:

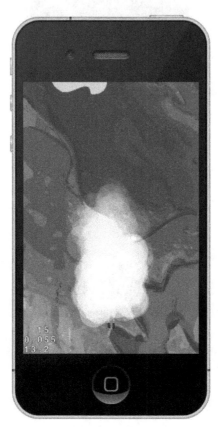

I just wanted to show you how powerful particle systems are in Cocos2d, but it doesn't stop there. Before proceeding, undo the last changes:

1. Delete `bubble.png` from the project, making sure that you choose the **Move to Trash** option.

2. Delete the line `_fire.texture = [CCTexture textureWithFile:@"bubble.png"];`.

CCParticleSystem modes

There are two modes of particle systems that depend on which way they emit particles:

- Gravity Mode
- Radius Mode

You can set the mode by assigning CCParticleSystemModeGravity or CCParticleSystemModeRadius to the emitterMode property of the particle system. These modes can be customized thanks to a broad set of properties, some of which are exclusive to each mode; that's why you need to pay attention or you will encounter NSInternalInconsistencyException.

CCParticleSystemModeGravity

This is the default mode and it creates particles that flow from a source point or that converge at a target point. You can set up a gravity particle, setting values for the following attributes:

- gravity: This indicates the acceleration of the particles in the x and y axes
- speed: This indicates the speed that each particle will have
- speedVar: This is the speed variance that each particle will have
- tangentialAccel: This indicates the velocity of the particles moving in a curved path
- tangentialAccelVar: This is the variance of the tangential acceleration
- radialAccel: This indicates the acceleration of a particle that moves at a constant speed along a circular path
- radialAccelVar: This is the variance of the radial acceleration

Better than reading, let's play a little with these attributes. Add the following lines to the init method, just before return self;:

```
_fire.emitterMode = CCParticleSystemModeGravity;
_fire.gravity = CGPointMake(0, -160);
_fire.speed = 50.0;
_fire.speedVar = 200.0;
_fire.tangentialAccel = 70.0;
_fire.tangentialAccelVar = 150.0;
_fire.radialAccel = 80.0;
_fire.radialAccelVar = 30.0;
```

Run the game and discover how these values affect the fire's behavior. I recommend you try your own setups to obtain your desired results.

CCParticleSystemModeRadius

This mode creates particles that move around a central point. The particular attributes for this mode are:

- startRadius: This determines the starting radius of the particles. In other words, the distance to the node's position.

- startRadiusVar: This is the starting radius variance of the particles.

- endRadius: This determines the final radius of the particles. It can be made equal to the starting radius by specifying CCParticleSystemStartRadiusEqualToEndRadius.

- endRadiusVar: This is the end radius variance of the particles.

- rotatePerSecond: This indicates the number of degrees the particles will rotate around the source.

- rotatePerSecondVar: This is the variance in degrees for each rotation per second.

Let's play a little with these attributes too. Replace the lines added in the gravity mode section with these ones:

```
_fire.emitterMode = CCParticleSystemModeRadius;
_fire.startRadius = 200.0;
_fire.startRadiusVar = 5.0;
_fire.endRadius = 30.0;
_fire.endRadiusVar = 3.0;
_fire.rotatePerSecond = 100.0;
_fire.rotatePerSecondVar = 12.0;
```

You can see the results in the following screenshots:

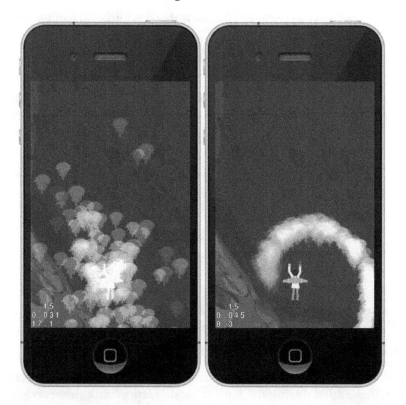

Common properties

Besides these specific attributes, `CCParticleSystem` objects have some common attributes among which I would like to stress the most interesting that you may want to know about:

- `totalParticles`: This is the maximum number of particles that will be on the screen at the same time.

- `life/lifeVar`: This is the time that each particle will take to move from the start to the end point. If this value is low enough, there will be more and more particles on the screen, but this will never exceed the `totalParticles` value.

- `emissionRate`: This indicates the number of particles that will be created per second. Usually, this value corresponds to `totalParticles/life`.

- `startSpin/startSpinVar`: This determines the initial spin value of each particle.

- `endSpin/endSpinVar`: This determines the final spin value of each particle.
- `startSize/startSizeVar`: This indicates the initial size of each particle.
- `endSize/endSizeVar`: This indicates the final size of each particle. You can keep the initial size at the end by using the `CCParticleSystemStartSizeEqualToEndSize` constant.
- `startColor/startColorVar`: This sets up the initial color of the particles. For example, you can tint your particles in green using `_fire.startColor = [CCColor greenColor]`.
- `endColor/endColorVar`: This sets the final color of each particle.
- `texture`: This specifies the texture used to render each particle.
- `angle/angleVar`: This determines the direction the particles will follow once emitted, where 0 means right, 90 means up, 180 means left, and 270 means down.
- `duration`: This is the time the emitter will run, not to be confused with the `life` attribute, where -1 and `CCParticleSystemDurationInfinity` means forever.
- `posVar`: This is the position variance of the emitter.
- `sourcePosition`: This indicates the offset position of the particles from the emitter.

However, you must be wondering how these properties affect our project visually. Replace the lines added during the Radius Mode section with these ones:

```
_fire.totalParticles = 200;
_fire.life = 3.3;
_fire.lifeVar = 0.5;
_fire.emissionRate = _fire.totalParticles/_fire.life;
_fire.startSpin = 13.0;
_fire.startSpinVar = 0.5;
_fire.endSpin = 50.0;
_fire.endSpinVar = 0.3;
_fire.startSize = 60.0;
_fire.startSizeVar = 5.0;
_fire.endSize = 10.0;
_fire.endSizeVar = 2.0;
_fire.startColor = [CCColor greenColor];
_fire.startColorVar = [CCColor blueColor];
_fire.endColor = [CCColor redColor];
```

```
_fire.endColorVar = [CCColor purpleColor];
_fire.angle = 270.0;
_fire.duration = CCParticleSystemDurationInfinity;
_fire.posVar = CGPointMake(10, 10);
_fire.sourcePosition = CGPointMake(0, 50);
```

Run the project again and look at the results.

Do you realize the potential these particles have thanks to these attributes? There are only a few changes required to achieve the result we are looking for in the backpack-reactor.

Replace the following properties from the previous block with the following ones:

```
// Configure the particle system
_fire.startSize = 50.0;
_fire.startSizeVar = 1.0;
_fire.posVar = CGPointMake(10, 0);
_fire.sourcePosition = CGPointMake(0, -10);
```

Add these new ones:

```
_fire.speed = 50.0;
_fire.speedVar = 1.0;
```

By modifying startSize and its variance, the position variance, and the source position, we have customized the particle node to behave as we want. Also, by setting its speed and speed variance, we made it look like a reactor, but we want the fire to follow the scientist so add these lines at the end of the update method:

```
// Make the fire follow the scientist
_fire.position = CGPointMake(_scientist.position.x,
_scientist.position.y);
```

Run the game and you will see the brand new invention of Dr. Fringe in action, the super BPR-200!

Particle Designer

It's important that as game developers we know as many tools as possible so in this section, I would like to introduce you to a very useful one: Particle Designer (http://71squared.com/en/particledesigner).

This editor, which has a trial and a paid version, allows us to customize our particle systems in real time without needing to run the Xcode project each time to see the resultant effect.

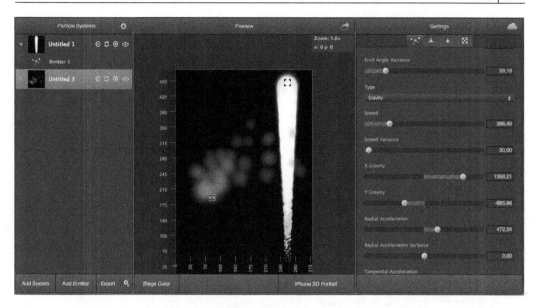

Particle Designer has a main view where you can see your particles (in the current version, you can work with multiple particle systems) in different screen modes: from iPhone SD Portrait to iPad HD Landscape and from Android Normal Portrait to Android X-Large Landscape. There you can change the stage color too, which will help you to reproduce your game's colors so you can achieve the proper effect.

On the left, you have your particle systems where you can edit its particlePositionType attribute (grouped or relative) and select other visual properties of the editor to show or hide the particle system.

On the right side, you will find four panel settings: **Emitter Settings**, **Particle Settings**, **Color Settings**, and **Texture Settings**. In these panels, you will be able to edit all the attributes of the particles while you see how this affects the visual result.

There is an interesting button with a cloud shape at the top-right corner of the editor. Clicking this shows the particles other users have shared, which you can export or just take a look at to get ideas.

Once you have set up your particles, if you have a licensed version, you can export them in the PEX, LAP, Plist, or JSON format. We won't cover how to integrate these files into Cocos2d in this book, but you will find a lot of documentation on the official website at http://71squared.com/particledesigner.

Extending CCSprite

Dr. Nicholas Fringe's enemies are an army of UFOs controlled by very intelligent extraterrestrial beings trying to wipe out all of mankind. That's why we're going to create them as a separate class that will derive from CCSprite, where we will define its evolved behavior.

Some developers prefer to derive this kind of class from CCNode and include a CCSprite instance as it offers more potential, but for the moment we are going to keep it simple and just extend CCSprite.

First of all, let's create the new class:

1. Right-click on the **Classes** group in the project navigator and select **New File...**.
2. Click on **iOS | cocos2d v3.x** and choose to create the new file from the CCNode class template.
3. Type CCSprite in the available field and click on **Next**.
4. Call the file as UFO and be sure that the **Classes** folder is selected before clicking on **Create**.

Then replace the contents of UFO.h with the following block of code:

```
#import <Foundation/Foundation.h>
#import "cocos2d.h"

@interface UFO : CCSprite {

}

// Declare property for number of hits
@property (readwrite, nonatomic) int numHits;

// Declare method to init UFOs
-(id) initWithHits:(int)hits;

@end
```

Replace the contents of UFO.m with these lines:

```
#import "UFO.h"

@implementation UFO
```

```
// Implement initWithHits
-(id) initWithHits:(int)hits{

    // Initialize UFO sprite specifying an image
    self = [super initWithImageNamed:@"ufo_green.png"];

    if (!self) return(nil);

    // Initialize number of hits
    _numHits = hits;

    return self;
}

@end
```

We declared a `readwrite` integer property to keep the control of the number of hits a UFO can receive before exploding, and as you can see, we're taking advantage of the auto-synthesized properties feature that will help us minimize coding.

We also declared a custom `init` method so we can assign initial values to each instance of the `UFO` class; in our case, we just want to specify the image to create the `UFO` object and the initial number of hits. Notice that we are calling the parent's `initWithImageNamed` method because if we don't, our class won't be properly initialized.

 It's important to call a parent's `init` method when initializing a derived class.

To conclude with the `UFO` class, you just need to add the corresponding image to the project:

1. In the project navigator, right-click on the **Resources** group and select **Add Files to "ExplosionsAndUFOs"...**.

2. In the **Resources** file, you will find `ufo_green.png`, so select it and click on **Add**.

Now let's put some enemies in the scene so Dr. Fringe can begin saving our planet. First, declare these two private instance variables by adding them in `GameScene.m`, after `CCParticleSystem *_fire;`:

```
// Declare an array of UFOs
NSMutableArray *_arrayUFOs;

// Max number of UFOs in scene
int _numUFOs;
```

Initialize them by adding the following lines in the `init` method, just before
`return self;`:

```
// Initialize the array of UFOs
_numUFOs = 3;
_arrayUFOs = [NSMutableArray arrayWithCapacity:_numUFOs];
```

We initialized the UFOs array to contain three objects for the moment, but things
will get harder for our scientist later.

Import the UFO class to `GameScene.m` by adding the following line at the top of the
class just after `#import "GameScene.h"`:

```
#import "UFO.h"
```

The next step is adding the enemies to the scene, and we're going to achieve this
by scheduling a spawn method where we will define their behavior. In the `init`
method, add the following line after the lines you added earlier:

```
// Schedule the UFOs spawn method
[self schedule:@selector(spawnUFO) interval:5.0f];
```

Implement the spawnUFO method by adding the following:

```
- (void) spawnUFO {

    if ([_arrayUFOs count] < _numUFOs){
        // Create a new UFO
        UFO *ufo = [[UFO alloc] initWithHits:3];

        // Set inital UFO position
        ufo.position = CGPointMake(ufo.contentSize.width / 2,
        _screenSize.height + ufo.contentSize.height / 2);

        // Adding the new UFO to the array
        [_arrayUFOs addObject:ufo];

        // Adding the UFO to the scene
        [self addChild:ufo];

        //Creating movement actions
        CCActionMoveTo *actionMoveInitialPosition =
        [CCActionMoveTo actionWithDuration:0.6
        position:CGPointMake(ufo.position.x, _screenSize.height -
        ufo.contentSize.height / 2)];
```

```
CCActionMoveTo *actionMoveRight1 = [CCActionMoveTo
actionWithDuration:0.3
position:CGPointMake(_screenSize.width -
ufo.contentSize.width / 2, _screenSize.height -
ufo.contentSize.height / 2)];

CCActionMoveTo *actionMoveDownLeft = [CCActionMoveTo
actionWithDuration:0.3
position:CGPointMake(ufo.contentSize.width / 2,
_screenSize.height - 2 * ufo.contentSize.height)];

CCActionMoveTo *actionMoveRight2 = [CCActionMoveTo
actionWithDuration:0.6
position:CGPointMake(_screenSize.width -
ufo.contentSize.width / 2, _screenSize.height - 2 *
ufo.contentSize.height)];

CCActionSequence *ufoSequence = [CCActionSequence
actionWithArray:@[actionMoveInitialPosition,
actionMoveRight1, actionMoveDownLeft, actionMoveRight2]];

// Repeat movement infinitely
CCActionRepeatForever *ufoLoop = [CCActionRepeatForever
actionWithAction:ufoSequence];

// Run the UFO movement
[ufo runAction:ufoLoop];
    }
}
```

I apologize for the big block of code, but don't worry, it's easy to understand what we've just done.

Once we get the array ready to receive objects, we schedule a method that will take care of the UFO spawn. I decided to leave 5 seconds between spawns to give the scientist a chance.

The first thing we do in spawnUFO is to check whether arrayUFOs is already filled with the maximum amount of objects, and if it's not, then we proceed with initializing the object by specifying the number of hits we want it to support before exploding (3 in this case). Then we place UFO off the top of the screen and we add it to both the array and the scene.

As we want the UFO objects to have some intelligence and be harder to kill, I decided to define a loop movement that consists of a four-movement sequence:

- `actionMoveInitialPosition`: This traces a path from outside the screen to its initial position, placed at the top-left corner of the screen
- `actionMoveRight1`: This moves the enemy to the right side of the screen, keeping the same `y` value, and performs a lateral displacement
- `actionMoveDownLeft`: This places the object on the left side of the screen again but a little lower than the initial position
- `actionMoveRight2`: This performs another lateral displacement, keeping the `y` value

As you can see, the duration of the movements is different because I wanted to make the movement a little unpredictable.

The last line just runs the `CCActionRepeatForever` action, similar to what we did in the particle effect section.

Now you can run the game and see how the spaceships draw a vertiginous zigzag pattern that is almost impossible to predict (I am joking).

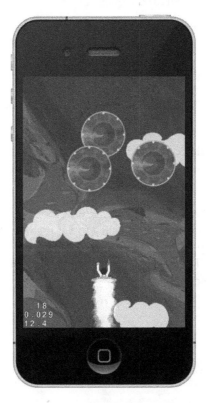

Let's extend the UFO class a little more so we can create instances of this class with a higher number of hits and a different texture image. First of all, add a couple more images for the new types of spaceship:

1. Right-click on the **Resources** group and select **Add Files to "ExplosionsAndUFOs"**....

2. In the Resources folder, you will find ufo_red.png and ufo_purple.png. Select them and click on **Add**.

To achieve this, we need to add a new property to UFO.h, so add the following property:

```
// Declare property for type of UFO
@property (readonly, nonatomic) UFOTypes ufoType;
```

However, you will need to define UFOTypes too. We will create an enumerated type for the different kinds of spaceships, so add the following lines just above the interface declaration @interface UFO : CCSprite {:

```
typedef enum {

    typeUFOGreen = 0,
    typeUFORed,
    typeUFOPurple

} UFOTypes;
```

Once we've specified the value for the first enumerated component (typeUFOGreen = 0), we don't need to specify the rest as it will follow an enumerated sequence.

Declare a new initializer method with the following line in UFO.h:

```
// Declare method to init UFOs with type
-(id) initWithType:(UFOTypes)type;
```

Implement this method in UFO.m with the following lines:

```
// Implement initWithType
-(id) initWithType:(UFOTypes)type {
    // Set the ufo type
    _ufoType = type;

    NSString *textureName;
    int numHits;

    switch (_ufoType) {
        case typeUFOGreen:
```

```
            // Assign textureName and numHits values
            textureName = @"ufo_green.png";
            numHits = 3;
            break;
        case typeUFORed:
            // Assign textureName and numHits values
            textureName = @"ufo_red.png";
            numHits = 5;
            break;
        case typeUFOPurple:
            // Assign textureName and numHits values
            textureName = @"ufo_purple.png";
            numHits = 7;
            break;

        default:
            break;
    }

    // Initialize UFO sprite specifying texture image
    self = [super initWithImageNamed:textureName];

    if (!self) return(nil);

    // Initialize number of hits
    _numHits = numHits;

    return self;
}
```

This method will receive the type as an input argument and depending on it, the method will create one kind of UFO or another. Notice that we're calling the [super initWithImageNamed:] method to properly create our instance.

Then, find the old initialization:

```
UFO *ufo = [[UFO alloc] initWithHits:3];
```

Replace it with the new initializer method:

```
int type = arc4random_uniform(3);
UFO *ufo = [[UFO alloc] initWithType:type];
```

We are passing a random number between 0 and 2 to create the UFO objects in an unpredictable manner. Come on, run the game and be scared of the almost indestructible spaceships with unknown technology!

Shooting some lasers

Did you think that the backpack-reactor was Dr. Fringe's only invention? You were wrong; he needs some kind of weapon to face the aliens and fortunately, he has developed some high tech lasers. So let's allow him to shoot them when we touch the screen.

First add the required image:

1. Right-click on the **Resources** group and select **Add Files to "ExplosionsAndUFOs"...**.

2. In the `Resources` folder, you will find `laser_green.png`, so select it and click on **Add**.

We're going to declare an array of lasers so we can keep control of them, so add these two private instance variables after `int _numUFOs;`:

```
// Declare array of green lasers
NSMutableArray *_arrayLaserGreen;

// Max number of lasers in scene
int _numLaserGreen;
```

Initialize the variables in the `init` method by adding the following code before `return self;`:

```
// Initialize the array of green lasers
_numLaserGreen = 5;
_arrayLaserGreen = [NSMutableArray
arrayWithCapacity:_numLaserGreen];
```

Dr. Nicholas Fringe's invention is still in the beta phase, that's why he can't shoot more than five laser beams at the same time. We need to enable touch interaction, something that we already know how to do. In the `init` method, add the following line at the end before `return self;`:

```
self.userInteractionEnabled = YES;
```

Implement `touchBegan` by adding these lines to `GameScene.m`:

```
-(void) touchBegan:(UITouch *)touch withEvent:(UIEvent *)event {

    if ([_arrayLaserGreen count] < _numLaserGreen){
        // Create green laser and setting its position
        CCSprite *laserGreen = [CCSprite
        spriteWithImageNamed:@"laser_green.png"];
```

```
         laserGreen.position = CGPointMake(_scientist.position.x +
         _scientist.contentSize.width / 4, _scientist.position.y +
         _scientist.contentSize.height / 2);
         // Add laser to array of lasers
         [_arrayLaserGreen addObject:laserGreen];

         // Add the laser to the scene
         [self addChild:laserGreen];

         // Declare laser speed
         float laserSpeed = 400.0;

         // Calculate laser's final position
         CGPoint nextPosition = CGPointMake(laserGreen.position.x,
         _screenSize.height + laserGreen.contentSize.height / 2);

         // Calculate duration
         float laserDuration = ccpDistance(nextPosition,
         laserGreen.position) / laserSpeed;

         // Move laser sprite out of the screen
         CCActionMoveTo *actionLaserGreen = [CCActionMoveTo
         actionWithDuration:laserDuration position:nextPosition];

         // Action to be executed when the laser reaches its final
         position
         CCActionCallBlock *callDidMove = [CCActionCallBlock
         actionWithBlock:^{

             // Remove laser from array and scene
             [_arrayLaserGreen removeObject:laserGreen];
             [self removeChild:laserGreen];

         }];

         CCActionSequence *sequenceLaserGreen = [CCActionSequence
         actionWithArray:@[actionLaserGreen, callDidMove]];

         [laserGreen runAction:sequenceLaserGreen];
    }
}
```

The very first thing we're doing is checking whether we have shot the maximum number of laser beams. If not, we create a new one, setting its position by the laser gun and adding it to the scene and the array of green lasers.

Each laser will trace a vertical path from its initial shooting position to the top, off the screen. That's why we're calculating the final position as the same *x* axis value and `_screenSize.height + laserGreen.contentSize.height / 2` on the *y* axis. This is the same approach we take every time we want to place some sprite off the screen, so it's nothing new to us.

As we want the laser to always move at the same speed, we specify its velocity to calculate the duration of the movement and we make this calculation in the same way we did in the previous chapter: divide the distance to be covered by the laser's speed.

Then we create a `CCActionMoveTo` instance with the calculated direction and the final position. Once the move action ends, we want the laser to disappear from both the scene and the array, so we implement a `CCActionCallBlock` action where we place this logic.

As the last instruction, we build a sequence with the movement action and the action block and run it. Build and run your game and look what we've just done.

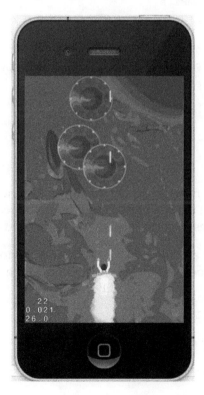

When UFOs collide

Despite being in the beta phase, Dr. Fringe's laser beams can destroy the alien's spaceships, so let's implement collision detection for this purpose.

When a laser beam hits a UFO, on one hand the spaceship's **number** of hits will decrease for one unit, and on the other hand, the laser will disappear from the scene. The same will happen to the UFO when its number of hits is 0.

First let's declare and implement an instance of the UFO method to check whether its number of hits has reached 0 or not. In UFO.h, add the following line just after the initWithHits method:

```
// Declare check method
-(BOOL) checkNumHits;
```

Then in UFO.m, implement checkNumHits by adding these lines at the bottom of the file, before the @end clause:

```
// Implement checkNumHits
-(BOOL) checkNumHits{

    if(_numHits == 0) {
        // Remove UFO from scene and return TRUE
        [self removeFromParent];
        return TRUE;
    }

    return FALSE;
}
```

This method will look at _numHits. If the _numHits instance variable equals 0, and in that case, it will remove the object from its parent (the scene) and return TRUE. For any other _numHits instance variable, it will return FALSE.

Back to GameScene.m. We are going to develop a method to wrap collision detection tasks. In the update method, add the following lines at the end:

```
// Collision detection
[self detectCollisions];
```

Implement the method by pasting the following lines:

```
-(void)detectCollisions {

    CCSprite *laserGreen;
```

```
// For each UFO on the scene
for(UFO *ufo in _arrayUFOs) {

    // For each laser beam shot
    for (laserGreen in _arrayLaserGreen){

        // Detect laserGreen-ufo collision
        if (CGRectIntersectsRect(ufo.boundingBox,
        laserGreen.boundingBox)) {

            CCLOG(@"COLLISION DETECTED");

            // Decrease UFO's number of hits
            ufo.numHits--;

            // Check if numHits is 0
            if ([ufo checkNumHits]) {
            CCLOG(@"UFO DESTROYED");
        }
            }
        }
    }
}
```

We're iterating the green lasers and the spaceships array and trying to detect a collision between their rectangles. When a collision happens, we decrease the UFO number of hits and we check whether it should be destroyed. In that case, we remove the object from the scene. However, at the moment it won't work properly. If you run the object, you will realize that's because once we destroy the first _numUFOs spaceships, no more are spawned.

This is due to the fact that we aren't removing the destroyed spaceships from the array. You may be thinking that making an object disappear from the scene has a straightforward solution: remove the object from the array and the child from the scene, but it's not that simple.

If you want to try it, add this line after CCLOG(@"UFO DESTROYED");:

```
[_arrayUFOs removeObject:ufo];
```

Run the project again and shoot until you destroy one UFO.

There you have it, the app crashed due to an uncaught exception:

```
Terminating app due to uncaught exception 'NSGenericException',
reason: '*** Collection <__NSArrayM: 0x17805b900> was mutated
while being enumerated.'
***
```

If you pay attention to the log message, it makes sense. It's warning us that we're modifying the array while it's being enumerated (iterated) and this is a forbidden action.

So, how can we deal with it? The approach followed by game developers is to create a separate array to store the objects we want to delete and then proceed to remove them as soon as the loop ends.

As we will have the same problem with laser beams if we try to remove them when a collision happens, we will apply a similar approach.

First of all, delete the line to remove the spaceship from `arrayUFOs` and declare two new arrays after `int _numLaserGreen;`:

```
// Array of removable laser beams
NSMutableArray *_lasersGreenToRemove;

// Array of removable UFOs
NSMutableArray *_ufosToRemove;
```

Initialize them at the end of the `init` method, just after `self.userInteractionEnabled = YES;`:

```
// Initialize removable objects arrays
_lasersGreenToRemove = [NSMutableArray array];
_ufosToRemove = [NSMutableArray array];
```

Then, in `detectCollisions`, find the following line:

```
CCLOG(@"COLLISION DETECTED");
```

Replace it with:

```
// Stopping laser beam actions
[laserGreen stopAllActions];

// Adding the object to the removable objects array
[_lasersGreenToRemove addObject:laserGreen];

// Remove the laser from the scene
[self removeChild:laserGreen];
```

Then find the line:

```
CCLOG(@"UFO DESTROYED");
```

Replace it with the following ones:

```
// Stopping ufo actions
[ufo stopAllActions];

// Adding the object to the removable objects array
[_ufosToRemove addObject:ufo];
```

Finally, add these lines after the `_arrayLaserGreen` loop:

```
for (CCSprite *laserGreen in _arrayLaserGreen){
  .
  .
  .
}
// Remove objects from array
[_arrayLaserGreen removeObjectsInArray:_lasersGreenToRemove];
```

Add this one after the `_arrayUFOs` loop:

```
for(UFO *ufo in _arrayUFOs) {
  .
  .
  .
}
// Remove objects from array
[_arrayUFOs removeObjectsInArray:_ufosToRemove];
```

Remember that we aren't removing UFOs from the scene in this method because we're already performing this task inside `checkNumHits`.

If you run the game now, you will find that each spaceship's spawn/destruction and the laser beam's shooting and disappearing functions are working correctly.

2-star challenge – create explosions

Now that we are able to detect when a UFO is destroyed, it would be more realistic to make them explode, and I think you're ready to develop this by yourself.

Create one explosion whenever a spaceship is destroyed by using the file `explosion.png` that you will find in the `Resources` folder.

The solution

You will need to go back a few pages to achieve this challenge because in this case, we're going to create a CCParticleSystemModeRadius particle.

First of all, add explosion.png to the project and then add the following lines inside the method detectCollisions, after [_ufosToRemove addObject:ufo];:

```
CCParticleExplosion *explosion = [CCParticleExplosion node];
    explosion.texture = [CCTexture
    textureWithFile:@"explosion.png"];
        explosion.emitterMode = CCParticleSystemModeRadius;
        explosion.startSize = 100.0;
        explosion.startRadius = 20.0;
        explosion.endSize = 1.0;
        explosion.endRadius = 100.0;
        explosion.totalParticles = 200;
        explosion.life = 2.0;
        explosion.lifeVar = 0.0;
    explosion.emissionRate =
    explosion.totalParticles/explosion.life;
    explosion.position = ufo.position;
        [self addChild:explosion z:1];
```

Now you will have an impressive explosion!

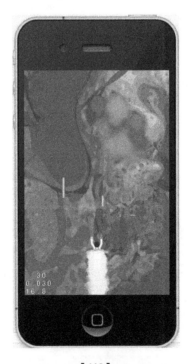

The attack of the aliens

Aliens have invaded the planet Earth to kill humanity and they have come fully armed with high technology red laser beams. In this section, we're going to implement their attack.

First of all, we need to add the image to create the red laser beams, so follow the next steps:

1. Right-click on the **Resources** group and select **Add Files to "ExplosionsAndUFOs"**....

2. In the `Resources` folder, you will find `laser_red.png`, so select it and click on **Add**.

Then we're going to proceed as in the green laser's case. Let's declare an array and a maximum number of red lasers. Add these lines after `NSMutableArray *_ufosToRemove;`:

```
// Declare array of red lasers
NSMutableArray *_arrayLaserRed;

// Max number of lasers in scene
int _numLaserRed;
```

Initialize them by adding the following in the `init` method, before the `return self;` statement:

```
// Initialize max number of red lasers
_numLaserRed = 15;

// Initialize the array of red lasers
_arrayLaserRed = [NSMutableArray
arrayWithCapacity:_numLaserRed];
```

For now, we are doing things we already know; we just initialized the maximum number of red lasers to be `15` and then initialized the red lasers array.

As we want the spaceships to shoot from time to time, we're going to schedule a method for this purpose. Include this line at the bottom of the `init` method, before `return self;`:

```
// Shoot red lasers
[self schedule:@selector(shootRedLaser:) interval:2.0f];
```

Implement it by adding the following block of code:

```
// Shoot red laser beams
-(void)shootRedLaser:(CCTime) delta {

    CCSprite *laserRed;

    // Shoot lasers if there are UFOs in scene and hasn't reached
    the max number of red lasers
    if ([_arrayUFOs count] > 0 && [_arrayLaserRed count] <
    _numLaserRed){

        // For each UFO on the scene
        for(UFO *ufo in _arrayUFOs) {

            // Create red laser sprite
            laserRed = [CCSprite
            spriteWithImageNamed:@"laser_red.png"];

            // Set red laser position
            laserRed.position = CGPointMake(ufo.position.x,
            ufo.position.y - ufo.contentSize.height / 2);

            // Add laser to array of lasers
            [_arrayLaserRed addObject:laserRed];

            // Add laser to scene
            [self addChild:laserRed];

            // Declare laser speed
            float laserSpeed = 600.0;

            // Calculate laser's final position
            CGPoint nextPosition =
            CGPointMake(laserRed.position.x, -
            laserRed.contentSize.height / 2);

            // Calculate duration
            float laserDuration = ccpDistance(nextPosition,
            laserRed.position) / laserSpeed;

            // Move red laser sprite out of the screen
            CCActionMoveTo *actionLaserRed = [CCActionMoveTo
            actionWithDuration:laserDuration
            position:nextPosition];
```

```
    // Action to be executed when the red laser reaches
    its final position
    CCActionCallBlock *callDidMove = [CCActionCallBlock
    actionWithBlock:^{

        // Remove laser from array and scene
        [_arrayLaserRed removeObject:laserRed];
        [self removeChild:laserRed];

    }];

    CCActionSequence *sequenceLaserRed = [CCActionSequence
    actionWithArray:@[actionLaserRed, callDidMove]];

    // Run action sequence
    [laserRed runAction:sequenceLaserRed];
    }

  }
}
```

This code is pretty easy to understand. The first thing we do is check whether there is a UFO in the scene and whether the number of existing red lasers in the scene is lower than the maximum number of red lasers allowed. If these conditions are met, then we iterate the UFO objects array and perform two main actions.

First, we create a new laser sprite with the image we just added to the project and set its initial position on the bottom-center point of the UFO and add it to the scene.

Second, we set up the movement action for the spaceship. We calculate the duration of the laser displacement to the bottom of the screen at a constant speed of 600 and then we use this value to create a CCActionMoveTo instance. We create a CCActionCallBlock instance where we will remove the laser from the scene and from the array of red lasers, and then we execute the actions sequence.

Run the project and take a look at the results!

We just need to implement the collisions between red lasers and Dr. Fringe so we're going to proceed in a similar manner as we did with green lasers and UFO objects.

First, declare the auxiliary array we will use to remove collided red lasers by adding the following line just after `int _numLaserRed;`:

```
// Array of removable laser beams
NSMutableArray *_lasersRedToRemove;
```

Initialize it in the `init` method by adding this line after `_ufosToRemove = [NSMutableArray array];`:

```
_lasersRedToRemove = [NSMutableArray array];
```

Then, in `detectCollisions`, add the following block of code at the end of the method:

```
CCSprite *laserRed;

// For each red laser beam shot
for (laserRed in _arrayLaserRed){

    // Detect laserRed-scientist collision
    if (CGRectIntersectsRect(_scientist.boundingBox,
    laserRed.boundingBox)) {

        // Stopping laser beam actions
        [laserRed stopAllActions];

        // Adding the object to the removable objects array
        [_lasersRedToRemove addObject:laserRed];

        // Remove the laser from the scene
        [self removeChild:laserRed];

        CCLOG(@"RED LASER COLLISION");
    }
}
// Remove objects from array
[_arrayLaserRed removeObjectsInArray:_lasersRedToRemove];
```

This code is very similar to the green laser-UFO case. We iterate the red lasers array and try to find out whether some of them collide with our scientist. In this case, we stop all red laser actions, add it to the removable objects array, and remove the child from the scene. Once the loop has finished, we can remove the collided lasers from their array.

Drawing and coloring

Usually, you will be working with sprites, nodes, and other high-level objects, but maybe sometimes you will want to draw some geometric primitives such as lines, circles, or squares. In our case, we're going to use them to represent our scientist's life bar.

Fortunately, Cocos2d allows us to perform these tasks easily by using any of these three options:

- The draw method: This CCNode class method is the one you should override in your classes derived from CCNode to customize drawing your nodes. It's important here not to call [super draw] or you will face unexpected behavior.

- The visit method: This CCNode class method gives you more control as it calls the draw method of the node and its children in the order they were added to it, taking into account the specified z-orders.

- CCDrawNode: This class, derived from CCNode, is the one that gives you full control over the primitives because they are treated as nodes themselves.

The draw method presents a problem when there are other children added to the scene because the primitives created in this method have z-order values of 0, so they won't be visible unless you set all the nodes you want to be behind your primitives to have negative z-order values.

On the other hand, visit doesn't present this issue because it will perform the draw of the nodes in the correct order.

 One common point these methods have is that you will need to import CCDrawingPrimitives.h to draw your primitives.

In CCDrawingPrimitives.h, you can find methods to draw any kind of primitive. Some examples are: ccDrawPoint, ccDrawPoints, ccDrawLine, ccDrawRect, ccDrawSolidRect, ccDrawPoly, ccDrawSolidPoly, ccDrawCircle, ccDrawQuadBezier, and ccDrawCubicBezier.

Let's make use of one of these methods and check the draw and visit behavior, implementing both methods in the same way. First, add the following line at the top of GameScene.m:

```
#import "CCDrawingPrimitives.h"
```

Then implement the `draw` method by adding:

```
-(void)draw
{
    // Draw a solid blue rectangle in the middle of the screen
    ccDrawSolidRect(CGPointMake(0, (_screenSize.height / 2) - 50),
    CGPointMake(_screenSize.width, _screenSize.height / 2 + 50.0),
    [CCColor blueColor]);
}
```

If you run the project, you will think that there is nothing being drawn, but this is not true. The solid blue rectangle has been drawn behind the parallax node, so if you want to see it, you will need to modify the z-order of `parallaxNode`. Find the line where we added the parallax node to the scene:

```
[self addChild:parallaxNode];
```

Replace it with this one in which we specify a negative z-order value:

```
[self addChild:parallaxNode z:-1];
```

Run the project again and you will be able to see the solid blue rectangle in the middle of the screen.

Undo the last changes and replace the `draw` method with the implementation of the `visit` method using this code block:

```
-(void)visit
{
    [super visit];

    // Draw a solid blue rectangle in the middle of the screen
    ccDrawSolidRect(CGPointMake(0, (_screenSize.height / 2) - 50),
    CGPointMake(_screenSize.width, _screenSize.height / 2 + 50.0),
    [CCColor blueColor]);
}
```

As you can see, this method requires the call `[super visit];`, if you don't add it you will just draw the solid rectangle.

Run the project one more time and you will see the rectangle over the rest of the nodes but it is being merged with their textures:

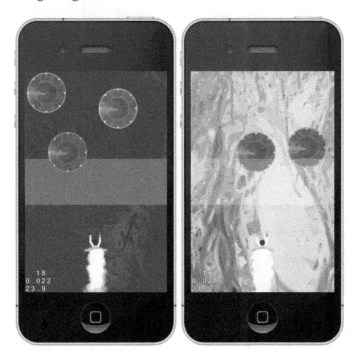

This is close but is not the desired effect because we want to have full control over the primitives, so let's try with the CCDrawNode class. First of all, delete the visit method implementation and the CCDrawingPrimitives import. Then add the following lines at the end of the init method, before return self;:

```
// Creating array of vertices
CGPoint vertices[4];
vertices[0] = CGPointMake(0, (_screenSize.height / 2) - 50);
vertices[1] = CGPointMake(0, (_screenSize.height / 2) + 50);
vertices[2] = CGPointMake(_screenSize.width,
_screenSize.height / 2 + 50.0);
vertices[3] = CGPointMake(_screenSize.width,
_screenSize.height / 2 - 50.0);

// Draw a polygon by specifying its vertices
CCDrawNode *rectNode = [CCDrawNode node];
[rectNode drawPolyWithVerts:vertices count:4
fillColor:[CCColor blueColor] borderWidth:0.0
borderColor:nil];
[self addChild:rectNode];
```

With this code, we can create a kind of primitive node that represents the same solid blue rectangle we wanted and also take advantage of all the `CCDrawNode` potential such as customizing its attributes or executing actions, where `vertices[0]` is the bottom-left vertex, `vertices[1]` is the top-left vertex, `vertices[2]` is the top-right vertex, and `vertices[3]` is the bottom-right vertex.

Run the project and you will see what I'm talking about.

Drawing primitives in the "primitive" way is expensive in terms of performance because `draw` and `visit` are called in each frame to keep things drawn. So you just need to count how many times you will be drawing the same thing and consider whether it's worth it. In our case, I think we can achieve what we need in a more efficient way.

Before proceeding, delete the block of code related to `rectNode`.

Drawing the life bar

We're going to draw a life bar composed of green rectangles using the last approach we saw. For this, we will need an integer counter to know the number of lives left and an array to store these rectangles in. Declare both variables by adding these lines after `NSMutableArray *_lasersRedToRemove;`:

```
// Declare number of lives
int _numLives;

// Array of life rectangles
NSMutableArray *_arrayLives;
```

Initialize them by adding the following lines at the end of `init`, before `return self;`:

```
// Initialize number of lifes and array
_numLives = 10;
_arrayLives = [NSMutableArray arrayWithCapacity:_numLaserRed];
```

Add the following method call at the end of the `init` method, just before `return self;`:

```
[self initLifeBar];
```

Implement it with these lines:

```
- (void)initLifeBar {

    //Initializing position and size values
    float positionX = 10.0;
```

```
float positionY = 40.0;
float rectHeight = 10.0;
float rectWidth = 0.0;

// Creating array of vertices
CGPoint vertices[4];

// Declaring draw node
CCDrawNode *rectNode;

for(int i = 0; i < _numLives; i++) {
    // Update position and width
    positionY += 15.0;
    rectWidth += 5.0;

    // Set values for next rectangle
    vertices[0] = CGPointMake(positionX, positionY); //bottom-
    left
    vertices[1] = CGPointMake(positionX, positionY +
    rectHeight); //top-left
    vertices[2] = CGPointMake(positionX + rectWidth, positionY
    + rectHeight); //top-right
    vertices[3] = CGPointMake(positionX + rectWidth,
    positionY); //bottom-right

    // Draw a polygon by specifying its vertices
    rectNode = [CCDrawNode node];
    rectNode.anchorPoint = CGPointMake(0.0, 0.0);
    [rectNode drawPolyWithVerts:vertices count:4
    fillColor:[CCColor greenColor] borderWidth:1.0
    borderColor:[CCColor blackColor]];

    // Add rectangle to scene
    [self addChild:rectNode];

    // Add rectangle to array
    [_arrayLives addObject:rectNode];

    }
}
```

This method will recursively create _numLives rectangles with different width values starting on the coordinate (10, 55). For this, we create an array of four vertices that will update their values at each iteration of the loop and a CCDrawNode instance that will draw them with a 1 pixel black border.

We set the anchor point of rectNode at (0, 0) to be sure that it's placed in the correct position and the rectangles grow up and rightward.

Then we just need to add the rectangle to the scene and to the array, but why do we need to keep them in an array? Well, it's just to facilitate managing them when a life is lost each time a red laser hits Dr. Nicholas Fringe.

In detectCollisions, find the log we left to know when a collision has happened:

```
CCLOG(@"RED LASER COLLISION");
```

Replace it with the following block of code:

```
// If there are lives left
if (_numLives > 0) {

    // Remove upper life rectangle
    [self removeChild:[_arrayLives objectAtIndex:_numLives-1]];

    // Remove rectangle from array
    [_arrayLives removeObjectAtIndex:_numLives-1];

    // Decrease number of lives
    _numLives--;
}
```

Come on, run the game and look at this beautiful and well-balanced life bar!

1-star challenge – collision detection between Dr. Fringe and the UFO

I'm sure you're now an expert at managing collisions, so I think we should detect collisions between our scientist hero and the spaceships or the game will lack realism.

Try to detect these collisions so we can't fly over the whole airspace and make the scientist blink as we did with the yeti in the previous chapter.

The solution

To achieve this challenge, you will need to take advantage of detectCollisions. How it's built makes our task very easy. As we want to detect collisions with UFOs, we will include our code inside the _arrayUFOs loop, and the best place is after this line:

```
[_arrayLaserGreen removeObjectsInArray:_lasersGreenToRemove];
```

Paste the following block of code there:

```
// Detect ufo-scientist collision
if (CGRectIntersectsRect(ufo.boundingBox, _scientist.
boundingBox)) {

    // Blink actions for both fire and scientist
    CCAction *actionDrBlink = [CCActionBlink
    actionWithDuration:0.8 blinks:2];
    CCAction *actionFireBlink = [CCActionBlink
    actionWithDuration:0.8 blinks:2];

    // Recover the visibility for both fire and scientist
    CCActionCallBlock *callDidDrBlink = [CCActionCallBlock
    actionWithBlock:^{
        // Recover the visibility of the scientist
        [_scientist setVisible:TRUE];

    }];
    CCActionCallBlock *callDidFireBlink =
     [CCActionCallBlock actionWithBlock:^{
        // Recover the visibility of the scientist
        [_fire setVisible:TRUE];

    }];
```

```
// Run actions
CCActionSequence *sequenceDr = [CCActionSequence
actionWithArray:@[actionDrBlink, callDidDrBlink]];
[_scientist runAction:sequenceDr];

CCActionSequence *sequenceFire = [CCActionSequence
actionWithArray:@[actionFireBlink, callDidFireBlink]];
[_fire runAction:sequenceFire];


}
```

Summary

In this chapter, you've learned how to link the CoreMotion framework to handle accelerometer input and how to convert them into movement. As the game developed is a shoot 'em up, you had to configure the project to be oriented in a portrait mode and you learned how to calibrate the accelerometer data to position the device in a comfortable way.

To simulate depth and speed, you implemented the parallax effect using several concatenated backgrounds and two cloud layers scrolled at different velocities.

Then you discovered how to make your games look like films by adding particle systems and how to customize them to achieve the desired effect. I then introduced you to a useful tool to create these particle systems: Particle Designer.

You learned to create a class derived from CCSprite to configure the behavior of the enemies' spaceships, implementing two different init methods. Also, I showed you the common mistake made when removing objects from NSMutableArray and how to deal with it. You also learned to shoot some laser beams and I challenged you to create explosions to make spaceship destructions more realistic.

To conclude the chapter, I taught you three ways of drawing geometrical primitives and how to use one of them (CCDrawNode) to draw a life bar for our scientist in a recursive way.

3
Your First Online Game

In these days of playing video games online, some readers might have never experienced watching a video game being played in an arcade, or have even played a game at a friend's house. But in the days before computer networks, that was the most social a video game could be.

The development of computer networks brought online video games to our devices and it resulted in a social boom. We can't imagine a game without online mode, or in its absence, a share button to let our friends around the world know our score record.

In this chapter, you will learn how to develop an online turn-based card game such as *Magic* or *Hearthstone: Heroes of Warcraft*. To achieve this, you will take advantage of the potential that Game Center offers to support online games.

Further into this chapter, you will learn to drag, scale, rotate, and move sprites, and how to implement and run actions in depth. In addition to that, you will see how to use bitmap fonts to load labels and scores.

You will learn the following things in this chapter:

- How to integrate Game Center
- How to develop a turn-based game
- How to drag, scale, rotate, and move sprites
- How to implement and run actions in depth
- How to use bitmap fonts in a game

Getting started with our project

We have planned to develop a card game similar to *Magic* and *Heroes of Warcraft* in which two elemental wizards will fight, invoking their minions thanks to a deck of cards. That's why we will create one independent class to implement the behavior and characteristics of these cards and another one to define the attributes of each wizard and keep the control of their deck.

As the aim of this chapter is to focus ourselves on the basis of online iOS games, we're taking an initial project as the starting point of our game. Open the code files of this chapter where you'll find `ElementalWizards_init.zip`, which contains the initial project.

This project includes `AppDelegate.h`, `AppDelegate.m`, `Card.h`, `Card.m`, `Wizard.h`, `Wizard.m`, `GameScene.h`, and `GameScene.m`.

We will ignore both `AppDelegate` files because they're exactly like those we saw in the previous chapter and they don't need any explanation. Let's take a look at `Card.h`:

```
#import <Foundation/Foundation.h>
#import "cocos2d.h"

typedef enum {
    fire = 0,
    air,
    water,
    earth
} ElementTypes;

@interface Card : CCSprite {
}
// Declare property for attack value
@property (readonly, nonatomic) unsigned int attack;
// Declare property for defense value
@property (readonly, nonatomic) unsigned int defense;
// Declare property for element type
@property (readonly, nonatomic) ElementTypes elementType;
// Declare property for element string
@property (readwrite, nonatomic) NSString *element;
// Declare property for image name
@property (readwrite, nonatomic) NSString *imageName;
```

```
// Declare method to init card with element type, attack and
defense
-(id) initWithType:(ElementTypes)type attack:(unsigned int)attack
defense:(unsigned int)defense image:(NSString *)image;

@end
```

The first interesting thing in this file is the `ElementTypes` enumeration that will define the different types a `Card` interface can be, as the actors on each match are elemental wizards that can control the nature elements: fire, air, water, and earth.

Each `Card` instance has two unsigned integer values; one concerns the attack value and the other one refers to the defense value. These attributes indicate how strong an elemental minion represented by a `Card` instance is and the damage each of them can receive before being killed.

As the `Card` class is defined by an `ElementTypes` enumeration, we will need a property to keep it so we can use this value during the battles, which will enter into action when a `Card` instance is confronted by its opposite element type.

We're also going to store the element type as a string in a `readwrite` variable to facilitate working with its value.

The last property is the name of the image used to represent this minion, which is `readwrite` as we will need to modify this object's attributes. If you take a look at the class we're deriving, you will realize that a `Card` class is a `CCSprite` instance. We're going to show this class on the screen. I'm sorry to say the images used in this game won't be as spectacular as the *Magic* ones; nevertheless, we will have a different texture for each `Card` instance that will represent its type, attack values, and defense values.

To conclude this header file, we declare an initializer method that will receive the type, attack values, and defense values, and the image of the `Card` class. If you keep reading, you will learn how this method works.

Let's take a look at `Card.m`; if you open it, you will see the following lines:

```
#import "Card.h"

@implementation Card

-(id) initWithType:(int)type attack:(unsigned int)attack
defense:(unsigned int)defense image:(NSString *)image{
    self = [super initWithImageNamed:image];
```

```
    if (!self) return(nil);

    _elementType = type;
    _attack = attack;
    _defense = defense;
    _imageName = image;

    switch (type) {
        case fire:
            _element = @"fire";
            break;
        case air:
            _element = @"air";
            break;
        case water:
            _element = @"water";
            break;
        case earth:
            _element = @"earth";
            break;
        default:
            break;
    }
    return self;
}


@end
```

In the initializer method, we first call the `initWithImageNamed` method of the `CCSprite` class; if you remember from the previous chapter, we're performing this step to avoid unexpected behavior when extending a class that, for example, does not appear in the scene.

Then, we initialize each property with the value passed as input arguments to the method and return the created object. If you pay attention to the `switch` statement, we use this approach to initialize the `element` string value.

Now that we know how a `Card` class is represented, we can define the `Wizard` class, so open `Wizard.h` and take a look at it:

```
#import <Foundation/Foundation.h>
#import "cocos2d.h"
#import "Card.h"
```

```
@interface Wizard : CCNode {
}

// Declare property for life points
@property (readwrite, nonatomic) int lifePoints;
// Declare property for element type
@property (readonly, nonatomic) ElementTypes elementType;

// Declare property for the array of cards
@property (readonly, nonatomic) NSMutableArray *cards;

// Declare property for card played
@property (readwrite, nonatomic) Card *cardPlayed;

// Declare method to init wizard with name, life points, element
type, cards and played card
-(id) initWithLifePoints:(int)lifePoints type:(ElementTypes)type
cards:(NSMutableArray *)cards cardPlayed:(Card *)cardPlayed;

@end
```

If you pay attention to the imports section, you will realize we're importing Card.h; this is due to two facts: first, this class defines the types of natural elements a Wizard instance can be and second, each instance of Wizard will handle a deck of several Card objects.

The next line shows the parent class we're extending. In this case, we just need our class to keep the information about each player; that's why we just need to extend CCNode.

We need to know how many life points each player has in order to control when they're defeated; that's why we declare a modifiable integer property.

Every player will choose the natural element it has more affinity with so we keep it on an ElementTypes property. We will make use of this property during the matches to give some advantages to Wizard instances when invoking elementals of the same type.

As each player will manage a deck of cards, we will store them in an array and keep the card the wizard has played too.

Finally, we declare a custom initializer that will set the initial values.

Open `Wizard.m` and you will see that it's pretty simple; this file just includes the implementation of the initializer method:

```
#import "Wizard.h"

@implementation Wizard

-(id) initWithLifePoints:(int)lifePoints type:(ElementTypes)type
cards:(NSMutableArray *)cards cardPlayed:(Card *)cardPlayed {

    self = [super init];

    if (!self) return(nil);

    _lifePoints = lifePoints;
    _elementType = type;
    _cards = cards;
    _cardPlayed = cardPlayed;

    return self;
}

@end
```

This file follows the same philosophy as `Card.m`; we first call the super class `init` method to initialize the instance properly and then we assign the different input values to the instance properties.

There is nothing important to highlight in `GameScene.h`; it only declares the `scene` and `init` methods. So let's focus on `GameScene.m`. Open it and you will see the following lines:

```
#import "GameScene.h"
#import "Card.h"
#import "Wizard.h"

// Number of common deck cards
#define DECK_NUM_CARDS 24

// Number of wizard cards
#define NUM_CARDS 5

// Initial life points
#define INIT_LIFE_POINTS 12
```

```
@implementation GameScene {
    // Declare common deck of cards
    NSMutableArray *_deckOfCards;
}


+ (GameScene *)scene
{
    return [[self alloc] init];
}


- (id)init
{
    // Apple recommends assigning self with supers return value
    self = [super init];
    if (!self) return(nil);

    [self initializeCards];

    return self;
}
@end
```

We import `Card.h` and `Wizard.h` because the scene will make use of these objects during the battle, and we define constant values for both the number of common cards and wizard deck cards, and a constant for the initial player's life points.

Then we declare an array of cards that will store the whole deck that we will use to extract a random group for each player.

The next thing to appoint is the `init` method; there we initialize the cards by calling the `initializeCards` method that looks like this:

```
- (void)initializeCards {

    NSString *cardPrefix = @"card_";
    NSString *typeDescription;
    Card *card;

    _deckOfCards = [NSMutableArray
    arrayWithCapacity:DECK_NUM_CARDS];

    for (int type = fire; type <= earth; type++) {
        switch (type) {
            case fire:
                typeDescription = @"fire";
```

```
                    break;
            case air:
                typeDescription = @"air";
                break;
            case water:
                typeDescription = @"water";
                break;
            case earth:
                typeDescription = @"earth";
                break;
            default:
                break;
        }
        card = [[Card alloc] initWithType:type attack:1 defense:2
        image:[NSString stringWithFormat:@"%@%@_%@", cardPrefix,
        typeDescription, @"12.png"]];
        [_deckOfCards addObject:card];

        card = [[Card alloc] initWithType: type attack:2 defense:1
        image:[NSString stringWithFormat:@"%@%@_%@", cardPrefix,
        typeDescription, @"21.png"]];
        [_deckOfCards addObject:card];
        card = [[Card alloc] initWithType: type attack:2 defense:3
        image:[NSString stringWithFormat:@"%@%@_%@", cardPrefix,
        typeDescription, @"23.png"]];
        [_deckOfCards addObject:card];
        card = [[Card alloc] initWithType: type attack:3 defense:2
        image:[NSString stringWithFormat:@"%@%@_%@", cardPrefix,
        typeDescription, @"32.png"]];
        [_deckOfCards addObject:card];
        card = [[Card alloc] initWithType: type attack:1 defense:3
        image:[NSString stringWithFormat:@"%@%@_%@", cardPrefix,
        typeDescription, @"13.png"]];
        [_deckOfCards addObject:card];
        card = [[Card alloc] initWithType: type attack:3 defense:1
        image:[NSString stringWithFormat:@"%@%@_%@", cardPrefix,
        typeDescription, @"31.png"]];
        [_deckOfCards addObject:card];
    }
}
```

This method is responsible for initializing the whole group of Card objects that will consist of four groups of six objects each.

At the beginning of the method, we declare two strings that we will use to store the element type and the image name. This name will have the `card_TYPEELEMENT_ATTACKDEFENSE.png` format.

We initialize the deck of cards to be an array of 24 objects (six minions for each of the four elemental types) and then we initialize the `Card` objects in a peculiar loop:

```
for (int type = fire; type <= earth; type++)
```

We iterate the enumerated types as if they were integers. Notice that we're indicating the stop condition as `<= earth` because we want to consider this possibility too.

Then we detect each of the types thanks to a `switch` statement in which we take advantage by storing the type string to build the image's filename.

After breaking out the `switch` statement, we create six `Card` objects in the same way and add them to the deck array. To achieve this, we pass the type description, the attack and defense values, and the formatted image name to the initialize method that we saw earlier in `Card.m`.

The last thing to do is add the image files for the different cards:

1. Right-click on the **Resources** group.
2. Choose **Add Files to "ElementalWizards"...**.
3. Finally, select the 24 `card_TYPEELEMENT_ATTACKDEFENSE.png` image files you will find in the `Resources` folder.

Initializing the game

Once we've set up everything, we can initialize the game by creating a new `Wizard` instance with its attributes and deck of cards.

First thing, declare two private instance variables by adding the following lines to the `@implementation` block in `GameScene.m`:

```
// Declare global variable for screen size
CGSize _screenSize;
// Declare current player instance
Wizard *_currentPlayer;
```

We want to store the screen size for later calculations and keep the information of the player executing the game; this is the aim of the previous variables.

We need to add a background image to the screen, but first we need to include it in the project, so follow these steps:

1. Right-click on the **Resources** group and select **Add Files to "ElementalWizards"...**.

2. Select the `background.png` image that you will find in the `Resources` folder.

3. Be sure that **Copy items into destination group's folder (if needed)** is selected and click on **Add**.

Once the image is available in the project, we can add the following lines in the `init` method after `[self initializeCards];`:

```
// Store the screen size for later calculations
_screenSize = [CCDirector sharedDirector].viewSize;
// Adding the background image
CCSprite *background = [CCSprite
spriteWithImageNamed:@"background.png"];
background.position = CGPointMake(_screenSize.width / 2,
_screenSize.height / 2);
[self addChild:background z:-1];
```

There is no mystery there, we just store the screen size by getting `viewSize` from `CCDirector` and we use this value to place the background sprite in the center of the screen.

Then we're going to show four buttons to allow the player to choose the natural element they want to control, but first we need to include the images that will represent each element:

1. Right-click again on **Resources** and select **Add Files to "ElementalWizards"...**.

2. Select `element_fire.png`, `element_air.png`, `element_water.png`, and `element_earth.png` images that you will find in the `Resources` folder and click on **Add**.

We need to declare some variables that we have to access during the development, so add these lines just after `Wizard *_currentPlayer;`:

```
// Declare element buttons
CCButton *_fireElementButton;
CCButton *_airElementButton;
CCButton *_waterElementButton;
CCButton *_earthElementButton;
```

You will realize that the project doesn't recognize the CCButton type; that's because you need to import the cocos2d-ui library. Add the following lines at the top of GameScene.h:

```
#import "cocos2d-ui.h"
```

Now you can add the following lines in the init method just before return self;:

```
// Create fire button
_fireElementButton = [CCButton buttonWithTitle:@""
spriteFrame:[CCSpriteFrame
frameWithImageNamed:@"element_fire.png"]];
_fireElementButton.positionType = CCPositionTypeNormalized;
_fireElementButton.position = ccp(0.2f, 0.30f);
[_fireElementButton setTarget:self
selector:@selector(initWizardWithTypeFire)];
[self addChild:_fireElementButton];

// Create air button
_airElementButton = [CCButton buttonWithTitle:@""
spriteFrame:[CCSpriteFrame
frameWithImageNamed:@"element_air.png"]];
_airElementButton.positionType = CCPositionTypeNormalized;
_airElementButton.position = ccp(0.4f, 0.30f);
[_airElementButton setTarget:self
selector:@selector(initWizardWithTypeAir)];
[self addChild:_airElementButton];

// Create water button
_waterElementButton = [CCButton buttonWithTitle:@""
spriteFrame:[CCSpriteFrame
frameWithImageNamed:@"element_water.png"]];
_waterElementButton.positionType = CCPositionTypeNormalized;
_waterElementButton.position = ccp(0.6f, 0.30f);
[_waterElementButton setTarget:self
selector:@selector(initWizardWithTypeWater)];
[self addChild:_waterElementButton];

// Create earth button
_earthElementButton = [CCButton buttonWithTitle:@""
spriteFrame:[CCSpriteFrame
frameWithImageNamed:@"element_earth.png"]];
_earthElementButton.positionType = CCPositionTypeNormalized;
_earthElementButton.position = ccp(0.8f, 0.30f);
[_earthElementButton setTarget:self
selector:@selector(initWizardWithTypeEarth)];
[self addChild:_earthElementButton];
```

Each button is created in the same way; we initialize it with the corresponding image we just added. We specify the button position type as `CCPositionTypeNormalized`, which means that we're going to set its position relative to the parent container, and we place each button in such a way that they cover the whole width of the screen. We specify the method that will be called when the button is pressed that matches the pattern `initWizardWithTypeELEMENT` and then we add the button to the scene.

You might be wondering what these methods do. Don't worry, add the following lines to `GameScene.m` and you will understand it shortly:

```
- (void)initWizardWithTypeFire {
    [self initWizardWithType:fire];
}

- (void)initWizardWithTypeAir {
    [self initWizardWithType:air];
}

- (void)initWizardWithTypeWater {
    [self initWizardWithType:water];
}

- (void)initWizardWithTypeEarth {
    [self initWizardWithType:earth];
}

- (void)initWizardWithType:(ElementTypes)type {

    // Initialize current player
    int initialLifePoints = INIT_LIFE_POINTS;
    NSMutableArray *randomDeck = [self createRandomDeckOfCards];
    _currentPlayer = [[Wizard alloc]
    initWithLifePoints:initialLifePoints type:type
    cards:randomDeck cardPlayed:NULL];

}
- (NSMutableArray *) createRandomDeckOfCards {

    NSMutableArray *deck = [NSMutableArray
    arrayWithCapacity:NUM_CARDS];
    int randomCard;

    for (int i = 0; i < NUM_CARDS; i++) {
        randomCard = arc4random_uniform(DECK_NUM_CARDS);
```

```
        [deck addObject:[_deckOfCards objectAtIndex:randomCard]];
    }
    return deck;
}
```

The `initWizardWithTypeELEMENT` method in fact calls another method, passing to it the corresponding element as an argument. This method, `initWizardWithType`, is responsible for initializing the first player with the element type, the initial life points, a default name, and a random deck of cards. The card played will remain `NULL` for the moment.

This random deck of cards is created in the `createRandomDeckOfCards` method, which initializes a new array of five cards and builds it with random `Card` objects taken from the common deck.

If you put the following lines at the end of `createRandomDeckOfCards` and before `return deck`, you will be able to log the cards created:

```
for (Card *card in deck){
        CCLOG(@"createRandomDeckOfCards - card type %u, card
        attack %d, card defense %d, card image %@",
        card.elementType, card.attack, card.defense,
        card.imageName);
}
```

We have written a lot, but we didn't see any results. Run the project and look at the initial screen of our game that we have so far:

Creating labels with CCLabelBMFont

In the *Adding labels* section of *Chapter 1*, *Sprites, Sounds, and Collisions*, you learned how to create labels thanks to the CCLabelTTF class and you found that it presented a performance problem due to the fact that every time you update a label, you create and fill a new CCLabelTTF texture. In this section, we're going to introduce CCLabelBMFont, where BM stands for bitmap, a class used to display bitmap font labels.

CCLabelBMFont has the advantage that it reduces the amount of memory overload when updating labels frequently. Thanks to CCLabelBMFont, we can treat each character as an independent sprite, which means that it will be accessed as a child of the label. It presents a little inconvenience because you will need to include a .fnt file created with some external software in order to render the label. But don't worry, there are several editors, both paid and free, for users to create their own bitmap font:

- bmGlyph is a paid desktop editor that offers a trial version
- Glyph Designer is another paid desktop editor that is widely used
- BMFont is a free desktop editor
- Littera is a free online product

Littera

To explain this section of creating labels with CCLabelBMFont, I chose Littera (http://kvazars.com/littera) as I think it provides an easy, fast, and free way to create our bitmaps.

If you access the previous URL, you will see a screen similar to the following one:

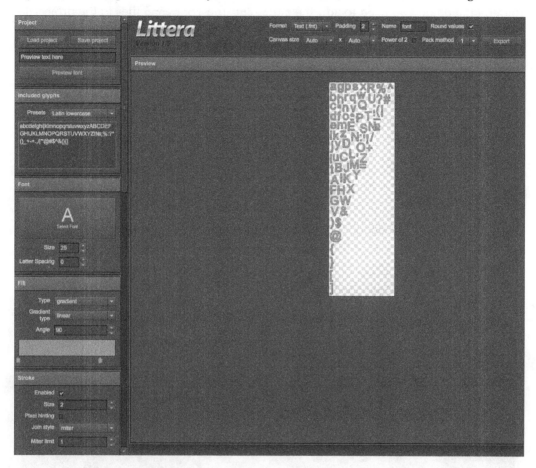

As you can see, it's composed of three sections:

- The central section shows a preview of the font we're building.

- On the left, we have several menus where we can edit several attributes, for example, the font size, letter spacing, color, stroke, shadow, or glow, to achieve the effect desired. I recommend you play with the different attributes to understand how each one affects the resultant font.

- The upper section allows us to export the font in different formats, padding, name, or canvas size.

I created a Text (`.fnt`) bitmap font called `font` that you will find in the `Resources` folder. First of all, you need to add the `font.fnt` and `font.png` files to the project so follow these steps:

1. On the navigator project on the left, right-click on the **Resources** group and select **Add Files to "ElementalWizards"...**.

2. Select `font.fnt` and `font.png` and click on **Add**.

As we will need to work with this label in several places in the code, we should declare it as an instance variable, so add the following lines after `CCButton *_earthElementButton;`:

```
// Declare label
CCLabelBMFont *_label;
```

Once the files are available in the project and the variable is declared, add the following lines to the `init` method just before `return self;`:

```
// Create CCLabelBMFont label
_label = [CCLabelBMFont labelWithString:@"Choose your element"
fntFile:@"font.fnt"];
_label.position = CGPointMake(_screenSize.width / 2,
_screenSize.height * 2 / 3);
[self addChild:_label];
```

If you run the project again, you will now see the label created with this bitmap font:

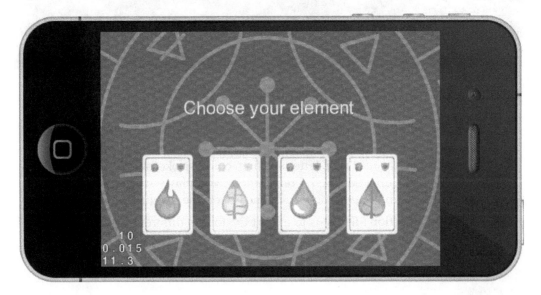

It's important to take into account that all the characters of a label created with `CCLabelBMFont` have their anchor point placed on (0.5, 0.5) and it's best not to change them to avoid unexpected behavior.

CCActions in depth

In the previous chapters, you learned how to create movement actions and sequences. But you may know that there are more types of actions, and we're going to see them in this section.

Actions are used to modify a node's properties such as its position, size, and rotation, or simulate some dynamic effects; that's why we can find in the order of tens of different actions.

We can categorize actions in three main groups depending on the kind of modification they apply to the node. In this way, we find:

*   **Interval actions**: This is the type of action that the actions we've been using in the previous chapters belong to. They get this name since you must specify the duration of the action.
*   **Instant actions**: These actions allow you to modify some node properties such as visibility or position, with the exception that this way you can perform these modifications in a sequence.
*   **Ease actions**: These actions apply a dynamic effect to the node and are widely used on transitions. All these actions inherit from `CCActionEase`.

Apart from the preceding groups, we find other types of actions that deserve to be highlighted:

*   **Sequences**: We've been using these to concatenate actions, as this is their purpose. Thanks to sequences, you can run actions one after another to achieve very interesting effects.
*   **Function calls**: By using a `CCActionCallFunc` call, we can call a custom function to be executed, for example, in the middle of a sequence of actions.
*   **Blocks**: `CCActionCallBlock` allows us to call a block of sentences to be executed in a sequence of actions.

By combining all these types of actions, you can achieve whatever effect you need. I recommend you play with them to understand their behavior and the effect produced.

We're going to use some actions to make the element buttons and the label disappear and to show the cards on screen. First add this line at the end of `initWizardWithType`:

```
// Hide buttons and label
[self hideElements];
```

Implement this new method by adding the following lines to `GameScene.m`:

```
-(void) hideElements {
    // Determine duration of interval actions
    float duration = ccpDistance(_label.position,
    CGPointMake(_label.position.x, _screenSize.height +
    _label.texture.contentSize.height / 2)) / 500;

    // Create move action for the label
    CCActionMoveTo *actionLabelMove = [CCActionMoveTo
    actionWithDuration:duration
    position:CGPointMake(_label.position.x, _screenSize.height +
    _label.texture.contentSize.height / 2)];
    // Combine move action with an ease action
    CCActionEaseBackInOut *easeLabel = [CCActionEaseBackInOut
    actionWithAction:actionLabelMove];

    // Create move action for the label
    CCActionMoveTo *actionFireMove = [CCActionMoveTo
    actionWithDuration:duration
    position:CGPointMake(_fireElementButton.position.x, -
    _fireElementButton.contentSize.height / 2)];
    // Combine move action with an ease action
    CCActionEaseSineIn *easeFire = [CCActionEaseSineIn
    actionWithAction:actionFireMove];

    // Create move action for the label
    CCActionMoveTo *actionAirMove = [CCActionMoveTo
    actionWithDuration:duration/2
    position:CGPointMake(_screenSize.width +
    _airElementButton.contentSize.width/2,
    _airElementButton.position.y)];
    // Combine move action with an ease action
    CCActionEaseOut *easeAir = [CCActionEaseOut
    actionWithAction:actionAirMove];

    // Create move action for the label
    CCActionMoveTo *actionWaterMove = [CCActionMoveTo
    actionWithDuration:duration
    position:CGPointMake(_waterElementButton.position.x, -
    _waterElementButton.contentSize.height / 2)];
```

```
    // Combine move action with an ease action
    CCActionEaseBackIn *easeWater = [CCActionEaseBackIn
    actionWithAction:actionWaterMove];

    // Create move action for the label
    CCActionMoveTo *actionEarthMove = [CCActionMoveTo
    actionWithDuration:duration
    position:CGPointMake(_earthElementButton.position.x, -
    _earthElementButton.contentSize.height / 2)];
    // Combine move action with an ease action
    CCActionEaseElasticIn *easeEarth = [CCActionEaseElasticIn
    actionWithAction:actionEarthMove];

    // Execute actions in parallel
    [_label runAction:easeLabel];
    [_fireElementButton runAction:easeFire];
    [_airElementButton runAction:easeAir];
    [_waterElementButton runAction:[CCActionCallFunc
    actionWithTarget:self selector:@selector(runEaseWater)]];
    [_earthElementButton runAction:[CCActionCallBlock
    actionWithBlock:^{
        [_earthElementButton runAction:easeEarth];
    }]];
}
```

The first thing we're doing in this method is initializing a duration variable to specify the same value to all the actions so they will finish at the same time. For that, we calculate the distance between the current label position and the place where we want to move it out of the screen, and we divide this value by the speed that we want for the action (500 in this case).

Then, we create a CCActionMoveTo instance that will place the label to the top of the screen, out of the view, in the time we have calculated as duration. We combine this action with a CCActionEaseBackInOut instance that will generate an attractive movement.

After that, we create a similar move action to displace the fire button at the bottom of the screen out of view and we use this action to generate a CCActionEaseSineIn class.

In a similar way, we create CCActionEaseOut, CCActionEaseBackIn, and CCActionEaseElasticIn to make the buttons disappear.

The last block of code runs each of these actions at the same time. Pay attention to the last two lines; we are executing a function through an action thanks to `CCActionCallFunc`. This class receives a target, that can be any object, and a selector, that corresponds to the method we're going to execute. This line could be replaced by the following one, but I just wanted to show you how to implement a `CCActionCallFunc` instance:

```
[self runEaseWater];
```

You just need to implement the `runEaseWater` method we're calling:

```
- (void) runEaseWater {
    // Determine duration of interval actions
    float duration = ccpDistance(_label.position,
    CGPointMake(_label.position.x, _screenSize.height +
    _label.texture.contentSize.height / 2)) / 500;
    // Create move action for the label
    CCActionMoveTo *actionWaterMove = [CCActionMoveTo
    actionWithDuration:duration
    position:CGPointMake(_waterElementButton.position.x, -
    _waterElementButton.contentSize.height / 2)];
    // Combine move action with an ease action
    CCActionEaseBackIn *easeWater = [CCActionEaseBackIn
    actionWithAction:actionWaterMove];
    [_waterElementButton runAction:easeWater];
}
```

The `CCActionCallBlock` call just runs the contents of a block as we've seen in the previous chapters.

Before proceeding, we're going to clean the code a little, so delete the `runEaseWater` method and let the actions execute as follows:

```
// Execute actions in parallel
[_label runAction:easeLabel];
[_fireElementButton runAction:easeFire];
[_airElementButton runAction:easeAir];
[_waterElementButton runAction:easeWater];
[_earthElementButton runAction:easeEarth];
```

Now that we have hidden the label and buttons, we need to show the random cards of the wizard. For that, call the following method by adding this line at the end of `initWizardWithType`, just after `[self hideElements];`:

```
// Show current player cards
[self dealCards];
```

Implement the method by adding the following lines:

```
-(void) dealCards {

    // Get an auxiliary card to get its width
    Card *cardAux = [_deckOfCards objectAtIndex:0];
    // Calculate gaps between cards to place them equidistantly
    float gapWidth = ((_screenSize.width - NUM_CARDS *
    cardAux.contentSize.width) / (NUM_CARDS + 1));
    // Initial x position for the cards
    float positionX = gapWidth + (cardAux.contentSize.width / 2);

    for (Card *card in _currentPlayer.cards){
        // Set the card position
        card.position = CGPointMake(_screenSize.width +
        card.contentSize.width/2, _screenSize.height -
        card.contentSize.height / 2);

        // Add the card to the scene
        [self addChild:card];

        // Generate a spin and displacement action
        CCActionMoveTo *actionMove = [CCActionMoveTo
        actionWithDuration:0.5 position:CGPointMake(positionX,
        card.contentSize.height / 2)];
        CCActionRotateBy *actionSpin = [CCActionRotateBy
        actionWithDuration:0.5 angle:720];

        CCLOG(@"dealCards - card type %u, card attack %d, card
        defense %d, card image %@, position x %f, position y %f",
        card.elementType, card.attack, card.defense,
        card.imageName, positionX,
        card.texture.contentSize.height);

        // Execute actions simultaneously
        [card runAction:actionSpin];
        [card runAction:actionMove];
        // Update next x position
        positionX += gapWidth + card.contentSize.width;
    }
}
```

This method will show the cards that belong to the wizard on the screen. As we want them to cover the whole width, we need to place them equidistantly; that's why we take an auxiliary card from the global deck in order to use its width.

We calculate the gap between cards, taking into account the screen and auxiliary card widths, and the number of cards. Then we initialize the `positionX` variable, which we will use to place each card in its proper position.

Then, for each wizard's card, we place it in the top-right corner out of view and we add it to the scene.

We want the cards to appear to move to their position in view while they rotate, so we create both `CCActionMoveTo` and `CCActionRotateBy` actions with the same duration. The movement action doesn't need explanation so take a look at the rotation; we just need to specify the duration of the movement and the degree of the angle the node will perform. In this case, `720` means that the card will describe two circumferences.

As we want both actions to be executed simultaneously, we run them without a `CCActionSequence` and then update the next card position.

Run the game and take a look at the actions we just created:

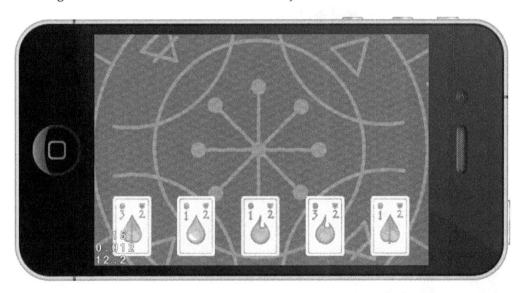

It's possible that you face an exception at this point when the same card is added to the player deck. As this `Card` instance is the same and we are trying to add it multiple times to the scene, it throws the following exception:

```
'NSInternalInconsistencyException', reason: 'child already added
to another node. It can't be added again'
```

To fix this, we should make a few changes. In `Card.h`, declare the following method:

```
// Declare method to init card by match card
-(id) initWithCard:(Card *)card;
```

Implement it by adding the following lines to `Card.m`:

```
-(id) initWithCard:(Card *)card {
    self = [self initWithType:card.elementType attack:card.attack
    defense:card.defense image:card.imageName];
    return self;
}
```

Now, in `GameScene.m`, replace the following line in `createRandomDeckOfCards`:

```
[deck addObject:[_deckOfCards objectAtIndex:randomCard]];
```

With these lines:

```
// Avoid adding a card multiple times
Card *card = [_deckOfCards objectAtIndex:randomCard];
[deck addObject:[[Card alloc] initWithCard:card]];
```

Check it; you won't have this problem again.

Drag, drop, and scale

During each turn, each player will select a card and use it to attack its adversary. In this section, we're going to implement how to drag and drop a sprite and how to scale its size.

First of all, you need to enable touch management, so in `GameScene.m`, add these lines at the end of the `init` method, before `return self;`:

```
// Enabling user interaction
self.userInteractionEnabled = TRUE;
```

We need to declare two variables to manage which card has been selected and its initial position. Add the following lines after `CCLabelBMFont *_label;`:

```
    // Declare card selected
    Card *_selectedCard;

    // Declare initial card position
    CGPoint _initialCardPosition;
```

We will use `_selectedCard` to know which card is being dragged, and `_initialCardPosition` will store its initial position so we can recover it if the player doesn't want to play this card.

Now implement the `touchBegan` method:

```
- (void) touchBegan: (UITouch *) touch withEvent: (UIEvent *) event {
    // Check what card has been touched
    CGPoint touchLocation = [touch locationInNode:self];
    [self checkCardTouched:touchLocation];
}
```

This method just takes the currently touched location and calls `checkCardTouched` to know which card has been touched. Implement this method with these lines:

```
- (void) checkCardTouched: (CGPoint) touchLocation{
    for (Card *card in _currentPlayer.cards) {
        if (CGRectContainsPoint(card.boundingBox, touchLocation)){
            // The touch location belongs to the card
            _selectedCard = card;

            // Store the initial card position
            _initialCardPosition = _selectedCard.position;

            // Scale the card and update its z-order value
            CCActionScaleTo *scale = [CCActionScaleTo
            actionWithDuration:0.5 scale:1.5];
            [_selectedCard runAction:scale];
            _selectedCard.zOrder = 1;

            break;
        }
    }
}
```

We iterate through all the player cards and check whether the touched point belongs to its bounding box. If so, we store the card in the `_selectedCard` variable and take note of its original position.

We want to highlight the selected card so that's why we scale it by using a `CCActionScaleTo` action. This action is an interval action that receives a `duration` argument and the `scale` factor that we want to apply to the node.

The last thing in this method is the zOrder value update. We want the card to be moved over the rest of the cards; that's why we set zOrder as 1.

Then we need to implement the drag action, which is as simple as defining the desired behavior in the touchMoved method:

```
- (void) touchMoved: (UITouch *) touch withEvent: (UIEvent *) event
{
    // Moving the card along the screen
    CGPoint touchLocation = [touch locationInNode:self];
    _selectedCard.position = touchLocation;
}
```

This is pretty simple; we're just defining the new card position to be the same as the touched location.

Now we should define what happens when the player drops the card. To achieve this, implement the touchEnded method by adding these lines:

```
- (void) touchEnded: (UITouch *) touch withEvent: (UIEvent *) event {
    // Define area to drop the card
    CGRect boardRect = CGRectMake (0,
    _selectedCard.contentSize.height, _screenSize.width, 3 *
    _selectedCard.contentSize.height);

    // Only drop card inside the defined area
    if (CGRectContainsPoint(boardRect, [touch
    locationInNode:self])) {
        _selectedCard.position = CGPointMake(_screenSize.width /
        2, 2 * _selectedCard.texture.contentSize.height);
    } else {
        _selectedCard.position = _initialCardPosition;
    }
    // Revert scalation
    CCActionScaleTo *scale = [CCActionScaleTo
    actionWithDuration:0.15 scale:1.0];
    [_selectedCard runAction:scale];
}
```

We want to define an area where the player can drop the card to be played. If the card is dropped out of this area, we will understand that the wizard decided not to play it and will recover its original position.

The droppable area is a rectangle that will cover the whole width of the screen and two times the card's height. If the last touched location belongs inside this droppable area, we update the card's position to be centered on the screen and above the player's cards.

If the card is dropped out of the area, we recover its position so it will appear at its initial position.

Once the drag and drop sequence ends, we need to recover the card's scale so we define another CCActionScaleTo instance with a scale factor of 1.0 and duration of almost 0. Note that this value is just saying that the node has to have the same size as at the beginning.

Run the game and play a little with this drag, scale, and drop behavior:

Game Center

The time when arcade regulars entered their initials when the game was over has gone. Today, almost every game has an online mode and today's players are not satisfied with just playing games; they like to share their achievements, compare trophies, challenge other players, and play with their friends.

Game Center is a network service provided by Apple to support interaction between gamers in a variety of ways such as storing scores and leaderboards, managing achievements, or multiplayer games.

Game Kit is the framework needed to make Game Center features available in your games, but you will need to perform some previous steps before coding, for example, your app should be configured in iTunes Connect to enable Game Center.

Configuring Game Center in iTunes Connect

We are going to specify the steps you will need to follow in order to configure your app in iTunes Connect, but I recommend you take a look at the following website if you want to find more information: `https://developer.apple.com/library/ios/documentation/NetworkingInternet/Conceptual/GameKit_Guide/Introduction/Introduction.html`.

Going back to iTunes Connect (`http://itunesconnect.apple.com`):

1. You first need to access the **My Apps** section.
2. Click on **+** at the top-left side of the screen and select **New iOS App**.
3. Make sure you fill out the **Name** and **Primary Language** fields and click on the link below **Bundle ID** to the **Developer** portal.
4. In **Developer** portal, fill out the name field in the **App ID Description** field.
5. Make sure you select **Explicit App Id** and that you use a unique value for **Bundle ID**. This value will need to match the Xcode project's **Bundle Identifier** from the **General** project properties tab. In my case, I chose `com.jjordanarenas.ElementalWizards`, but you will need to specify a different identifier as it has to be unique.
6. Still in the **Registering an App ID** screen, make sure **Game Center** is selected before clicking on **Continue**.
7. Go back to the new app information screen, and be sure that you set newly created **Bundle ID**.
8. Follow the steps to finish creating the new app. If you need more information on these steps, you can find support at `https://developer.apple.com/library/ios/documentation/LanguagesUtilities/Conceptual/iTunesConnect_Guide/Chapters/About.html`.

Once your app has been created in iTunes Connect, you will have to configure the project in Xcode.

Configuring the game in Xcode

The first thing you have to do in Xcode is set up the same bundle ID you used to create the app in iTunes Connect. For that, go to the **General** tab on the Xcode project and set your ID in the **Bundle Identifier** field (in my case, com.jjordanarenas. ElementalWizards):

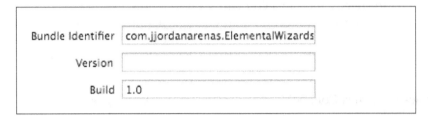

Note that the same property can be modified in the Info.plist file placed under the **Resources** group:

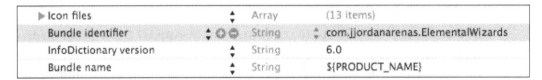

Now we will configure our game to require Game Kit to run on devices. To achieve this is easy: just go to the **Capabilities** section in the project's settings and turn on the **Game Center** button:

This will automatically add GameKit.framework to the project. This framework allows our game to connect players with their friends, create online matches, keep leaderboards and achievements, create turn-based matches, and challenge other players.

On the other hand, thanks to Game Kit we can create ad hoc networks (both Bluetooth and wireless) and provide in-game voice chat. This is an amazing service, isn't it?

So what are we waiting for? Let's make it work in our game!

Checking Game Center's availability

When running a Game Center-aware game, we must be sure that the operating system installed on the device is 4.1 or later. To perform this and other Game Center checks, we're going to create a helper class that will centralize these tasks.

First of all, let's create a new class:

1. Right-click on the **Classes** group in the project navigator and select **New File...**.
2. Click on **iOS | Cocoa Touch | Objective-C**, call it `GameCenterHelper`, and make it a subclass of `NSObject`.
3. Click on **Next**, choose where to save it, and click on **Create**.

Then replace `GameCenterHelper.h` with the following lines:

```
#import <Foundation/Foundation.h>
#import <GameKit/GameKit.h>
#import "cocos2d.h"

@interface GameCenterHelper : NSObject {
}

// Property to store Game Center availability
@property (assign, readonly) BOOL isGameCenterAvailable;

// Method that retrieves the singleton instance
+ (GameCenterHelper *)sharedGameCenterInstance;

// Check Game Center availability
(BOOL) checkGameCenterAvailable;
@end
```

We're importing the `GameKit` library and declaring a Boolean read-only property that will store information on whether Game Center is available.

We also declare a class method that will retrieve the singleton instance of the class. We implement the singleton pattern in this class, as we want to centralize the check tasks on just one object.

On the other hand, we declare a method that will check the Game Center availability.

Now we can implement our new helper class. Open `GameCenterHelper.m` and replace its contents with the following lines of code:

```
#import "GameCenterHelper.h"

@implementation GameCenterHelper
static GameCenterHelper *singletonHelper = nil;

+ (GameCenterHelper *) sharedGameCenterInstance {
    if (!singletonHelper) {
        // Create singleton of GameCenterHelper
        singletonHelper = [[GameCenterHelper alloc] init];
    }
    return singletonHelper;
}

- (id)init {
    if ((self = [super init])) {
      CCLOG(@"Helper initialized successfully");
    }
    return self;
}

- (BOOL) checkGameCenterAvailable {
    // Check for presence of GKLocalPlayer API
    Class gcClass = (NSClassFromString(@"GKLocalPlayer"));

    // check if the device is running iOS 4.1 or later
    NSString *reqSysVer = @"4.1";
    NSString *currSysVer = [[UIDevice currentDevice]
    systemVersion];
    BOOL osVersionSupported = ([currSysVer compare:reqSysVer
    options:NSNumericSearch] != NSOrderedAscending);

    _isGameCenterAvailable = (gcClass && osVersionSupported);
    CCLOG(@"Game Center is available: %@ ", _isGameCenterAvailable
    ? @"Yes" : @"No");
    return _isGameCenterAvailable;
}
@end
```

At the top of the file, we're declaring a static variable that will keep the singleton instance of the helper class, which it has instantiated in the `sharedGameCenterInstance` class method.

The `init` method doesn't deserve any mention as it's pretty simple, but we should pay attention to the `checkGameCenterAvailable` method. This method checks whether there is a class from Game Kit (`GKLocalPlayer`) available and then compares the device operating system installed with the minimum version (4.1).

Note that we're comparing both versions with the `compare` method and checking whether `currSysVer` is smaller than `regSysVer` thanks to `NSOrderedAscending`.

Add the following line in `AppDelegate.m` at the end of `didFinishLaunchingWithOptions`:

```
[[GameCenterHelper sharedGameCenterInstance]
checkGameCenterAvailable];
```

Import the Game Center helper library to the `AppDelegate.m` by adding the next line at the top of the file:

```
#import "GameCenterHelper.h"
```

Run the game and you can check whether Game Center is available by just looking at the logs.

Authenticating the player

The first thing you need to do when your game starts is to authenticate the player or they won't be able to retrieve any information from the server such as games, leaderboards, or achievements.

Following the guides Apple provides, let's declare the following method by adding the following line in `GameCenterHelper.h`:

```
// Authenticate local player
(void) authenticateLocalPlayer;
```

Implement it by adding the following block of code to `GameCenterHelper.m`:

```
- (void) authenticateLocalPlayer {

    if (!_isGameCenterAvailable) return;

    GKLocalPlayer *localPlayer = [GKLocalPlayer localPlayer];
    [localPlayer authenticateWithCompletionHandler:^(NSError
    *error) {
        if (localPlayer.isAuthenticated)
        {
```

```
            CCLOG(@"The player %@ has successfully authenticated",
            localPlayer.alias);
        }
    }];
}
```

In the `init` method, find this log line:

```
CCLOG(@"Helper initialized successfully");
```

Replace it with the following statement:

```
[self checkGameCenterAvailable];
```

The last thing is to find the following line in `AppDelegate.m`:

```
[[GameCenterHelper sharedGameCenterInstance]
checkGameCenterAvailable];
```

Replace it with this one:

```
[[GameCenterHelper sharedGameCenterInstance]
authenticateLocalPlayer];
```

These lines are pretty easy to understand; we first check the availability of Game Center, and if it is available, we instantiate new `GKLocalPlayer`. A Game Center `init` session will appear in case you're not logged in with your user, but if you are, you'll see a welcome message:

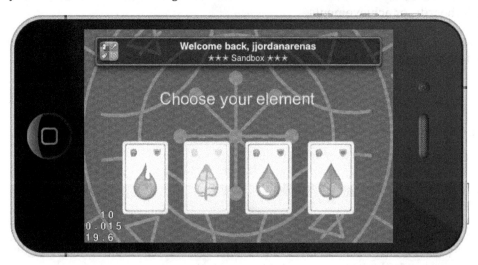

There is one last thing to take into account when managing user authentication, namely, what happens when an authenticated player logs off or logs in again. In those cases, we should update the `_isPlayerAuthenticated` value.

To achieve that, add the following block of code in the `init` method of `GameCenterHelper.m`, just after `[self checkGameCenterAvailable];`:

```
// If authenticated user changes
if (_isGameCenterAvailable) {
    NSNotificationCenter *nc =
    [NSNotificationCenter defaultCenter];
    [nc addObserver:self
            selector:@selector(authenticationChanged)
            name:GKPlayerAuthenticationDidChangeNotificationName
            object:nil];
}
```

Declare a new property by adding the following lines to `GameCenterHelper.h`:

```
// Property to know whether the player is authenticated or not
@property (assign, readonly) BOOL isPlayerAuthenticated;
```

Implement the method by adding:

```
- (void)authenticationChanged {

    if ([GKLocalPlayer localPlayer].isAuthenticated &&
        !_isPlayerAuthenticated) {
        CCLOG(@"Now player is authenticated");
        _isPlayerAuthenticated = TRUE;
    } else if (![GKLocalPlayer localPlayer].isAuthenticated &&
                _isPlayerAuthenticated) {
        CCLOG(@"Player has logged off");
        _isPlayerAuthenticated = FALSE;
    }
}
```

When initializing the game, or even if we switched to another app and went back to the game, we check whether the authentication has changed. This could happen if, for example, the player was not authenticated and had to go out of the game to log in or create a new Game Center account. In this case, `_isPlayerAuthenticated` is FALSE but the player just logged in so `[GKLocalPlayer localPlayer].isAuthenticated` is TRUE, so we need to update `_isPlayerAuthenticated`.

The opposite case is if the player is logged in and decides to log out of Game Center or even change the user ID.

Turn-based games

Once we're sure that Game Center is available and that the user is logged in, we can pay attention to the game itself.

[It's very important that at this point, your game has an authenticated user.]

We're developing a turn-based game in which the different players do not need to play concurrently; in fact, just one player can play during a turn. You perform your movement or action, pass the turn to your opponent, and wait for them to take theirs.

These turns can happen in a short period or may take several days, but the match data will stay updated during its whole lifetime. Even if a player is involved in several matches with different challengers, all of these matches will stay atomic.

This behavior is possible thanks to some specific Game Kit classes:

- `GKMatchRequest`: This is the class that contains the information required to create a new match. This class is common to all kinds of matches in Game Center.

- `GKTurnBasedMatch`: This is the main class, and is in charge of storing information about the match such as the players involved, the player owner of the turn, and the data needed to represent the match. Each instance of this class has an ID that will be useful to distinguish between matches and a status that will be useful to know the state of the game.

- `GKTurnBasedParticipant`: Each player involved in a game is an instance of this class that will be stored in an array. This array stores user information such as the user's identifier, status, and the outcome of the match.

- `GKTurnBasedMatchmakerViewController`: This class is used to display a screen (`UIViewController`) where players can manage their turn-based games. Players can decide to create a new match, take the turn on a specific game, or even quit from a match.

- `GKTurnBasedMatchmakerViewControllerDelegate`: This protocol will respond to the events generated by the `GKTurnBasedMatchmakerViewController` instance such as `didFindMatch`, `playerQuitForMatch`, `didFailWithError`, or `turnBasedMatchmakerViewControllerWasCancelled`.

- `GKTurnBasedEventListener`: The purpose of this is to manage the events happening in a turn-based match such as match ending, turn becoming active, or initiating a match.

Now that we know the tools needed to implement a turn-based match, let's apply it to our game.

The first step is to create the match, so add a new instance variable in `GameCenterHelper.h`:

```
// Declare view controller to load Game Center
UIViewController *gameCenterViewController;
```

We have

declared a `UIViewController` instance that will help us show the Game Center menu to manage new and existing matches.

Declare the following method in the same header file:

```
// Create a turn-based match
- (void)createMatchWithMinPlayers:(int)minPlayers
    maxPlayers:(int)maxPlayers
    viewController:(UIViewController *)viewController;
```

Implement it by adding the following lines to `GameCenterHelper.m`:

```
- (void)createMatchWithMinPlayers:(int)minPlayers
                maxPlayers:(int)maxPlayers
                viewController:(UIViewController *)viewController {
    if (!_isGameCenterAvailable) return;

    // Set the view to show the Game Center screen
    gameCenterViewController = viewController;

    // Create the match request
    GKMatchRequest *request = [[GKMatchRequest alloc] init];
    request.minPlayers = minPlayers;
    request.maxPlayers = maxPlayers;

    // Show the Game Center screen
    GKTurnBasedMatchmakerViewController *turnBasedViewController =
    [[GKTurnBasedMatchmakerViewController alloc]
     initWithMatchRequest:request];
    turnBasedViewController.turnBasedMatchmakerDelegate = self;
    turnBasedViewController.showExistingMatches = YES;

    [gameCenterViewController
    presentModalViewController:turnBasedViewController
    animated:YES];
}
```

This method first checks whether Game Center is available. If so, it will create a match request for the number of players specified and we instantiate a new `GKTurnBasedMatchmakerViewController` instance with the match request information. We load this view into the game thanks to the view controller we received as the argument at the beginning of the method. We specify `showExistingMatches` to `YES` so we can play several matches at the same time.

We will need to reorganize some methods in `GameScene.m` to show the Game Center screen, so replace the contents of the `init` method by these following lines:

```
// Apple recommends assigning self with supers return value
self = [super init];
if (!self) return(nil);

// Store the screen size for later calculations
_screenSize = [CCDirector sharedDirector].viewSize;

// Adding the background image
CCSprite *background = [CCSprite
spriteWithImageNamed:@"background.png"];
background.position = CGPointMake(_screenSize.width / 2,
_screenSize.height / 2);
[self addChild:background z:-1];
// Enabling user interaction
self.userInteractionEnabled = TRUE;
[self createPlayButton];

return self;
```

Add this line after `CGPoint _initialCardPosition`:

```
// Declare button to create a new game
CCButton *_createGameButton;
```

Implement the following method:

```
- (void)createPlayButton {
    _createGameButton = [CCButton buttonWithTitle:@"Play"
    fontName:@"Verdana-Bold" fontSize:28.0f];
    _createGameButton.positionType = CCPositionTypeNormalized;
    _createGameButton.position = ccp(0.5f, 0.5f);
    [_createGameButton setTarget:self
    selector:@selector(startMatch:)];
    [self addChild:_createGameButton];
}
```

There is nothing to appoint here; when the game initializes, we will show the play button that will start the match by calling the `startMatch` method.

Add these lines to implement `startMatch`:

```
- (void)startMatch:(id)sender
{
    [[GameCenterHelper sharedGameCenterInstance]
     createMatchWithMinPlayers:NUM_PARTICIPANTS
     maxPlayers:NUM_PARTICIPANTS viewController:[CCDirector
     sharedDirector]];
    [self removeChild:_createGameButton];
}
```

Declare the `NUM_PARTICIPANTS` constant adding the following line at the top of `GameScene.m`, just above `@implementation GameScene`:

```
// Number of participants in the match
#define NUM_PARTICIPANTS 2
```

Import `GameCenterHelper.h` by adding the following line at the top of `GameScene.h`:

```
#import "GameCenterHelper.h"
```

If you run the game now, you will see the **Play Now** button that will load the following Game Center screen when touched:

This screen shows the status of previous matches and allows us to create a new one. As there is no existing match, the screen directly takes you to the menu to start a new game. If you click on the **Invite Friends** button, you will be able to select one of our friends who has the game installed to start a match. If you choose **Play Now**, it will select a random Game Center user as your opponent. You can see that there is just one empty slot because we have defined a two-player game, and one of them is ourselves.

Once there is an existing match, the initial screen looks like the following one and you will need to push the **+** button to show the preceding screen.

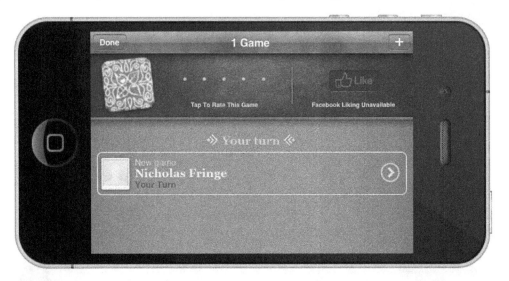

As you can see from the screenshot, I'm playing against Dr. Nicholas Fringe in our game and you will need to install the game on a friend's device and/or to use two sandbox Game Center accounts to test this game properly.

The next step is implementing the GKTurnBasedMatchmakerViewControllerDelegate protocol. Go back to GameCenterHelper.h and modify the @interface GameCenterHelper : NSObject to look like:

```
@interface GameCenterHelper : NSObject
<GKTurnBasedMatchmakerViewControllerDelegate> {
```

Implement the following methods of the protocol by adding these lines to GameCenterHelper.m:

```
- (void)turnBasedMatchmakerViewController:
(GKTurnBasedMatchmakerViewController *)viewController
                 didFindMatch:(GKTurnBasedMatch *)match {
```

```
    [gameCenterViewController
    dismissModalViewControllerAnimated:YES];
    CCLOG(@"Match %@ found", match);
}


- (void)turnBasedMatchmakerViewController:
(GKTurnBasedMatchmakerViewController *)viewController
                    playerQuitForMatch:(GKTurnBasedMatch *)match {
    CCLOG(@"Player %@ has quit from the match %@",
        match.currentParticipant, match);
}


- (void)turnBasedMatchmakerViewController:
(GKTurnBasedMatchmakerViewController *)viewController
                        didFailWithError:(NSError *)error {
    [gameCenterViewController
     dismissModalViewControllerAnimated:YES];
    CCLOG(@"Error trying to find a match: %@",
    error.localizedDescription);
}


- (void)turnBasedMatchmakerViewControllerWasCancelled:
(GKTurnBasedMatchmakerViewController *)viewController {
    [gameCenterViewController
     dismissModalViewControllerAnimated:YES];
    CCLOG(@"Match has been cancelled");
}
```

The didFindMatch method is called when a player selects a match from Game Center and it receives a GKTurnBasedMatch instance as input. The playerQuitForMatch method is called when a player chooses to quit the match. The didFailWithError method is called when some error occurs and wasCancelled is called when a match is canceled.

These methods should be implemented in order to manage the different situations in a multiplayer game such as if the player owner of the turn quits or cancels a match. All the methods dismiss the view in a modal way, which means that the user input (touches) will only apply to the Game Center view and not in the game itself until the player closes that view.

If you run the game and create a new match, you will see logs like the following ones that correspond to the call to the `didFindMatch` method:

```
2014-06-30 20:33:56.360 ElementalWizards[311:60b] Match
<GKTurnBasedMatch 0x1702520f0 - matchID:8e4ebb89-2862-4eb2-8ac5-
9efb91d241a3 bundleID:com.jjordanarenas.ElementalWizards status:G
KTurnBasedMatchStatusOpen message:(null) creationDate:2014-06-30
18:33:52 +0000 currentParticipant:<GKTurnBasedParticipant 0x17000f070
- playerID:G:982034245 (local player) status:Active matchOutcome:None
lastTurnDate:(null) timeoutDate:(null)> participants:<GKTurnBase
dParticipant 0x17000f070 - playerID:G: 982034245 (local player)
status:Active matchOutcome:None lastTurnDate:(null) timeoutDate:(
null)>,<GKTurnBasedParticipant 0x17000f060 - playerID:G:819246524
status:Invited matchOutcome:None lastTurnDate:(null)
timeoutDate:(null)> matchData.length:0 matchDataMaximumSize:65536
exchanges:(null)> found
```

If you pay attention to the log, you will notice that we're getting important information such as the match ID, status of the match, the current player owner of the turn with its player ID and status, the list of participants, the last turn date (`null` until a turn happens), and the match outcome. The invited user is Dr. Fringe's ID as I decided to play with him instead of creating a game with a random user.

I recommend you practice creating new matches, canceling matches, or quitting matches so you can get familiar with the data shown in each case.

The first turn

As we created the match, we're the owners of the first turn. In each turn, we will need to play a card before passing the turn to our opponent. To record the state of the match, we will build an `NSData` instance with all the information needed to represent the new status.

To keep the information of the match, we're going to declare a `GKTurnBasedMatch` instance, so add the following lines to `GameCenterHelper.h`:

```
// Property to keep the information of the match
@property (retain) GKTurnBasedMatch *activeMatch;
```

The first thing we have to do with it is assign the match information in `didFindMatch`, so add these lines at the end of `didFindMatch` in `GameCenterHelper.m`:

```
_activeMatch = match;

// Get first participant last turn date
GKTurnBasedParticipant *firstParticipant =
```

```
[match.participants objectAtIndex:0];

if (firstParticipant.lastTurnDate) {
    CCLOG(@"It's an already created match");
} else {
    CCLOG(@"It's a new match");
}
```

We assign the match information to our newly created property and get the first participant of the match. We use the `lastTurnDate` property to find out whether it is a new game or an existing one. If `lastTurnDate` is NULL, we can assume that nobody played before us so it's the first turn of the match. You can check this by creating a new match and looking at the logs.

Once we are sure it's a new match, we need to load the initial screen on the game so the player can choose their element and receive a deck of random cards to start playing. For this purpose, we need to link `GameCenterHelper` and `GameScene`; that's why we're going to implement our own protocol.

In `GameCenterHelper.h`, add the following lines at the beginning of the class, just after the imports section:

```
@protocol GameCenterHelperDelegate
- (void) initializeNewGame:(GKTurnBasedMatch *)match;
- (void) receiveTurn:(GKTurnBasedMatch *)match;
- (void) matchOver:(GKTurnBasedMatch *)match;
@end
```

Add the following property:

```
// Delegate property
@property (nonatomic, retain) id <GameCenterHelperDelegate>
delegate;
```

We have declared three protocol methods and a new property. The purpose of these protocol methods is the following:

- `initializeNewGame`: This method is called in `didFindMatch`, and will perform the actions needed to set up a new match

- `receiveTurn`: This method is called in `didFindMatch` too, and it will configure the view for a match in which we're owners of the turn

- `matchOver`: This method will be responsible for checking the end of the game

So now we can update the `didFindMatch` method by finding `CCLOG`:

```
CCLOG(@"It's an already created match");
```

Replace it with the following call:

```
[_delegate receiveTurn:match];
```

Find the following log:

```
CCLOG(@"It's a new match");
```

Replace it with the following `delegate` method call:

```
[_delegate initializeNewGame:match];
```

Before proceeding, we need to make `GameScene` implement the `GameCenterHelperDelegate` protocol. To achieve this, replace the `@interface GameScene` line in `GameScene.h` with the following one:

```
@interface GameScene : CCScene <GameCenterHelperDelegate>{
```

Now we can implement the protocol methods, so in `GameScene.m`, add the following lines:

```
- (void) initializeNewGame:(GKTurnBasedMatch *)match {
    CCLOG(@"Initializing new game");
}

- (void) receiveTurn:(GKTurnBasedMatch *)match {
    CCLOG(@"Turn received");
}
```

We just show a log message in both methods in order to know which one is accessed.

The last thing left is initializing the `delegate` property, which we will do by adding the following lines at the end of the `init` method before `return self;`:

```
// Initializing the delegate property
[GameCenterHelper sharedGameCenterInstance].delegate = self;
```

Again, you can check this by running the project and looking at the logs after creating a new game.

Now that we have linked `GameCenterHelper` and `GameScene`, in other words, the Game Center view and our game, we can start implementing the game's functionality. Once we create a new match, we should show the `init` screen with the elemental buttons, so replace the contents of `initializeNewGame` in `GameScene.m` with this line:

```
[self showInitScreen];
```

Implement it by adding the following block of code:

```
- (void)showInitScreen {
    // Create fire button
    _fireElementButton = [CCButton buttonWithTitle:@""
    spriteFrame:[CCSpriteFrame
    frameWithImageNamed:@"element_fire.png"]];
    _fireElementButton.positionType = CCPositionTypeNormalized;
    _fireElementButton.position = ccp(0.2f, 0.30f);
    [_fireElementButton setTarget:self
    selector:@selector(initWizardWithTypeFire)];
    [self addChild:_fireElementButton];

    // Create air button
    _airElementButton = [CCButton buttonWithTitle:@""
    spriteFrame:[CCSpriteFrame
    frameWithImageNamed:@"element_air.png"]];
    _airElementButton.positionType = CCPositionTypeNormalized;
    _airElementButton.position = ccp(0.4f, 0.30f);
    [_airElementButton setTarget:self
    selector:@selector(initWizardWithTypeAir)];
    [self addChild:_airElementButton];

    // Create water button
    _waterElementButton = [CCButton buttonWithTitle:@""
    spriteFrame:[CCSpriteFrame
    frameWithImageNamed:@"element_water.png"]];
    _waterElementButton.positionType = CCPositionTypeNormalized;
    _waterElementButton.position = ccp(0.6f, 0.30f);
    [_waterElementButton setTarget:self
    selector:@selector(initWizardWithTypeWater)];
    [self addChild:_waterElementButton];

    // Create earth button
    _earthElementButton = [CCButton buttonWithTitle:@""
    spriteFrame:[CCSpriteFrame
    frameWithImageNamed:@"element_earth.png"]];
    _earthElementButton.positionType = CCPositionTypeNormalized;
    _earthElementButton.position = ccp(0.8f, 0.30f);
    [_earthElementButton setTarget:self
    selector:@selector(initWizardWithTypeEarth)];
    [self addChild:_earthElementButton];

    // Create CCLabelBMFont label
    _label = [CCLabelBMFont labelWithString:@"Choose your element"
    fntFile:@"font.fnt"];
```

```
_label.position = CGPointMake(_screenSize.width / 2,
_screenSize.height * 2 / 3);
[self addChild:_label];

[self initializeCards];
}
```

This should be familiar to you, as we're just doing the same steps that we performed at the beginning of the chapter; we show the four element buttons and initialize the label and the common cards. If you run the game again, you will see that we've implemented the same functionality we already had, but this time we link it to Game Center.

Passing the turn

Now that we have a new match created, we need a button to pass the turn to our opponent and a way to send the data from the match. It looks hard the first time but it's actually pretty easy.

First, let's create the button to pass the turn. Add the following lines to GameScene.m just after CCButton *_createGameButton;:

```
// Declare button to pass the turn
CCButton *_passTurnButton;
```

For the moment, we're going to create this button at the end of the initWizardWithType method, as we're going to show it after the player chooses an element. Add the following method to GameScene.m:

```
-(void) initializePassTurnButton {
    // Add pass turn button to the scene
    _passTurnButton = [CCButton buttonWithTitle:@"Pass Turn"
    fontName:@"Verdana-Bold" fontSize:20.0f];
    _passTurnButton.position = CGPointMake(_screenSize.width - 70,
    _screenSize.height/2);
    [_passTurnButton setTarget:self
    selector:@selector(passTurn:)];
    [self addChild:_passTurnButton];
}
```

Call it from the end of initWizardWithType by adding these lines at the bottom of the method:

```
//Initialize pass turn button
[self initializePassTurnButton];
```

We're just creating a button and setting its position on the middle-right side of the screen. This button will call the `passTurn` method that we're going to implement with the following lines:

```
- (void) passTurn: (id) sender {
    if (_selectedCard != NULL){
        // Retrieve active match information
        GKTurnBasedMatch *currentMatch =
        [[GameCenterHelper sharedGameCenterInstance] activeMatch];
        // Encode turn data
        NSData *turnData = [NSKeyedArchiver
        archivedDataWithRootObject:_selectedCard];
        // Player index
        NSUInteger currentPlayerIndex = [currentMatch.participants
                    indexOfObject:currentMatch.currentParticipant];

        // Retrieving next player from participants
        GKTurnBasedParticipant *nextPlayer;
        nextPlayer = [currentMatch.participants objectAtIndex:
                    ((currentPlayerIndex + 1) %
                    [currentMatch.participants count])];
        // End turn
        [currentMatch endTurnWithNextParticipant:nextPlayer
        matchData:turnData completionHandler:^(NSError *error) {
            if (error) {
                CCLOG(@"Some error happened passing the turn %@",
                error);
            }
        }];
        CCLOG(@"Passing the turn %@ to next player %@", turnData,
        nextPlayer);
        _passTurnButton.visible = FALSE;
    }
}
```

This method first checks whether there is a card selected because it's a necessary condition to pass the turn to the opponent. Then we retrieve the match information from the helper class as we're going to need its attributes in the process.

The next thing is to encode the data related to the current turn, which should be encoded in an `NSData` object. Once we have the data ready, we get the next player by searching the next index in the array of participants using the modulo operator. This task is easy because our game is a two-player game, but if your game is more complex, this is the point where you will need to calculate who should take the next turn.

Then, we call the `endTurnWithNextParticipant` method of our match object passing in the next participant, the turn data, and a completion handler. This handler is a block that will be called when the end turn method finishes in order to detect success or failure. We only want to know when an error occurred so we can log it on the output.

To avoid passing the turn several times, we hide the button as soon as the turn has passed.

If you run the game and pass the turn, you will face an error because we still haven't implemented the encoding method. But don't worry, we will fix that in the following steps. Just add the following method declaration to `Card.h`:

```
// Declare encode method
- (void)encodeWithCoder:(NSCoder *)coder;
// Declare decode method
- (id)initWithCoder:(NSCoder *)decoder;
```

Implement it by adding the following lines to `Card.m`:

```
- (void)encodeWithCoder:(NSCoder *)coder{
    [coder encodeInteger:_elementType forKey:@"elementType"];
    [coder encodeInteger:_attack forKey:@"attack"];
    [coder encodeInteger:_defense forKey:@"defense"];
    [coder encodeObject:_element forKey:@"element"];
    [coder encodeObject:_imageName forKey:@"imageName"];
}

- (id)initWithCoder:(NSCoder *)decoder {
    if (self = [super init]) {
        _elementType = [decoder decodeIntForKey:@"elementType"];
        _attack = [decoder decodeIntForKey:@"attack"];
        _defense = [decoder decodeIntForKey:@"defense"];
        _element = [decoder decodeObjectForKey:@"element"];
        _imageName = [decoder decodeObjectForKey:@"imageName"];
    }
    return self;
}
```

The first method encodes the different properties of the object. You must pay attention to the type of data you're encoding, for example, _elementType, _attack, and _defense are integers, but _imageName and _element are strings, so they're treated as objects.

In the `decoder` method, we do the opposite; we decode the values for each property of the `Card` instance.

If you run the game, create a new match, and pass the turn, you should see something like this:

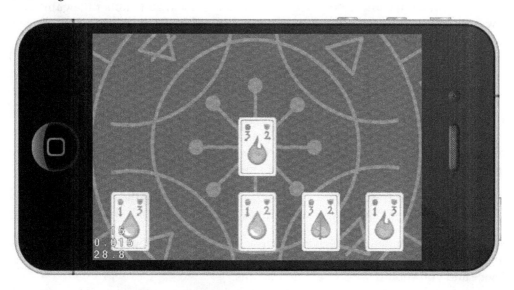

You should see a log similar to the following one:

```
2014-07-01 22:58:49.405 ElementalWizards[6791:60b] Passing the turn
<62706c69 73743030 d4010203 0405061e 1f582476 65727369 6f6e5824
6f626a65 63747359 24617263 68697665 72542474 6f701200 0186a0a4
07081314 55246e75 6c6cd509 0a0b0c0d 0e0f1011 125b656c 656d656e
74547970 65576465 66656e73 6559696d 6167654e 616d6556 61746461
636b5624 636c6173 73120024 b5201003 80021001 80035f10 11636172
645f6561 7274685f 31332e70 6e67d215 1617185a 24636c61 73736e61
6d655824 636c6173 73657354 43617264 a5191a1b 1c1d5443 61726458
43435370 72697465 5643434e 6f64655b 43435265 73706f6e 64657258
4e53466f 6a656374 5f100f4e 534b6579 65644172 63686976 6572d120
2154726f 6f748001 00080011 001a0023 002d0032 0037003c 0042004d
00590061 006b0072 0079007e 00800082 00840086 009a009f 00aa00b3
00b800be 00c300cc 00d300df 00e800fa 00fd0102 00000000 00000201
00000000 00000022 00000000 00000000 00000000 00000104> to next
player <GKTurnBasedParticipant 0x178002f00 - playerID:G:891054215
status:Invited matchOutcome:None lastTurnDate:(null)
timeoutDate:(null)>
```

Here we can see the serialized turn data and the next player.

At this moment, the next player can't receive the turn and play it. We are going to implement them being able to receive the turn and play it in the following section.

Receiving the turn

If you remember, we implement didFindMatch to recognize whether the game is a new or existing game by looking at lastTurnDate of the first participant. Once we have arrived at this point, we're going to need two different sandbox Game Center accounts to check when we created the game or whether we have been challenged. It would be really helpful to have two devices, but we can switch from one account to the other without problems.

If you open the game with the opponent's Game Center account and push the play button, it will show you the list of active games and you will be able to select the match you created with the previous account and take your turn. In this case, Dr. Fringe is handling the other account, so he will do this task for me.

If you look at the output logs, you will notice that it's showing the expected messages, so we can be assured that it's working properly.

Now we should implement receiveTurn so we can receive the data of the match, in other words, the card played by the first player. Run the game in the second player device and you should see something like this:

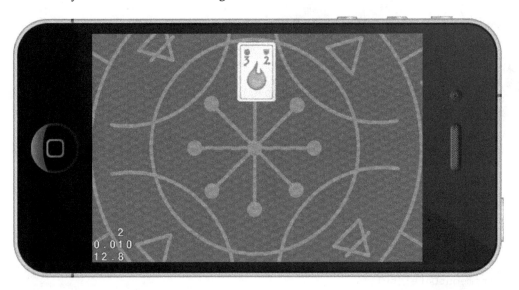

Amazing, isn't it? For the moment, we have developed a game that allows us to create a turn-based match with another Game Center user and to pass one turn. The game is not fully functional but don't worry, we will implement it now.

We need to implement a way to show the initial screen to the second player to allow the user to select their element and receive the card played by the first player.

Also, we will need to send more data than just the card played; that's why we're going to implement a new object that will store all the relevant information, so let's start at this point:

1. Right-click on the **Classes** group in the project navigator and select **New File…**.

2. Click on **iOS | cocos2d v3.x | CCNode class** and make this class a subclass of CCNode.

3. Call this class MatchStatus and click on **Create**.

Then replace MatchStatus.h with the following lines:

```
#import <Foundation/Foundation.h>
#import "cocos2d.h"
#import "Wizard.h"
#import "Card.h"

@interface MatchStatus : CCNode {
}

// Declare Wizard property for player1
@property (readwrite, nonatomic) Wizard *player1;

// Declare Wizard property for player2
@property (readwrite, nonatomic) Wizard *player2;

// Declare method to init MatchStatus with two wizards
-(id) initWithPlayer1:(Wizard *)player1 player2:(Wizard *)player2;

// Declare encode method
- (void)encodeWithCoder:(NSCoder *)coder;

// Declare decode method
- (id)initWithCoder:(NSCoder *)decoder;

@end
```

In this header, we're declaring two Wizard properties that we will use to keep the information of both players. Also in this file, we declare an initializer method and the serializer methods.

Replace the contents on `MatchStatus.m` with the following ones:

```objc
#import "MatchStatus.h"

@implementation MatchStatus

-(id) initWithPlayer1:(Wizard *)player1 player2:(Wizard *)player2 {
    self = [super init];
    if (!self) return(nil);

    _player1 = player1;
    _player2 = player2;

    return self;
}

- (void)encodeWithCoder:(NSCoder *)coder{
    [coder encodeObject:_player1 forKey:@"player1"];
    [coder encodeObject:_player2 forKey:@"player2"];
}

- (id)initWithCoder:(NSCoder *)decoder {
    if (self = [super init]) {
        _player1 = [decoder decodeObjectForKey:@"player1"];
        _player2 = [decoder decodeObjectForKey:@"player2"];
    }
    return self;
}
@end
```

Here, we're implementing the initializer by setting the `Wizard` objects to our properties so we can pass the data between turns and implement the `encodeWithCoder` and `initWithCoder` methods in the same way we did with `Card`. Thanks to them, this data can travel through a Game Center match.

You might now realize, we will also need to encode the `Wizard` instances to serialize them, so in `Wizard.h`, declare the serialize methods by adding these lines:

```objc
// Declare encode method
- (void)encodeWithCoder:(NSCoder *)coder;
// Declare decode method
(id)initWithCoder:(NSCoder *)decoder;
```

Implement them with the following lines in `Wizard.m`:

```objc
- (void)encodeWithCoder:(NSCoder *)coder{
    [coder encodeObject:_name forKey:@"name"];
    [coder encodeInteger:_lifePoints forKey:@"lifePoints"];
    [coder encodeInteger:_elementType forKey:@"elementType"];
    [coder encodeObject:_cards forKey:@"cards"];
    [coder encodeObject:_cardPlayed forKey:@"cardPlayed"];
}

- (id)initWithCoder:(NSCoder *)decoder {
    if (self = [super init]) {
        _name = [decoder decodeObjectForKey:@"name"];
        _lifePoints = [decoder decodeIntForKey:@"lifePoints"];
        _elementType = [decoder decodeIntForKey:@"elementType"];
        _cards = [decoder decodeObjectForKey:@"cards"];
        _cardPlayed = [decoder decodeObjectForKey:@"cardPlayed"];
    }
    return self;
}
```

Now that the status class has been created, let's involve it in the game. First, declare it by adding the following lines in `GameScene.m` after `CCButton *_passTurnButton;`:

```objc
// Declare the match status variable
MatchStatus *_matchStatus;
```

Import the header class by adding the following line in `GameScene.h`:

```objc
#import "MatchStatus.h"
```

Then go back to `GameScene.m` and add the following block of code at the very top of `initializeNewGame`:

```objc
if(!_matchStatus){
    _matchStatus = [[MatchStatus alloc] init];
}
```

This will initialize the `MatchStatus` object as soon as the match is created.

Let's build this object's information in order to send it instead of just the selected card. To achieve this, replace the contents of `passTurn` with the following lines of code:

```objc
if (_selectedCard != NULL){
    // Retrieve active match information
    GKTurnBasedMatch *currentMatch =
```

```
    [[GameCenterHelper sharedGameCenterInstance] activeMatch];
    // Player index
    NSUInteger currentPlayerIndex = [currentMatch.participants
            indexOfObject:currentMatch.currentParticipant];

    // If it's player 1 who passes the turn
    if((currentPlayerIndex + 1) % [currentMatch.participants
    count ] == 1) {
        _matchStatus.player1 = _currentPlayer;
        _matchStatus.player1.cardPlayed = _selectedCard;
        [_matchStatus.player1.cards
        removeObjectAtIndex:[_matchStatus.player1.cards
        indexOfObject:_selectedCard]];

        CCLOG(@"Player 1 selected card - card type %u, card
        attack %d, card defense %d, card image %@",
        _matchStatus.player1.cardPlayed.elementType,
        _matchStatus.player1.cardPlayed.attack,
        _matchStatus.player1.cardPlayed.defense,
        _matchStatus.player1.cardPlayed.imageName);
    } else {
        _matchStatus.player2 = _currentPlayer;
        _matchStatus.player2.cardPlayed = _selectedCard;
        [_matchStatus.player2.cards
        removeObjectAtIndex:[_matchStatus.player2.cards
        indexOfObject:_selectedCard]];

        CCLOG(@"Player 2 selected card - card type %u, card
        attack %d, card defense %d, card image %@",
        _matchStatus.player2.cardPlayed.elementType,
        _matchStatus.player2.cardPlayed.attack,
        _matchStatus.player2.cardPlayed.defense,
        _matchStatus.player2.cardPlayed.imageName);
    }

    // Encode turn data
    NSData *turnData = [NSKeyedArchiver
    archivedDataWithRootObject:_matchStatus];
    // Retrieving next player from participants
    GKTurnBasedParticipant *nextPlayer;
    nextPlayer = [currentMatch.participants objectAtIndex:
                ((currentPlayerIndex + 1) %
                [currentMatch.participants count])];
    // End turn
    [currentMatch endTurnWithNextParticipant:nextPlayer
    matchData:turnData completionHandler:^(NSError *error) {
```

```
            if (error) {
                CCLOG(@"Some error happened passing the turn %@",
                error);
            }
    }];
    CCLOG(@"Passing the turn %@ to next player %@", turnData,
    nextPlayer);
    _passTurnButton.visible = FALSE;
}
```

Let's look at this code. After checking that the player has selected a card, we retrieve the current match information and get the index of the current participant. Thanks to this, we know which of the players on the status object we have to update. In both cases, we set its `Wizard` object as the current player and set its `cardPlayed` as the selected card.

Then we remove the selected card from the player's array of cards, so we can know when the game is over.

If you run the game now, create a new game, and send the first turn, you will see different match data information. It's bigger than before because we're passing more information than just a card.

Now we need to implement what happens when the invited player receives their first turn. Replace the `receiveTurn` method contents with the following lines:

```
if ([match.matchData bytes]) {
    // Decode the card played by the opponent
    _matchStatus = [NSKeyedUnarchiver
    unarchiveObjectWithData:match.matchData];

    // If it's player 2's first turn
    if (match.currentParticipant.lastTurnDate == NULL) {
        if ([match.currentParticipant.playerID
                isEqualToString:[GKLocalPlayer
                localPlayer].playerID]) {
                    [self showInitScreen];
        }
    }
}
```

If the match data exists, we deserialize it so we can use the information stored in it. We check whether it's the first turn for the second player and, in this case, show the initial screen to it.

Let's make a small change in `showInitScreen`. Add the following lines:

```
// Show player1 first card played
if (_matchStatus.player1.cardPlayed) {
        _opponentCard = [[Card alloc]
        initWithCard:_matchStatus.player1.cardPlayed];
        _opponentCard.position = CGPointMake(_screenSize.width/2,
        5 * _opponentCard.texture.contentSize.height / 2);
        [self addChild:_opponentCard];
}
```

Declare an instance variable for the opponent card to show it to the current player. Add the following lines after `MatchStatus *_matchStatus;`:

```
// Declare opponent card
Card *_opponentCard;
```

This will take the `player1` card played and show it on the screen after `player2` selects their element type and receives their deck of cards.

Let's go run the game on the second player's device and choose your element; you should see a screen similar to the following one:

Now that you understand how to retrieve and send the match data for the first turn on both devices, we need to implement what happens when it's not the first turn. We need to modify again the `receiveTurn` method so we can support new and already created matches.

Replace the contents of `receiveTurn` with these lines:

```
if ([match.matchData bytes]) {
        // Decode the card played by the opponent
        _matchStatus = [NSKeyedUnarchiver
        unarchiveObjectWithData:match.matchData];
            // If it's player 2's first turn
            if (match.currentParticipant.lastTurnDate == NULL) {
                if ([match.currentParticipant.playerID
                    isEqualToString:[GKLocalPlayer
                    localPlayer].playerID]) {
                        // Player 2 first turn
                        [self showInitScreen];
                }
            } else {

                if ([match.currentParticipant.playerID
                    isEqualToString:[GKLocalPlayer
                    localPlayer].playerID]) {
                        // Your turn
                        [self updateViewWithMatch:match];
                }

            }
}
```

In this case, when the match has been created and it's the turn of `player1`, we call to the `updateViewWithMatch` method that will set the screen with the information received. Implement this method by adding the following lines to `GameScene.m`:

```
- (void) updateViewWithMatch:(GKTurnBasedMatch *)match {

    [self initializePassTurnButton];
    // Player index
    NSUInteger currentPlayerIndex = [match.participants
                indexOfObject:match.currentParticipant];
    // Auxiliary Card to paint player cards
    Card *cardAux;

    // If it's player 1's turn
    if((currentPlayerIndex + 1) % [match.participants count ] ==
    1) {

        // Set player1 the current player
        _currentPlayer = _matchStatus.player1;
```

```
            _opponentCard = [[Card alloc]
            initWithCard:_matchStatus.player2.cardPlayed];

        } else {
            // Set player1 the current player
            _currentPlayer = _matchStatus.player2;
            _opponentCard = [[Card alloc]
            initWithCard:_matchStatus.player1.cardPlayed];

            _opponentCard.position = CGPointMake(_screenSize.width /
            2, 5 * _opponentCard.contentSize.height / 2);

            // We only show the opponent card for player 2
            [self addChild:_opponentCard];
        }
        // Initialize the auxiliary card
        cardAux = _opponentCard;
        // Calculate gaps between cards to place them equidistantly
        float gapWidth = ((_screenSize.width - NUM_CARDS *
        cardAux.contentSize.width) / (NUM_CARDS + 1));

        // Initial position for the cards
        float positionX = gapWidth + (cardAux.contentSize.width / 2);
        float positionY = cardAux.contentSize.height / 2;

        for(int i = 0; i < _currentPlayer.cards.count; i++) {
            cardAux = [[Card alloc] initWithCard:[_currentPlayer.cards
            objectAtIndex:i]];

            if (cardAux) {
                // Set the card position
                cardAux.position = CGPointMake(positionX, positionY);
                cardAux.imageName = [NSString
                stringWithFormat:@"card_%@_%d%d%@", [NSString
                stringWithFormat:@"%@", cardAux.element],
                cardAux.attack, cardAux.defense, @".png"];

                // Add the card to the scene
                [self addChild:cardAux];
                [_currentPlayer.cards replaceObjectAtIndex:
                i withObject:cardAux];
            }
            // Update the next x position
            positionX += gapWidth + cardAux.contentSize.width;
        }
    }
```

This method has two parts, firstly in which we retrieve the information related to the current player and the card played by the opponent. We check it in the same way as we're doing in the `passTurn` method, so nothing new at this point. We also set the button to pass the turn.

The second part of this method regards the disposition of the left cards of the `Wizard` instance and it's similar to what we did in `dealCards`. The only difference is that we're showing the cards one beside the other instead of leaving a blank space for the played cards.

If you run the game, you will be able to choose a card and pass the turn between both players, but we need some method to know which card wins each battle, and this is covered in the next section.

Fighting cards

To implement a method to know which card wins, add the following lines into `passTurn` before `// Encode turn data` in `GameScene.m`:

```
if (_matchStatus.player2.cardPlayed &&
_matchStatus.player1.cardPlayed && !((currentPlayerIndex + 1) %
[currentMatch.participants count ] == 1)) {
        [self
        fightSelectedCard:_matchStatus.player2.cardPlayed
        againstOpponentCard:_matchStatus.player1.cardPlayed];
}
```

With this conditional block, we're indicating that we will fight `player1` and `player2` cards only when they exist and when it's the turn of `player2`.

We need to implement `fightSelectedCard: againstOpponentCard` so add the following block of code to `GameScene.m`:

```
-(void) fightSelectedCard:(Card *)selectedCard
againstOpponentCard:(Card *)opponentCard {
    if ((selectedCard.defense > opponentCard.
        attack) || (selectedCard.defense == opponentCard.attack
        && [self oppositeElementType:_currentPlayer.elementType
        toType:opponentCard.elementType])) {
        // P2 wins this turn
        _matchStatus.player1.lifePoints -= selectedCard.attack;
        CCLOG(@"P1 lost with damage %d", selectedCard.attack);
    } else {
        // P1 wins this turn
```

```
            _matchStatus.player2.lifePoints -= opponentCard.attack;
            CCLOG(@"P2 lost with damage %d", opponentCard.attack);
        }
    }
```

The second player will win when their card defense value is bigger than that of the opponent card's attack value. On the other hand, if these values are the same and the element type of the player 2 is the opposite of the opponent card type, the second player will also win. To know whether this last condition is true, we need the following method:

```
-(BOOL) oppositeElementType:(ElementTypes *)attackerType
toType:(ElementTypes *)defensorType {

    if((((int)attackerType == fire && (int)defensorType == air) ||
       ((int)attackerType == water && (int)defensorType == fire) ||
       ((int)attackerType == earth && (int)defensorType == water) ||
       ((int)attackerType == air && (int)defensorType == earth)) {
        return true;
    } else {
        return false;
    }
}
```

This means that the fire type wins over the air type, water wins over fire, earth wins over water, and air wins over earth.

Run the game again and check the logs to find out which player wins each turn!

Labels for life points

Now that we have a way to find out which player wins, let's add a few labels to show each player's life points. First of all, add the declaration for the labels by adding the following lines after `Card *_opponentCard;`:

```
// Declare player 1 label
CCLabelBMFont *_currentPlayerLabel;
// Declare player 2 label
CCLabelBMFont *_opponentPlayerLabel;
```

Implement this method that will show the labels:

```
-(void)showLifePointsLabels:(int)currentPlayerIndex {
    if (_matchStatus.player1 && _matchStatus.player2) {

        // If current player it's player 1
        if((currentPlayerIndex + 1) % NUM_PARTICIPANTS == 1) {
```

```
        // Set player 1 life points label
        _currentPlayerLabel = [CCLabelBMFont
        labelWithString:[NSString stringWithFormat:@"%d",
        _matchStatus.player1.lifePoints] fntFile:@"font.fnt"];
        // Set player 2 life points label
        _opponentPlayerLabel = [CCLabelBMFont
        labelWithString:[NSString stringWithFormat:@"%d",
        _matchStatus.player2.lifePoints] fntFile:@"font.fnt"];
    } else {
        // Set player 1 life points label
        _currentPlayerLabel = [CCLabelBMFont
        labelWithString:[NSString stringWithFormat:@"%d",
        _matchStatus.player2.lifePoints] fntFile:@"font.fnt"];
        // Set player 2 life points label
        _opponentPlayerLabel = [CCLabelBMFont
        labelWithString:[NSString stringWithFormat:@"%d",
        _matchStatus.player1.lifePoints] fntFile:@"font.fnt"];
    }

} else { // It's a newly created match
    // Set player 1 life points label
    _currentPlayerLabel = [CCLabelBMFont
    labelWithString:[NSString stringWithFormat:@"%d",
    INIT_LIFE_POINTS] fntFile:@"font.fnt"];

    // Set player 2 life points label
    _opponentPlayerLabel = [CCLabelBMFont
    labelWithString:[NSString stringWithFormat:@"%d",
    INIT_LIFE_POINTS] fntFile:@"font.fnt"];
}
_currentPlayerLabel.position = CGPointMake(30,
(_screenSize.height / 2) - 30);
[self addChild:_currentPlayerLabel];
_opponentPlayerLabel.position = CGPointMake(30,
(_screenSize.height / 2) + 30);
[self addChild:_opponentPlayerLabel];
}
```

If there are two players in the match, we set their current value as the `lifePoints` attribute of the objects. In this case, we're using the `NUM_PARTICIPANTS` constants as we don't have any match information other than the status.

If the current player is the one who created the match, we will show their label on _currentPlayerLabel, but if the current player is the invited player, we will show their life points in _currentPlayerLabel. This way, the player will always see their information on the bottom half of the screen.

If there are not two players, this means that it's a new match so we will show their initial life points.

Finally, we place each label on the left side of the screen, with the current player a little below the middle of the screen and the opponent's label a little above the middle of the screen.

To show the labels, add the following line at the end of initWizardWithType:

```
[self showLifePointsLabels:0];
```

Add the following lines at the end of updateViewWithMatch:

```
// Show life points labels
[self showLifePointsLabels:(int)currentPlayerIndex];
```

The last thing to do is update the labels when two cards fight. So find the following line:

```
CCLOG(@"P1 lost with damage %d", selectedCard.attack);
```

Replace it with this one:

```
[_opponentPlayerLabel setString:[NSString stringWithFormat:@"%d",
_matchStatus.player1.lifePoints]];
```

Find the following line:

```
CCLOG(@"P2 lost with damage %d", opponentCard.attack);
```

Replace it with this one:

```
[_currentPlayerLabel setString:[NSString stringWithFormat:@"%d",
_matchStatus.player2.lifePoints]];
```

If you run the game now and take some turns, you will see how the labels update with each fight.

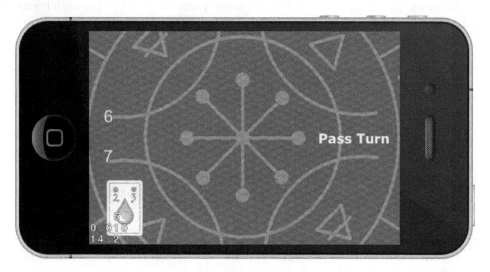

Match over

What happens when both players play their five cards? The match should be over and the winner will the player with more life points.

First, we need to check when a match has finished, so add the following lines to passTurn just before // Encode turn data in GameScene.m:

```
// End match
if (_matchStatus.player1.cards.count <= 0 &&
_matchStatus.player2.cards.count <= 0){
    [self matchOver:currentMatch];
    // Encode turn data
    NSData *turnData = [NSKeyedArchiver
    archivedDataWithRootObject:_matchStatus];
    [currentMatch endMatchInTurnWithMatchData:turnData
                    completionHandler:^(NSError *error) {
                        if (error) {
                            CCLOG(@"%@", error);
                        }
                    }];
} else {
```

Wrap all the endTurnWithNextParticipant code in the else statement. This checks whether the number of cards has reached 0 and if so, we call the matchOver method that will set the screen up to show the last state. Then we serialize the match status data and end the match by calling endMatchInTurnWithMatchData, which will finish the match on Game Center.

You will need to implement matchOver by adding the following lines to GameScene.m:

```
- (void)matchOver:(GKTurnBasedMatch *)match {
    GKTurnBasedParticipant *player1;
    GKTurnBasedParticipant *player2;

    // Player index
    NSUInteger currentPlayerIndex = [match.participants
                indexOfObject:match.currentParticipant];

    // Current player is player 1
    if((_matchStatus.player1.lifePoints >=
    _matchStatus.player2.lifePoints) && ((currentPlayerIndex + 1)
    % [match.participants count ] == 1)) {
        // You win
        CCLOG(@"YOU WIN");
        // Create CCLabelBMFont label
        _label = [CCLabelBMFont labelWithString:@"YOU WIN"
        fntFile:@"font.fnt"];

        player1 = [match.participants objectAtIndex:0];
        player1.matchOutcome = GKTurnBasedMatchOutcomeWon;

        player2 = [match.participants objectAtIndex:1];
        player2.matchOutcome = GKTurnBasedMatchOutcomeLost;

        // Show life points labels
        [self showLifePointsLabels:0];

    } else if ((_matchStatus.player2.lifePoints >
        _matchStatus.player1.lifePoints) && ((currentPlayerIndex +
        1) % [match.participants count ] == 0)) {
        // You win
        CCLOG(@"YOU WIN");
        // Create CCLabelBMFont label
        _label = [CCLabelBMFont labelWithString:@"YOU WIN"
        fntFile:@"font.fnt"];
```

```
        player2 = [match.participants objectAtIndex:1];
        player2.matchOutcome = GKTurnBasedMatchOutcomeWon;

        player1 = [match.participants objectAtIndex:0];
        player1.matchOutcome = GKTurnBasedMatchOutcomeLost;

        // Show life points labels
        [self showLifePointsLabels:1];
    }
}
```

This method checks whether `player1` or `player2` wins the match. In both cases, we set the player information of the match, set the match outcome too, and create a label to show the result. This property refers to the result of the player in the match. In the first case, player 1 won so we set their `matchOutcome` value to `GKTurnBasedMatchOutcomeWon` and the `matchOutcome` value of player 2 to `GKTurnBasedMatchOutcomeLost`.

The second part of the method checks whether the second player won.

Now to check whether the current player lost, add the following lines at the very end of `matchOver`:

```
else if ((_matchStatus.player1.lifePoints <
_matchStatus.player2.lifePoints) && ((currentPlayerIndex + 1) %
[match.participants count ] == 1)){
        // Player 1 lose
        // You lose
        CCLOG(@"YOU LOSE");

        _label = [CCLabelBMFont labelWithString:@"YOU LOSE"
        fntFile:@"font.fnt"];

        player1 = [match.participants objectAtIndex:0];
        player1.matchOutcome = GKTurnBasedMatchOutcomeLost;

        player2 = [match.participants objectAtIndex:1];
        player2.matchOutcome = GKTurnBasedMatchOutcomeWon;

        // Show life points labels
        [self showLifePointsLabels:0];

    } else { // Player 2 lose
        // You lose
        CCLOG(@"YOU LOSE");
        _label = [CCLabelBMFont labelWithString:@"YOU LOSE"
        fntFile:@"font.fnt"];
```

```
        GKTurnBasedParticipant *player2 = [match.participants
        objectAtIndex:1];
        player2.matchOutcome = GKTurnBasedMatchOutcomeLost;
        GKTurnBasedParticipant *player1 = [match.participants
        objectAtIndex:0];
        player1.matchOutcome = GKTurnBasedMatchOutcomeWon;

        // Show life points labels
        [self showLifePointsLabels:1];

    }
    _label.position = CGPointMake(_screenSize.width / 2,
    _screenSize.height / 2);
    [self addChild:_label];
    [self removeChild:_selectedCard];
    [self removeChild:_opponentCard];
    [self removeChild:_passTurnButton];
```

These lines do something similar to the previous ones, but they check which player loses and update their matchOutcome value accordingly.

The last thing they do is remove the unnecessary nodes such as the last played cards and the pass turn button.

Play a complete game and try to win!

The last thing to do is ensure that we can't perform any action when we receive the turn and the match is over. To achieve this, put the block of code that exists in the body of the `if ([match.matchData bytes]) {` statement of `receiveTurn` into a new `if` statement:

```
if (!(match.status == GKTurnBasedMatchStatusEnded)) {
```

Viewing the status when it's not our turn

It's possible that you will want to check your last turn passed and show the status of the match when it's not your turn.

Add the following method to `GameScene.m`:

```
- (void) updateViewAsViewer:(GKTurnBasedMatch *)match {

    if (!(match.status == GKTurnBasedMatchStatusEnded)) {

        // Auxiliary Card to paint player cards
        Card *cardAux;
        // Player index
        NSUInteger currentPlayerIndex = [match.participants
                    indexOfObject:match.currentParticipant];

        // If it's player 2 the viewer
        if((currentPlayerIndex + 1) % [match.participants count ]
        == 1) {
            _currentPlayer = _matchStatus.player2;
            cardAux = [[Card alloc]
            initWithCard:_currentPlayer.cardPlayed];
            // Show life points labels
            [self showLifePointsLabels:1];
        } else {
            _currentPlayer = _matchStatus.player1;
            _selectedCard = [[Card alloc]
            initWithCard:_matchStatus.player1.cardPlayed];
            cardAux = _selectedCard;
            _selectedCard.position = CGPointMake(_screenSize.width
            / 2, (3 * _selectedCard.contentSize.height) / 2);

            [self addChild:_selectedCard];
            // Show life points labels
            [self showLifePointsLabels:0];
        }
    }
}
```

This piece of code sets the current player as the participant that just passed their turn; that's why the condition checks whether the viewer is player 2. Then we get their played card and show the life points labels.

You also need to add these lines after the `else` clause on `updateViewAsViewer`:

```
// Calculate gaps between cards to place them
equidistantly
float gapWidth = ((_screenSize.width - NUM_CARDS *
cardAux.contentSize.width) / (NUM_CARDS + 1));
// Initial x position for the cards
float positionX = gapWidth + (cardAux.contentSize.width /
2);
// y position
float positionY = cardAux.contentSize.height / 2;

for(int i = 0; i < _currentPlayer.cards.count; i++) {
    cardAux = [[Card alloc]
    initWithCard:[_currentPlayer.cards objectAtIndex:i]];
    if (cardAux) {
        // Set the card position
        cardAux.position = CGPointMake(positionX,
        positionY);
        cardAux.imageName = [NSString
        stringWithFormat:@"card_%@_%d%d%@", [NSString
        stringWithFormat:@"%@", cardAux.element],
        cardAux.attack, cardAux.defense, @".png"];
        // Add the card to the scene
        [self addChild:cardAux];
        [_currentPlayer.cards replaceObjectAtIndex:i
        withObject:cardAux];
    }
    // Update next x position
    positionX += gapWidth + cardAux.contentSize.width;
}
```

This block is the same as in `dealCards`; it places the cards of the participant on the screen.

To finish, we need to indicate when we should call the just implemented method. Go to the `receiveTurn` method and replace the `// If it is player 2's first turn` block of code with the following lines:

```
// If it is player 2's first turn
if (match.currentParticipant.lastTurnDate == NULL) {
    if ([match.currentParticipant.playerID
            isEqualToString:[GKLocalPlayer localPlayer].playerID]) {
        [self showInitScreen];
    } else {
        // Not your turn
        [self updateViewAsViewer:match];
    }
} else {
    if ([match.currentParticipant.playerID
        isEqualToString:[GKLocalPlayer localPlayer].playerID]){
        // Your turn
        [self updateViewWithMatch:match];
    } else {
        // Not your turn
        [self updateViewAsViewer:match];
    }
}
```

Find the following lines at the end of the `receiveTurn` method:

```
    }
}
```

Replace them with the following block:

```
    } else {
        [self updateViewAsViewer:match];
    }
}
```

Execute the game, play your turn, and then take a look at this match; it should look like this:

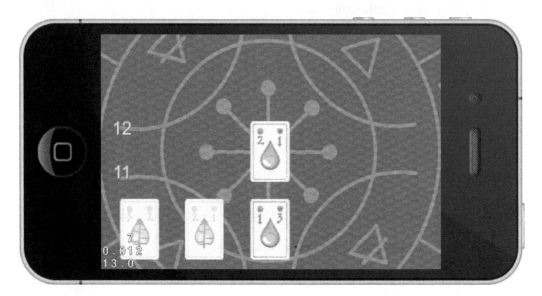

Summary

In this chapter, I showed you how to create labels using `CCLabelBMFont` and how to use a free editor to create your own fonts. Thanks to this, you will be able to update labels in a more efficient way.

You also learned to create complex actions such as spin, which we combined between them to run several actions into nodes on the game. You also learned how to drag a sprite and how to drop it in the desired place.

Then I showed you the steps needed to configure your game to include Game Center both in iTunes Connect and Xcode. Once the game was configured, you learned to check the availability of Game Center and to authenticate the user.

Finally, we created a turn-based match and you learned how to deal with turns, passing and receiving them until the match ends due to some condition. Then we updated the `matchOutcome` value of each participant and ended the match.

In the next chapter, we will develop a beat 'em up game using some of the knowledge you have acquired so far.

4
Beat All Your Enemies Up

Thinking about my favorite games before the appearance of the 32-bit video consoles, I can remember several beat 'em up titles such as *Teenage Mutant Ninja Turtles*, *Captain Commando*, *Target Renegade*, *Double Dragon*, *Final Fight*, *Battletoads*, *Golden Axe*, and *Streets of Rage*.

This genre of games became very popular during the 80s and 90s, but even though they lost popularity due to the rise of the fifth generation of video consoles, they are still alive on smartphones. However, this presents a handicap: the lack of game controllers on these devices; that's why it's common to include a virtual joystick in the game to control the main character.

In this chapter, you will learn how to create a beat 'em up game available just for iPad devices. Sometimes you will need to restrict your game to the iPad family devices, for example, because you need a bigger screen. In our case, the reason is we want to show a virtual game pad.

Throughout the chapter, I will show you how to load multiple image files and how to optimize the development of the game using sprite sheets and batch nodes. Then you will learn to manage several images to animate some sprites to simulate movements.

To represent the enemies and the game pad of this game, you will learn to create classes that subclass CCNode in spite of CCSprite to take advantage of the potential it provides.

The following is the list of topics covered in this chapter:

- How to build an iPad-only game
- How to develop a virtual game pad
- How to optimize handling images by using sprite sheets and batch nodes
- How to create classes that subclass CCNode
- How to load multiple image files to animate sprites

Creating an iPad-only game

In this chapter, we don't need to follow each step needed to configure a project to be executed only on iPad devices; we will just cover the specific steps.

When creating a new project, after selecting the template, you will see a screen like the following one where you will be able to specify the family of devices that will support this game. Then follow these steps:

1. Specify `HumanApocalypse` as **Product Name**.
2. Fill out **Organization Name** and **Company Identifier**.
3. In **Device Family**, choose **iPad** before clicking on **Next**.
4. Then choose the place where you want the project to be saved before clicking on **Create**.

We can see all of this information in the following screenshot:

Once the project has been created, you can check whether it's an iPad-only game by looking at the **Devices** menu under **General | Deployment Info**.

Now that the project is ready, we need to think about the singularities a game made for iPad will have.

Image sizes and names

If you remember, we were talking about image sizes and names in the *Placing things in context* section of *Chapter 1, Sprites, Sounds, and Collisions*, but in this chapter, we're going to focus on the case of iPad and iPad Retinas:

	iPad	iPad Retina
Devices	iPad, iPad 2, iPad Mini	iPad Air, iPad Mini Retina
Resolution	1024 x 768	2048 x 1536
Cocos2d file suffix	`file-ipad.png`	`file-ipadhd.png`

The resolution property indicates the maximum size of an image, which can entirely cover the screen. So, for example, if you're designing a background image for a game, you should take into account that the maximum size you're going to see on the screen is 1024 pixels for the width and 768 pixels for the height (2048 and 1536 on Retina devices).

In fact, if you use sizes bigger than the following ones, some parts of the background won't be visible or won't be placed in the expected area. So users will face undesired behavior if you don't anticipate it.

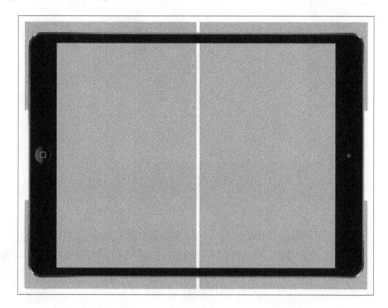

As you can see in the preceding image, goals have been placed out of view and it won't make sense when a goal is scored. On the other hand, boundaries don't correspond with reality so it will be confusing if you expected them to be in a different place.

I recommend you always take control of what is visible in your game, specifically critical areas, by designing all of your images focusing on the proper resolutions. This way, you can decide what and when things are going to be visible. For example, in *Chapter 2, Explosions and UFOs*, we designed parallax layers to fit within the screen width and longer than the screen height and set their anchor points at (0, 0), being aware that we were going to scroll the parallax layers.

The other important point to take into account is the image's filename. When designing Cocos2d games for iPad family devices, we need to specify all the filenames as `image-ipad.png` for non-Retina devices and `image-ipadhd.png` for Retina devices.

Using the previous example, let's imagine that we don't have iPad-specific images available. In this case, our scene will try to load the lower-resolution files (`image-iphone5hd.png`, `image-hd.png`, or `image.png`) and it will be placed on the center of the screen, maintaining the resolution, and as a result there will be blank spaces:

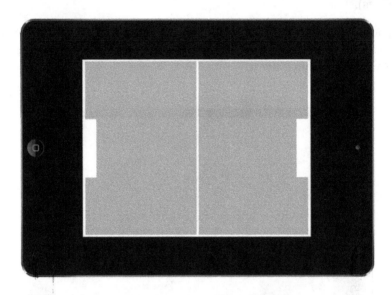

On the other hand, let's imagine that we fix this problem by adding a 1024 x 768 pixel `background-ipad.png` image and try to run the game on an iPad Air. In this case, the device will try to scale the background by duplicating the pixels in each axis (4x at the end), resulting in a loss of quality.

Now that we're aware of the common issues related to images when developing iPad games, we can load some of them as usual. For this chapter, you better use the initial project you will find in the code bundle of this chapter.

Open the initial project and perform the following steps:

1. In the project navigator, select the **Resources** group.
2. Right-click and select **Add Files to "HumanApocalypse"...**.
3. Look for the `background0-ipad.png`, `background0-ipadhd.png`, `background1-ipad.png`, `background1-ipadhd.png`, `background2-ipad.png`, `background2-ipadhd.png`, `background3-ipad.png`, `background3-ipadhd.png`, `zombie-ipad.png`, and `zombie-ipadhd.png` files on the `Resources` folder you unzipped.
4. Be sure that **Copy items into destination group's folder (if needed)** is selected and click on **Add**.

Replace the contents of GameScene.m with the following lines:

```
#import "GameScene.h"

@implementation GameScene{
    // Declare global variable for screen size
    CGSize _screenSize;
    // Declaring a private CCSprite instance variable
    CCSprite *_zombie;
    // Declare sprites for the background
    CCSprite *_background0;
    CCSprite *_background1;
    CCSprite *_background2;
    CCSprite *_background3;
}

+ (GameScene *)scene
{
    return [[self alloc] init];
}

- (id)init {
    // Apple recommends assigning self with super's return value
    self = [super init];
    if (!self) return(nil);
    // Initializing the screen size variable
    _screenSize = [CCDirector sharedDirector].viewSize;
    // Adding the background images
    _background0.anchorPoint = CGPointMake(0.0, 0.0);
    _background0 = [CCSprite
    spriteWithImageNamed:@"background0.png"];
    _background0.position =
    CGPointMake(_background0.contentSize.width / 2,
    _screenSize.height / 2);
    _background1.anchorPoint = CGPointMake(0.0, 0.0);
    _background1 = [CCSprite
    spriteWithImageNamed:@"background1.png"];
    _background1.position =
    CGPointMake(_background0.contentSize.width / 2 +
    _background0.contentSize.width, _screenSize.height / 2);
    _background2.anchorPoint = CGPointMake(0.0, 0.0);
    _background2 = [CCSprite
    spriteWithImageNamed:@"background2.png"];
    _background2.position =
    CGPointMake(_background0.contentSize.width / 2 +
    _background0.contentSize.width +
    _background1.contentSize.width, _screenSize.height / 2);
    _background3.anchorPoint = CGPointMake(0.0, 0.0);
```

```
_background3 = [CCSprite
spriteWithImageNamed:@"background3.png"];
_background3.position =
CGPointMake(_background0.contentSize.width / 2 +
_background0.contentSize.width +
_background1.contentSize.width +
_background2.contentSize.width, _screenSize.height / 2);
[self addChild:_background0 z:-1];
[self addChild:_background1 z:-1];
[self addChild:_background2 z:-1];
[self addChild:_background3 z:-1];

// Initialize the main character
_zombie = [CCSprite spriteWithImageNamed:@"zombie.png"];
_zombie.position = CGPointMake(2 * _zombie.contentSize.width,
_zombie.contentSize.height);
[self addChild:_zombie];
return self;
}
@end
```

We're initializing the background and the main character. You will realize that the background has been composed on four images because of the 4096 x 4096 size restriction and placed one after the other as we did when we developed the parallax effect.

Run the project and look at the scene:

You might have realized that our main character in this game is a zombie; do you remember the name we gave to our project? In this game, we will control a zombie that is being attacked by a horde of humans trying to kill him; terrifying!

Developing virtual game controls

I think that one of the reasons why beat 'em up games have lost popularity on smartphones is the fact that there is no game pad to control the character's movements. Touchable screens have conditioned games to be played by using the accelerometer or handling touches; that's why it's not usual to find titles like the classic arcade games. In the case of existing games, their playability is not comparable to handling a joystick and beating almost-indestructible buttons.

Despite this, we can emulate game pads by designing some places on the screen to react to touches and convert them into movements and actions. These touchable areas must be well-defined to track fingers moving on them, so let's get to work and make our own controller.

We're going to create a separate class to specify the pad's behavior due to the amount of methods and variables we will need to manage:

1. Right-click on the **Classes** group in the project navigator and select **New File...**.
2. Click on **iOS | cocos2d v3.x | CCNode class**.
3. Make this class a subclass of CCNode.
4. Call it GamePad and click on **Create**.

Note that we're extending CCNode because despite the controller having a visual representation, it would be enough to derive from CCSprite. We will also need some of the features provided by CCNode such as adding sprite children, which will make its representation more complete.

 It's not mandatory to extend CCSprite every time you need a node with a visual representation; it will depend on the purpose of the node. You can extend CCNode and add some CCSprite children if you need some specific features from CCNode.

Open `GamePad.h` and replace its contents with the following:

```
#import <Foundation/Foundation.h>
#import "cocos2d.h"

typedef enum {
    directionCenter = 0, directionRight, directionUpRight,
    directionUp, directionUpLeft, directionLeft,
    directionDownLeft, directionDown, directionDownRight
} GamePadDirections;

@class GamePad;

@protocol GamePadDelegate <NSObject>
- (void)gamePad:(GamePad *)gamePad
didChangeDirectionTo:(GamePadDirections)newDirection;
- (void)gamePad:(GamePad *)gamePad
isHoldingDirection:(GamePadDirections)holdingDirection;
- (void)gamePadTouchEnded:(GamePad *)gamePad;
@end

@interface GamePad : CCNode {
    // Declare a sprite to represent the pad
    CCSprite * padSprite;
}
@property (weak, nonatomic) id <GamePadDelegate> delegate;
@property (assign, nonatomic) GamePadDirections direction;
@property (assign, nonatomic) GamePadDirections previousDirection;
@property (assign, nonatomic) BOOL isHeld;
@property (assign, nonatomic) CGFloat padRadius;
@property (assign, nonatomic) NSUInteger touchHash;
// Declare init method
(GamePad *) initWithRadius:(CGFloat)radius;

@end
```

In this file, we're declaring the `GamePadDirections` enumeration for the different directions the game pad will support.

 Note that we even specify `directionCenter` as it will be a state that the pad should be aware of, despite it not being a movement.

We add the @class GamePad; line because we need to indicate that a class called GamePad exists before the declaration of the interface. This is due to the fact that we are defining some methods in the GamePadDelegate protocol that receives GamePad instances.

If you remember, we declared a protocol in *Chapter 3, Your First Online Game,* too. The purpose of using protocols is sharing the responsibility of some functionality with another class, its delegate, which will be responsible for implementing the methods specified. This delegation pattern allows you to reuse this class and implement the protocol methods in a more convenient way.

To visually represent the pad, we declare a CCSprite instance variable; this way we don't need to derive our class from CCSprite.

We declare two GamePadDirections properties (direction and previousDirection) to keep the previous and new directions so we can react to any change. We declare isHeld, a Boolean property that will indicate whether the pad is being held or not, and padRadius, a float property to store its radius value. The last property is an unsigned integer to keep the identifier of the touch hash so we can focus just on the one we want. Then we declare an initializer method that will set up our object.

Now implement GamePad.m, replacing its content with the following lines:

```
#import "GamePad.h"

@implementation GamePad

-(GamePad *) initWithRadius:(CGFloat)radius {
    self = [super init];
    if (!self) return(nil);

    // Initialize properties
    _padRadius = radius;
    _direction = directionCenter;
    _isHeld = FALSE;
    // Initialize sprite
    padSprite = [[CCSprite alloc]
    initWithImageNamed:@"gamepad.png"];
    padSprite.position = CGPointMake(padSprite.contentSize.width /
    2, padSprite.contentSize.height / 2);
    // Set content size
    self.contentSize = CGSizeMake(padSprite.contentSize.width,
    padSprite.contentSize.height);
    // Add sprite to game pad
```

```
        [self addChild:padSprite];
        // Enable user interaction
        self.userInteractionEnabled = TRUE;

        return self;
    }

@end
```

The initializer method calls its parent `init` method as usual. Then if the node has been properly created, we initialize the radius to the value received as input and we set center as the initial position. We also initialize `isHeld` as `FALSE` as there is no touch for the moment.

We initialize the sprite with an image (which we will add to the project in a few lines) and set its position to be placed at the bottom-left corner of the screen (I decided to place the pad in this position to take up the minimum space).

We need to set the game pad content size to detect whether a touch is placed inside it. Then we add the sprite to the node and we enable user interaction. Now follow the next steps:

1. Right-click on the **Resources** group and select **Add Files to "HumanApocalypse"…**.
2. Look for the `gamepad.png` file in the `Resources` folder.
3. Be sure that **Copy items into destination group's folder (if needed)** is selected and click on **Add**.

Now that user interaction is enabled, let's implement the corresponding methods to handle touches. Add the following lines to `GamePad.m`:

```
- (void)touchBegan:(UITouch *)touch withEvent:(UIEvent *)event
{
    // If there is no previous touch
    if (_touchHash == 0) {
        // Get the touch location
        CGPoint touchLocation = [touch
        locationInNode:self.parent];
        // Calculate the distance between touch and sprite
        CGFloat distance = ccpDistance(touchLocation,
        padSprite.position);
        // If the touch is inside the pad
        if (distance <= _padRadius * _padRadius) {
            // Store current touch hash
            _touchHash = touch.hash;
```

```
                    // Update direction
                    [self updateDirectionForTouchLocation:touchLocation];
                    // It's been held
                    _isHeld = TRUE;
                }
            }
        }
```

When a touch is received, we only pay attention to it if there is no previous touch stored. We take the touch and check whether it's placed inside the non-rectangular bounds of the game pad by calculating its distance to the center of the pad.

If the distance is less than or equal to the radius, we can assume that the touch was inside the pad so we store its `hash` value and call the `updateDirectionForTouchLocation` method before setting the `isHeld` property to `TRUE`.

 A `touchhash` value uniquely identifies a touch so we can track a specific touch among all the events raised by multiple touches.

The `updateDirectionForTouchLocation` method will be implemented soon, so don't worry if you get an error message from Xcode.

Now add the following method to `GamePad.m`:

```
- (void)touchMoved:(UITouch *)touch withEvent:(UIEvent *)event{
    // If it's the same touch as stored
    if (touch.hash == _touchHash) {
        // Get the touch location
        CGPoint touchLocation = [touch
        locationInNode:self.parent];
        // Update direction
        [self updateDirectionForTouchLocation:touchLocation];
    }
}
```

If we detect a touch moved event, this means that the user is moving their finger while touching the screen. We check whether the touch corresponds to our previously stored hash, as this way we can be sure that it is the same touch and the same finger that began the touch.

In this method, we just take the current touch location and call to
updateDirectionForTouchLocation to update the direction.

The last method to implement to handle touches is touchEnded, so add the following
lines to GamePad.m:

```
- (void)touchEnded:(UITouch *)touch withEvent:(UIEvent *)event {
    // Reset direction
    _direction = directionCenter;
    // Is no more held
    _isHeld = FALSE;
    // If it's the same touch as stored
    if (touch.hash == _touchHash)
    {
        // Call delegate touch end method
        [_delegate gamePadTouchEnded:self];
        // Reset hash value
        _touchHash = 0;
    }
}
```

This method will be called when the touch has ended, so we reset the direction
value to its initial value. We also set the initial value to isHeld and then we call the
delegate gamePadTouchEnded method if the touch matches the stored one. The last
line resets the hash value too so we can be ready to manage future touches.

Now add the update method by adding the following lines to GamePad.m:

```
- (void)update:(NSTimeInterval)delta
{
    // if it's being held
    if (_isHeld) {
        // Call delegate holding method
        [_delegate gamePad:self
               isHoldingDirection:_direction];
    }
}
```

This method will be called every frame and will constantly call the
isHoldingDirection method if the user holds the game pad.

Now let's implement updateDirectionForTouchLocation, so add the following lines to GamePad.m:

```
- (void)updateDirectionForTouchLocation:(CGPoint)touchLocation {

    // Get the difference between the touched location and the
    pad's center
    CGPoint point = CGPointMake(touchLocation.x -
    padSprite.position.x, touchLocation.y - padSprite.position.y);
    // Convert point to radians
    CGFloat radians = ccpToAngle(point);
    // Calculate degrees
    CGFloat degrees = CC_RADIANS_TO_DEGREES(radians);
    // Update previous direction
    _previousDirection = _direction;
    // Calculate direction
    if (degrees <= 22.5 && degrees >= -22.5) {
        _direction = directionRight;
        CCLOG(@"New direction RIGHT - %d", _direction);
    } else if (degrees > 22.5 && degrees < 67.5) {
        _direction = directionUpRight;
        CCLOG(@"New direction UP RIGHT - %d", _direction);
    } else if (degrees >= 67.5 && degrees <= 112.5) {
        _direction = directionUp;
        CCLOG(@"New direction UP - %d", _direction);
    } else if (degrees > 112.5 && degrees < 157.5) {
        _direction = directionUpLeft;
        CCLOG(@"New direction UP LEFT - %d", _direction);
    } else if (degrees >= 157.5 || degrees <= -157.5) {
        _direction = directionLeft;
        CCLOG(@"New direction LEFT - %d", _direction);
    } else if (degrees < -112.5 && degrees > -157.5) {
        _direction = directionDownLeft;
        CCLOG(@"New direction DOWN LEFT - %d", _direction);
    } else if (degrees <= -67.5 && degrees >= -112.5) {
        _direction = directionDown;
        CCLOG(@"New direction DOWN - %d", _direction);
    } else if (degrees < -22.5 && degrees > -67.5) {
        _direction = directionDownRight;
        CCLOG(@"New direction DOWN RIGHT - %d", _direction);
    }

    if (_isHeld) {
        if (_previousDirection != _direction) {
```

```
            [_delegate gamePad:self
                didChangeDirectionTo:_direction];
        }
    } else {
        [_delegate gamePad:self
            didChangeDirectionTo:_direction];
        }
    }
}
```

This method takes the touched location and calculates the vector between the location of the center of the pad and the touch location.

Then we take this vector and convert it to an angle using `ccpToAngle`, a function that returns an angle value in radians. We convert this value to degrees thanks to the `CC_RADIANS_TO_DEGREES` macro and use this value in degrees to determine the direction selected by the user.

Before proceeding, we store the current direction as the previous direction because we're about to change it.

The next block of conditional clauses just takes the angle and checks which direction it is set in. We have to take into account that 0 degrees is placed on the *x* axis and that it increases counterclockwise to a maximum of 180. After this value, it falls into negative values.

Once we know the next direction, we check whether the direction has changed or not. It's easy to detect this: it's a direction change when the pad is being held and the previous direction was different than the new one or when the pad is not being touched (no direction exists).

In `GameScene.h`, add the following import:

```
#import "GamePad.h"
```

In `GameScene.m`, declare a new game pad object by adding the following lines after `CCSprite *_background3;`:

```
// Declare a variable for game pad
GamePad *_gamePad;
```

The very last thing to do is create the game pad and add it to the scene, so add the following lines to the `init` method in `GameScene.m` just before `return self;`:

```
// Set radius as the image width
CGFloat radius = 192;
// Initialize game pad
```

```
_gamePad = [[GamePad alloc] initWithRadius:radius];
// Add the game pad to the scene
[self addChild:_gamePad];
```

We will create the pad with a radius equal to the texture width; that's why we specify this value as 192. Then, we call the initWithRadius method and add the object to the scene.

 We haven't enabled user interaction in the scene as we don't need to handle these touches, we just need to focus on the touches received by the game controller.

Ok, enough writing! Run the game now and look at the brand new controller. Play with it and look at the logs to check how it's responding:

Moving the zombie

Now that the game pad is working, it's time to use the touch events received to move our zombie. In this section we're just going to change its position on the screen, but in further sections we will animate it so it looks like the real living dead.

What we need to do to achieve this is implement the `GamePadDelegate` protocol as per our will. So in `GameScene.h`, find the following line:

```
@interface GameScene : CCScene {
```

Replace it with this one:

```
@interface GameScene : CCScene <GamePadDelegate>{
```

In `GameScene.m`, add the following lines at the end of the `init` method, just before `return self;`:

```
// Set GameScene as the GamePad delegate
_gamePad.delegate = self;
```

This will convert our scene class into a delegate of the protocol so we can implement the protocol methods. For the moment, we're just going to implement `didChangeDirectionTo` and `isHoldingDirection`, so add the following lines to `GameScene.m`:

```
- (void)gamePad:(GamePad *)gamePad
didChangeDirectionTo:(GamePadDirections)newDirection {
    CGPoint nextPosition = [self
    calculateNextPosition:newDirection isHeld:FALSE];
    [self moveWithDirection:nextPosition];
}
- (void)gamePad:(GamePad *)gamePad
isHoldingDirection:(GamePadDirections)holdingDirection {
    CGPoint nextPosition = [self
    calculateNextPosition:holdingDirection isHeld:TRUE];
    [self moveWithDirection:nextPosition];
}
- (void)gamePadTouchEnded:(GamePad *)gamePad {
}
```

Both methods call another method that will calculate the new position for the zombie depending on whether the pad is held or not and they will also call `moveWithDirection`, passing the new position as an argument.

We will leave `gamePadTouchEnded` blank as it's not important right now.

Add the following method:

```
- (void)moveWithDirection:(CGPoint)nextPosition {
    _zombie.position = CGPointMake(_zombie.position.x +
    nextPosition.x, _zombie.position.y + nextPosition.y);
}
```

This method updates the character's position by adding the calculated values to the current position.

Now we just need to implement the `calculateNextPosition` method, so add the following lines to `GameScene.m`:

```
- (CGPoint) calculateNextPosition:
(GamePadDirections)zombieDirection isHeld:(BOOL)isHeld{
    CGFloat incrX;
    CGFloat incrY;
    if (isHeld) {
        incrX = 1.5f;
        incrY = 1.125f;
    } else {
        incrX = 1.0f;
        incrY = 0.75f;
    }
    switch (zombieDirection) {
        case directionCenter:
            return CGPointZero;
            break;
        case directionUp:
            return CGPointMake(0.0, incrY);
            break;
        case directionUpRight:
            return CGPointMake(incrX, incrY);
            break;
        case directionRight:
            return CGPointMake(incrX, 0.0);
            break;
        case directionDownRight:
            return CGPointMake(incrX, -incrY);
            break;
        case directionDown:
            return CGPointMake(0.0, -incrY);
            break;
        case directionDownLeft:
            return CGPointMake(-incrX, -incrY);
            break;
        case directionLeft:
            return CGPointMake(-incrX, 0.0);
            break;
        case directionUpLeft:
            return CGPointMake(-incrX, incrY);
            break;
```

```
        default:
            return CGPointZero;
            break;
    }
}
```

This method just defines increment values for both the *x* and *y* axes depending on whether the pad is being held or not. It will take the direction the zombie is following and will create a new point that will be used (as we saw in didChangeDirectionTo and isHoldingDirection) to calculate the next position.

 Depending on the direction, the new point will have zero, positive, or negative increment values on its axis.

It's time to run the game and enjoy the work we have done until this moment. Run it and move the zombie in every direction so you can check it's working properly:

Now that we're able to move the main character across the screen, we can start thinking about animating it. As an animation consists of several images repeated constantly, we have to load all the images needed to simulate the character's movements, but this will increase the burden our device has to support each time it loads a texture.

CCSpriteBatchNode

To improve the tasks involved in drawing a texture on the screen, we can take advantage of the `CCSpriteBatchNode` class, which wraps the multiple sprite renders in just one execution.

The only objects that can be added to `CCSpriteBatchNode` are `CCSprite` instances or any other class derived from `CCSprite`. There is another restriction: every child in the batch must make use of the same texture, but we will see in the next section that this isn't in fact a weakness.

Let's learn how to use this class by adding several enemies to the scene, so let's add the image that will represent them:

1. Right-click on the **Resources** group and select **Add Files to "HumanApocalypse"...**.

2. Look for the `human-ipad.png` and `human-ipadhd.png` files in the `Resources` folder.

3. Be sure that **Copy items into destination group's folder (if needed)** is selected and click on **Add**.

Define a constant value for the number of human enemies that will be loaded by adding the following line to `GameScene.m` after the imports section:

```
// Number of human enemies
const int NUM_HUMANS = 10;
```

 We are not using `#define` as it does not provide type safety; that's why it's a good practice to declare constant variables.

Add the call to the method that will create the enemies, adding the following lines at the end of the `init` method just before `return self;`:

```
// Load enemies
[self createEnemies];
```

Implement this method by adding the following block of code:

```
- (void)createEnemies {

    // Initialize the batch node with an image
    CCSpriteBatchNode *batchNode = [CCSpriteBatchNode
    batchNodeWithFile:@"human.png"];
    // Add the batch node to the scene
```

```
    [self addChild:batchNode];
    CCSprite *human;
    for (int i = 0; i < NUM_HUMANS; i++) {
        // Create a new human sprite
        human = [CCSprite spriteWithImageNamed:@"human.png"];
        // Set the human position
        human.position = CGPointMake((i + 1) *
        human.contentSize.width, _screenSize.height / 2);
        // Add the human to the batch
        [batchNode addChild:human];
    }
}
```

This method initializes a batch node using a filename. Note that a batch node can be initialized using a texture, but we will use a filename for now. Once it's initialized, it must be added to the scene and then we can create all the enemy sprites we need. For that reason, we iterate NUM_HUMANS times and create a new sprite using the same image in each iteration.

We just set the human position to be centered on the screen so we can see the results, and then add the sprite to the scene. These few lines are enough to load several sprites with the same image. Run the game and look at the results:

If you look at the bottom-left corner of the screen, you will see the number of draw actions needed to load all of these images. Yes, it's 7: one for each file of the background, one for the zombie, one for the game pad, and the last one is for the batch node.

Now replace the contents of `createEnemies` with this block:

```
CCSprite *human;
for (int i = 0; i < NUM_HUMANS; i++) {
    // Create a new human sprite
    human = [CCSprite spriteWithImageNamed:@"human.png"];
    // Set the human position
    human.position = CGPointMake((i + 1) *
    human.contentSize.width / 2, _screenSize.height / 2);
    // Add the human to the scene
    [self addChild:human];
}
```

If you look at the number of draw actions needed, you will realize it's bigger (16) than before. This is the result of loading 10 enemies, but try to imagine a case in which the enemies are animated and need several images to simulate the animation. In this case, the number of draw actions could cause performance issues in your game and we don't want these kinds of problems.

 Using a batch node lets you load one asset into the memory rather than lots of little images. This way, the benefits of using a batch node are bigger, and the bigger the number of draw calls needed.

So now that you understand the importance of reducing draw calls to improve the performance, undo the last change so `createEnemies` uses a batch node to load the image.

As you can see, we're loading the enemies in the `init` method; this way there won't be delays when trying to load them for the first time during the game execution. There will be a delay in the initialization instead; that's why we see progress bars in some games.

Now we will take advantage of using `CCSpriteBatchNode` to create our animations, but how can we do this if for each animation, we need several different images, but we can only load one texture in a batch? The answer is just on the next line.

Texture atlases

Texture atlases are a way to combine several images into a bigger one that will contain them, and will improve our game performance.

These files rely on the fact that any texture loaded takes a power of two values as the width and height in the internal memory. For example, let's imagine we have a texture whose dimensions are 150 x 150, and will take 256 x 256 in memory, so you can have an idea of the loss of resources we will face if we load several images like this:

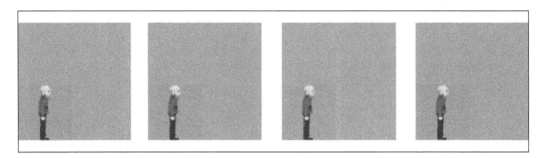

In fact, texture atlases are very similar to sprite sheets, but they differ in two aspects:

- Texture atlases can contain images that are not to the power of two in the same file, whereas sprite sheets can't
- Sprite sheets need to load several files, whereas texture atlases just need one to have all the artwork available in your game

But how can we create these texture atlases? There are several tools to create and edit texture atlases such as the AtlasMaker script for Photoshop or NVIDIA Texture Atlas Tools, but one of the most widely used in Cocos2d game development is TexturePacker.

Creating texture atlases with TexturePacker

TexturePacker (https://www.codeandweb.com/texturepacker) is a tool that allows us to create texture atlases and make it easier to export tasks.

The tool has a free and a paid version. You can use the non-paid version to build your atlases, but it won't allow you to save high-resolution files (for Retina devices). Don't worry about this, as in this chapter, I will provide you with Retina and non-Retina files.

To create a texture atlas, you need to organize your images in a tree hierarchy. You will need to create a new folder (anywhere in Finder) called `Assets` and inside it, a subfolder with all the images you want to be contained in the same atlas.

If you take a look in the `Resources` folder, you will see an `Assets` folder that contains `HumanApocalypseAtlas` with all the images needed for this chapter.

Note that there is no `-hd` suffix in the filenames because TexturePacker treats all the images as the high-definition version and downscales each one automatically.

If you drag the `Assets` folder and drop it into TexturePacker, it will organize them in a single atlas:

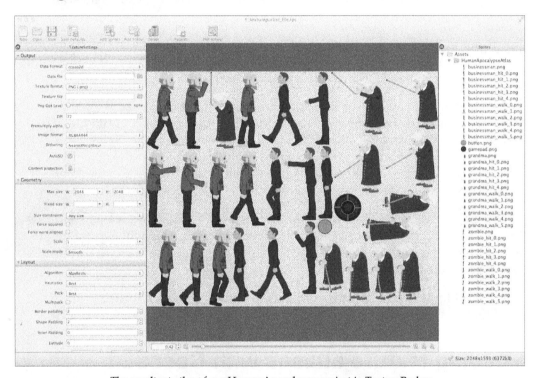

The resultant atlas of our HumanApocalypse project in TexturePacker

As you can see in the previous screenshot, here are all the enemy images. But if you pay attention, you will realize these are not all the human images. TexturePacker avoids duplicating textures thanks to its **stacking** feature and you can check which textures reference more than one image by clicking the following icon placed over the corresponding texture:

We're not adding the background images to this atlas because they are too big to fit in just one texture and even though TexturePacker allows multiple textures, we won't cover it in this chapter.

You may have realized that some images have been rotated, optimizing the atlas space. You don't need to worry about this because Cocos2d will know how to deal with them.

TexturePacker also removes (trims) the blank borders, reducing the image size to the minimum thanks to the default **Trim mode** selected. In fact, the space left between the images and the border of the atlas corresponds to the **Border padding** and **Shape Padding** values under the **Layout** configuration menu. These default values are optimal so you can leave them as they are.

If you look at the bottom-right corner of the editor, you will see the size of the resulting atlas and the memory it will consume (these values are for the high-definition version; the standard definition will consume four times less).

Other options that you can set are **Data Format** (the default **cocos2d** is what we want) that will allow us to create the atlas for other frameworks. In **Data file**, specify where you want the atlas to be saved, and call it `humanApocalypse-hd.plist`. We specify here the `-hd` suffix, as we want TexturePacker to know that it's the high-definition texture. Xcode will deal with it to downgrade it to the standard definition version.

The **Image format** field allows us to specify the number of bits we want to dedicate to each color and the alpha channel. The election of this setting will depend on the number of colors we want to work with. Change the default value to **RGBA4444** and see how the file size decreases.

Leave **PNG (.png)** as the **Texture format** field and click on the **Publish** icon; if everything works, you will have both `.png` and `.plist` files where you expected.

Loading texture atlases with Cocos2d

Now that the texture atlas is created, we need to add the published files to our project:

1. Right-click on the **Resources** group and select **Add Files to "HumanApocalypse"**....

2. Look for the `humanApocalypse-hd.png` and `humanApocalypse-hd.plist` files on the folder you chose and click on **Add**.

Before proceeding, delete the old files we have added since the beginning of the chapter: `human-ipad.png`, `human-ipadhd.png`, `gamepad.png`, `zombie-ipad.png`, and `zombie-ipadhd.png`, so they don't disturb us.

We're going to use the texture atlas for all the animations and sprites so we will need to make a few changes. Start declaring a new private instance by adding the following lines after `GamePad *_gamePad;` in `GameScene.m`:

```
// Declare global batch node
CCSpriteBatchNode *_batchNode;
```

Load the atlas with the following lines in the `init` method just after `if (!self) return(nil);`:

```
// Load texture atlas
[[CCSpriteFrameCache sharedSpriteFrameCache]
addSpriteFramesWithFile: @"humanApocalypse-hd.plist"];
// Load batch node with texture atlas
_batchNode = [CCSpriteBatchNode
batchNodeWithFile:@"humanApocalypse-hd.png"];
// Add the batch node to the scene
[self addChild:_batchNode];
```

This block will load the texture atlas information stored in the `.plist` file by using a `CCSpriteFrameCache` singleton and then we initialize the batch node in a very similar way as we saw before, but in this case, we use the texture atlas file. Then we add the batch node to the scene.

Now we need to replace the following lines in the `init` method. Find this line:

```
_zombie = [CCSprite spriteWithImageNamed:@"zombie.png"];
```

Replace it with this line:

```
_zombie = [CCSprite
spriteWithImageNamed:@"HumanApocalypseAtlas/zombie.png"];
```

In the `initWithRadius` method in `GamePad.m`, find this line:

```
padSprite = [[CCSprite alloc] initWithImageNamed:@"gamepad.png"];
```

Replace it with the next one:

```
padSprite = [[CCSprite alloc]
initWithImageNamed:@"HumanApocalypseAtlas/gamepad.png"];
```

If you take a look at the contents of humanApocalypse-hd.plist, you will understand why we did this. If you remember the hierarchy tree we set before dragging and dropping the images into TexturePacker, we set all the images under a folder called HumanApocalypseAtlas to group them in the same atlas. We will need to indicate to Cocos2d the exact route where it should look for the images.

The last change we need to make is replacing the contents of the createEnemies method in GameScene.m with the following piece of code:

```
CCSprite *human;
for (int i = 0; i < NUM_HUMANS; i++) {
    // Create a new human sprite
    human = [CCSprite spriteWithImageNamed:
    @"HumanApocalypseAtlas/businessman.png"];
    // Set the human position
    human.position = CGPointMake((i + 1) *
    human.contentSize.width / 2, _screenSize.height / 2);
    // Add the human to the batch
    [_batchNode addChild:human];
}
```

We removed the creation of the batch node as we have done it before, and we have specified the exact route for the human.png file.

Run the game and note that everything stays equal before introducing the texture atlas, even the number of draw calls!

Creating your first animation

Now that we have a way to load a large amount of images efficiently, we can go further using these images to animate our sprites.

An animation is the simulation of a movement by displaying sequences of static images that will make our brain think that it's looking at a smooth motion.

If you think about it, we already have the knowledge and the tools to create them because for this purpose, we need a sequence of static images that will be displayed in a loop that could be endless or not.

To begin, we need to import the CCAnimation class, so add the following code to the imports section in GameScene.h:

```
#import "CCAnimation.h"
```

Now let's declare a constant for the number of frames that will take part in the animation by adding the following lines to GameScene.m after the import section:

```
// Number of walk animation frames
const int NUM_WALK_FRAMES = 6;
```

This doesn't need an explanation, as it's just a constant declaration. Now add the following lines at the end of the init method, just after [self createEnemies]:

```
// Animate the zombie
[self animateZombie];
```

Implement the method by adding the following lines:

```
- (void)animateZombie {
    // Initialize an array of frames
    NSMutableArray *zombieFrames = [NSMutableArray
    arrayWithCapacity: NUM_WALK_FRAMES];

    for (int i = 0; i < NUM_WALK_FRAMES; i++) {
        // Create a sprite frame
        CCSpriteFrame *zombieFrame = [[CCSpriteFrameCache
        sharedSpriteFrameCache] spriteFrameByName:[NSString
        stringWithFormat:
        @"HumanApocalypseAtlas/zombie_walk_%i.png", i]];
        // Add sprite frame to the array
        [zombieFrames addObject:zombieFrame];
    }
    // Create an animation with the array of frames
    CCAnimation *zombieAnimation = [CCAnimation
    animationWithSpriteFrames:zombieFrames delay:0.2];
```

```
    // Create an animate action with the animation
    CCActionAnimate *zombieWalkAnimation = [CCActionAnimate
    actionWithAnimation:zombieAnimation];
    // Create an endless action
    CCActionRepeatForever *repeatWalkAction =
     [CCActionRepeatForever actionWithAction:zombieWalkAnimation];
    //Run the endless action
    [_zombie runAction:repeatWalkAction];
}
```

This block of code first initializes an array that will store the images that will conform to the animation. We use the previously declared NUM_WALK_FRAMES to define the array's capacity.

Then, in a loop that will be iterated as many times as the number of frames we will need, we declare a CCSpriteFrame instance, which is a class that contains a texture and its associated rectangle, and add it to the array of frames.

If you pay attention, we're creating CCSpriteFrame by taking advantage of the CCSpriteFrameCache singleton, as we did when loading the .plist file of the texture atlas that loads the corresponding frame file.

 When naming frame images, it is a good choice to use the same prefix followed by an integer value that could be easily replaced with the iteration value.

Once the frames array is ready, we create an animation thanks to the frames and a delay value. This delay value represents the time in seconds that will elapse between each image apparition. The smoothness of our animation will depend on this value, so it's important to try different values until we get the desired effect.

With this animation object, we can create an animation action easily and use it to create a CCActionRepeatForever action to make the zombie move every time. Then we just need to run the endless action to make our zombie walk.

Come on, run the game and take a look at our first animation!

Ok, he is not going to perform the thriller dance, but it's quite good, isn't it? Now that we know how to create animations, we can take advantage of this to create different movements such as walk, attack, or remain still.

3-star challenge – hitting the air

Besides moving the zombie, we will need to allow him to punch his enemies, so we should add a button to the game pad to defend him.

For this purpose, add a new sprite and perform a few modifications in the GamePad and GameScene classes. You can use the button.png image file included in the texture atlas.

The solution

To achieve this challenge, first let's declare a new sprite for the button by adding the following lines in GamePad.h after CCSprite *padSprite;:

```
// Declare a sprite to represent the button
CCSprite *buttonSprite;
```

There is nothing special here, just a CCSprite declaration. Then we want another CGFloat property to store the new button radius, so add the next line in the properties section:

```
@property (assign, nonatomic) CGFloat buttonRadius;
```

As we need to initialize a new sprite, we should modify the initializer method. Replace the initWithRadius method declaration with the following line:

```
(GamePad *) initWithPadRadius:(CGFloat)padRadius
buttonRadius:(CGFloat)buttonRadius;
```

Implement it by replacing the old initWithRadius method with these lines:

```
- (GamePad *) initWithPadRadius:(CGFloat)padRadius
buttonRadius:(CGFloat)buttonRadius {
    self = [super init];
    if (!self) return(nil);

    // Initialize properties
    _padRadius = padRadius;
    _buttonRadius = buttonRadius;
    _direction = directionCenter;
    _isHeld = FALSE;
    // Initialize pad sprite
    padSprite = [[CCSprite alloc]
    initWithImageNamed:@"HumanApocalypseAtlas/gamepad.png"];
    padSprite.anchorPoint = CGPointMake(0.5f, 0.5f);
    padSprite.position = CGPointMake(padSprite.contentSize.width /
    2, padSprite.contentSize.height / 2);
    // Initialize button sprite
    buttonSprite = [[CCSprite alloc]
    initWithImageNamed:@"HumanApocalypseAtlas/button.png"];
    buttonSprite.anchorPoint = CGPointMake(0.5, 0.5);
    buttonSprite.position = CGPointMake([[CCDirector
    sharedDirector].viewSize.width -
    (buttonSprite.contentSize.width / 2),
    buttonSprite.contentSize.height / 2);
    // Set content size
    self.contentSize = CGSizeMake(16000,
    padSprite.contentSize.height);
    // Add pad sprite to game pad
    [self addChild:padSprite];
    // Add button sprite to game pad
    [self addChild:buttonSprite];
    // Enable user interaction
```

```
self.userInteractionEnabled = TRUE;
// Enable multi touch interaction
self.multipleTouchEnabled = TRUE;

return self;
}
```

Here we have some important changes. The first one is that we initialize the `_buttonRadius` property with the new input of the method.

Then we initialize `buttonSprite` thanks to the `button.png` image placed in our texture atlas; we initialize its `anchorPoint` value in the same way we did with `padSprite` and finally, we place the button at the bottom-right corner of the screen.

We have to initialize `contentSize` in another way so the game pad covers the whole background space. That's why we set the `contentSize` width as a value bigger than the sum of the different background images' widths. You will understand why we do this in a later section.

The next step is adding the button sprite to the game pad and enabling multiple touches. We need to enable multiple touch recognition because we're going to allow users to touch the screen with several fingers at the same time: one to control the pad and another one to hit the button. Without this feature, our game would just listen to one of these events.

The last modification needed in `GamePad.m` is replacing `touchBegan` with the following block of code:

```
-(void)touchBegan:(UITouch *)touch withEvent:(UIEvent *)event
{
    // Get the touch location
    CGPoint touchLocation = [touch locationInNode:self.parent];

    // If the touch is inside the pad
    if (CGRectContainsPoint(padSprite.boundingBox, touchLocation))
    {
        // Store current touch hash
        _touchHash = touch.hash;
        // Update direction
        [self updateDirectionForTouchLocation:touchLocation];
        // Touch is being held
        _isHeld = TRUE;
    } else if (CGRectContainsPoint(buttonSprite.boundingBox,
    touchLocation)) {
        CCLOG(@"PUNCH!");
    }
}
```

In this case, we removed the `touchHash` check because we need to work with more than one touch; however, we still keep the property as it's important in `touchMoved`.

We now check whether the touch is placed inside the pad or the button by using the already-known `CGRectContainsPoint` method, and we no longer require a distance calculation. If the touch belongs to the button, we just throw a log that will let us know everything works properly.

Finally, in `GameScene.m`, find the following line in the `init` method:

```
_gamePad = [[GamePad alloc] initWithRadius:radius];
```

Replace it with the following ones:

```
CGFloat buttonRadius = 100;
// Initialize game pad
_gamePad = [[GamePad alloc] initWithPadRadius:radius
buttonRadius:buttonRadius];
```

We're initializing a variable for the button radius and then we call the new initializer.

Run the project now and take a look at both sprites' behavior:

Keep this challenge code for the rest of the chapter.

Creating the zombie class

As our zombie is going to perform several movements such as walk, run, or hit and it will have some attributes as the life points, we will create a class for it. Follow these steps:

1. Right-click on the **Classes** group in the project navigator and select **New File...**.

2. Click on **iOS | cocos2d v3.x | CCNode class**.

3. Make this class a subclass of CCNode, call it Zombie, and click on **Create**.

Replace the contents of Zombie.h with:

```
#import <Foundation/Foundation.h>
#import "cocos2d.h"
#import "CCAnimation.h"

typedef enum {
    stateStill = 0,
    stateWalking,
    stateRunning,
    stateHitting
} ZombieStates;

@interface Zombie : CCNode {
}

@property (readwrite, nonatomic) int lifePoints;
@property (readwrite, nonatomic) ZombieStates *state;
@property (readwrite, nonatomic) CCSprite *zombieSprite;
@property (readonly, nonatomic) CCActionAnimate *actionStill;
@property (readonly, nonatomic) CCActionRepeatForever *actionWalk;
@property (readonly, nonatomic) CCActionRepeatForever *actionRun;
@property (readonly, nonatomic) CCActionAnimate *actionHit;

// Declare init method
- (Zombie *) initZombie;
@end
```

If you pay attention, you will realize that we're importing CCAnimation.h because we're going to initialize the different actions in this class. Next, we declare an enumeration of states that we will use to control which action should be running. We have defined states for walking, running, hitting, and standing still. Then we declare properties for the life points, the zombie state, the sprite that will represent the zombie, and the four different actions that we're going to support. Note that we have declared the zombie sprite as a property because we need to access it from another classes.

There are two types of animations declared: CCActionAnimate and CCActionRepeatForever. This is due to the fact that walk and run actions will need to constantly be repeated until we stop walking or running, while hitting and remaining still actions are instant actions; in other words, they just take place once. We declared an initializer method too.

Then we replace Zombie.m with the following lines:

```
#import "Zombie.h"

// Number of walk animation frames
const int NUM_WALK_FRAMES = 6;
// Number of hit animation frames
const int NUM_HIT_FRAMES = 5;

@implementation Zombie
- (Zombie *) initZombie {
    self = [super init];
    if (!self) return(nil);

    // Initialize zombie sprite
    _zombieSprite = [[CCSprite alloc]
    initWithImageNamed:@"HumanApocalypseAtlas/zombie.png"];
    // Set content size
    self.contentSize = CGSizeMake(_zombieSprite.contentSize.width,
    _zombieSprite.contentSize.height);
    // Set initial state
    _state = stateStill;
    // Initialize life points
    _lifePoints = 15;
    // Add sprite to zombie
    [self addChild:_zombieSprite];

    return self;
}

@end
```

In this file, we're defining two constants for the number of walk and hit frames that will help us when initializing the different actions. Then we implement the `initZombie` method that will initialize the sprite using the `zombie.png` image placed in the texture atlas. After setting the anchor point, we set the zombie content size, initialize the state to be still as the zombie didn't move, and set the initial life points. Finally, we add the sprite to the class to be correctly displayed.

Now we need to initialize the actions, so in the same `initZombie` method, add the following block of code before `return self;`:

```
// Initialize an array of frames
NSMutableArray *zombieWalkFrames = [NSMutableArray
arrayWithCapacity: NUM_WALK_FRAMES];

for (int i = 0; i < NUM_WALK_FRAMES; i++) {
    // Create a sprite frame
    CCSpriteFrame *zombieWalkFrame = [[CCSpriteFrameCache
    sharedSpriteFrameCache] spriteFrameByName:[NSString
    stringWithFormat:
    @"HumanApocalypseAtlas/zombie_walk_%i.png", i]];
    // Add sprite frame to the array
    [zombieWalkFrames addObject:zombieWalkFrame];
}

// Create an animation with the array of frames
CCAnimation *zombieWalkAnimation = [CCAnimation
animationWithSpriteFrames:zombieWalkFrames delay:0.2];
// Create an animate action with the animation
CCActionAnimate *zombieWalkAction = [CCActionAnimate
actionWithAnimation:zombieWalkAnimation];
// Create walk action
_actionWalk = [CCActionRepeatForever
actionWithAction:zombieWalkAction];
// Create walk action
_actionRun = [CCActionRepeatForever
actionWithAction:zombieWalkAction];
```

We initialize an array with the capacity of NUM_WALK_FRAMES. Then we need to initialize the frames that will take part in the animation. This is why in a loop, we create the different sprite frames using the images in the texture atlas and we add it to the array of frames.

Once the array of frames contains all the images we need, we create a `CCAnimation` instance using this array and we specify a delay. Then we create a `CCActionAnimate` instance with the previously created action and we use it to create a `CCActionRepeatForever` instance to initialize both walk and run actions.

We use the same frames for walking and running because in our case, the only difference between both actions is the velocity, but you can create a different one with other frames for the running action.

Now there is one last thing to do and that's initialize the hitting and still actions, so add the following lines at the end of `initZombie` just before `return self;`:

```
// Initialize an array of frames
NSMutableArray *zombieHitFrames = [NSMutableArray
arrayWithCapacity: NUM_HIT_FRAMES];

for (int i = 0; i < NUM_HIT_FRAMES; i++) {
    // Create a sprite frame
    CCSpriteFrame *zombieHitFrame = [[CCSpriteFrameCache
    sharedSpriteFrameCache] spriteFrameByName:[NSString
    stringWithFormat:
    @"HumanApocalypseAtlas/zombie_hit_%i.png", i]];
    // Add sprite frame to the array
    [zombieHitFrames addObject:zombieHitFrame];
}

// Create an animation with the array of frames
CCAnimation *zombieHitAnimation = [CCAnimation
animationWithSpriteFrames:zombieHitFrames delay:0.1];
// Create an animate action with the animation
_actionHit = [CCActionAnimate
actionWithAnimation:zombieHitAnimation];
// Initialize an array of frames
NSMutableArray *zombieStillFrames = [NSMutableArray
arrayWithCapacity: 1];
// Create a sprite frame
CCSpriteFrame *zombieStillFrame = [[CCSpriteFrameCache
sharedSpriteFrameCache]
spriteFrameByName:@"HumanApocalypseAtlas/zombie.png"];
// Add sprite frame to the array
[zombieStillFrames addObject:zombieStillFrame];
// Create an animation with the array of frames
CCAnimation *zombieStillAnimation = [CCAnimation
animationWithSpriteFrames:zombieStillFrames delay:0.1];
// Create an animate action with the animation
_actionStill = [CCActionAnimate
actionWithAnimation:zombieStillAnimation];
```

This block is pretty similar to the previous one. We initialize an array with the capacity of the number of hit images we declared at the beginning of the file. We take advantage of a loop to initialize each frame and we add it to the array. With this array, we create an animation where we specify a different delay than the one we set for the walk and run actions. Then we use this action to initialize `actionHit`.

The next lines initialize the still action with a single image. We could create an animation that would represent the character as if, for example, it was breathing, but our zombie doesn't breathe anymore, so we will just use the `zombie.png` image.

> In `initZombie`, we initialized the actions so we can make use of them whenever we want without needing to create the animation each time. This way, we will improve the performance of our game.

The last thing we need to do is to make some modifications to `GameScene`. In `GameScene.h`, replace the `CCAnimation.h` import with `Zombie.h`.

In `GameScene.m`, we delete the definition of `NUM_WALK_FRAMES`, and in the `init` method, we remove the call to the method `animateZombie` and also remove the method implementation.

We need to declare a `Zombie` instance, so find these lines:

```
// Declaring a private CCSprite instance variable
CCSprite *_zombie;
```

Replace them with the following ones:

```
// Declare a variable for the zombie
Zombie *_zombie;
```

In the `init` method, find the following line:

```
_zombie = [CCSprite
spriteWithImageNamed:@"HumanApocalypseAtlas/zombie.png"];
```

Replace it with the following line:

```
_zombie = [[Zombie alloc] initZombie];
```

This will just create the zombie as a new instance of our `Zombie` class.

Now replace the contents of `didChangeDirectionTo` with this block of code:

```
CGPoint nextPosition= [self
calculateNextPosition:newDirection isHeld:FALSE];
// If zombie is still, running, or hitting
if ((int)_zombie.state == stateStill || (int)_zombie.state ==
stateRunning || (int)_zombie.state == stateHitting) {
    // Stop actions and init walk action
    [_zombie.zombieSprite stopAllActions];
    _zombie.state = stateWalking;
    [_zombie.zombieSprite runAction:_zombie.actionWalk];
} else if ((int)_zombie.state == stateWalking) {
    // Keep walking
    [self moveWithDirection:nextPosition];
}
```

We calculate the next position as we did before. If the zombie state is still, running, or hitting, we stop all the actions, set the state as walking, and run the walk action. If the zombie was walking, then we keep walking and moving to the next position.

Note that we're casting the zombie state to an integer, as we want to compare the integer value in spite of the `ZombieStates` value.

Now it's time to replace the contents of `isHoldingDirection` with the following lines:

```
 CGPoint nextPosition = [self
calculateNextPosition:holdingDirection isHeld:TRUE];
// If zombie is still or walking
if ((int)_zombie.state == stateStill || (int)_zombie.state ==
stateWalking) {
    // Init run action
    _zombie.state = stateRunning;
    [_zombie.zombieSprite runAction:_zombie.actionRun];
} else if ((int)_zombie.state == stateRunning) {
    // Keep running
    [self moveWithDirection:nextPosition];
}
```

The `nextPosition` calculation is the same as when we created the `Zombie` class before.

If the zombie state is still or walking, we set the state to running and begin the run action. If not, we just keep moving in the desired direction.

If you remember, we left the `gamePadTouchEnded` method blank, but now we are going to implement it with the following lines:

```
// Stop actions and init still action
[_zombie.zombieSprite stopAllActions];
_zombie.state = stateStill;
[_zombie.zombieSprite runAction:_zombie.actionStill];
```

When no button is touched, we stop all the actions, update the state to be still, and run `actionStill`.

The last modification we need to perform is add a method to control the button, so add the following line in the `GamePadDelegate` protocol definition of `GamePad`:

```
- (void)gamePadPushButton:(GamePad *)gamePad;
```

Find the following line in the `touchBegan` method in `GamePad.m`:

```
CCLOG(@"PUNCH!");
```

Replace it with the following one:

```
[_delegate gamePadPushButton:self];
```

Implement the `gamePadPushButton` method by adding the following block of code in `GameScene.m`:

```
- (void)gamePadPushButton:(GamePad *)gamePad {
    // If zombie is not hitting
    if ((int)_zombie.state != stateHitting) {
        _zombie.state = stateHitting;
    }
    // Stop actions and init hitting action
    [_zombie.zombieSprite stopAllActions];
    [_zombie.zombieSprite runAction:_zombie.actionHit];
}
```

If the state was different to `stateHitting`, we update it to be hitting, we stop all the actions as we don't want our zombie to walk or run while it hits, and then we run the hitting action.

A lot of coding, but at the end it has been easy, right? Come on, run the project and play a little with the pad and the button!

Creating the human enemies class

We need a new class to keep the information on each human enemy, who will try to search and kill the zombie before dying. In this section, you will understand how we're going to implement all of this behavior. Perform the following steps:

1. First of all, right-click on the **Classes** group in the project navigator and select **New File...**.

2. Click on **iOS | cocos2d v3.x | CCNode class**.

3. Make this class a subclass of CCNode, call it Human, and click on **Create**.

Once the class has been created, open Human.h and replace its contents with the following lines:

```
#import <Foundation/Foundation.h>
#import "cocos2d.h"
#import "CCAnimation.h"
```

```
typedef enum {
    humanStateStill = 0, humanStateWalking, humanStateHitting,
    humanStateDamaged
} HumanStates;
typedef enum {
    grandma = 0, businessman
} HumanType;
typedef enum {
    humanDecisionStill = 0, humanDecisionWalk, humanStateRun
} HumanDecisions;

@class Human;
// Protocol to implement the human behavior
@protocol HumanDelegate <NSObject>
- (void) decideWalkToPosition:(CGPoint)position human:
(Human *)human;
- (void) decideAttackToZombieHuman:(Human *)human;
- (void) decideStayStillHuman:(Human *)human;
@end
```

We import `CCAnimation.h` because we want the enemies to run actions such as walk and attack. We also defined types for the different states, kind of human, and decisions a human can have or take; you will understand their purpose later.

Then we declare a protocol that will take control of the actions each human can take. Its delegate will implement these methods so the enemies can walk, attack, and stay still as we want.

Add the following block of code after the previous lines in the same `Human.h` file:

```
@interface Human : CCNode {
}

// Properties to store the sprite and life points
@property (readwrite, nonatomic) int lifePoints;
@property (readwrite, nonatomic) CCSprite *humanSprite;
// Properties for the state, type, and decision
@property (readwrite, nonatomic) HumanStates *state;
@property (readwrite, nonatomic) HumanType *humanType;
@property (readwrite, nonatomic) HumanDecisions *decision;
// Properties for each human action
@property (readonly, nonatomic) CCActionAnimate *actionStill;
@property (readonly, nonatomic) CCActionRepeatForever *actionWalk;
@property (readonly, nonatomic) CCActionAnimate *actionHit;
// Declare init method
```

```
- (Human *) initHumanWithType:(HumanType)humanType;
// Declare custom method to set the position
- (void) setPosition:(CGPoint)position;

@end
```

We declare properties to keep the information on the life points and the sprite that will represent the enemy on the screen. We also declare properties to store the state, type, and decision taken by the human and then we declare properties for each action that the enemies can run.

The initializer and `setPosition` methods are the only two methods that will be implemented in `Human.m`, so open this file and replace its contents with the following code:

```
#import "Human.h"

@implementation Human
// Number of walk animation frames
const int NUM_WALK_FRAMES = 6;
// Number of hit animation frames
const int NUM_HIT_FRAMES = 5;

- (Human *) initHumanWithType:(HumanType)humanType {
    self = [super init];
    if (!self) return(nil);
    NSString *prefix;
    switch (humanType) {
        case grandma:
            // Assign textureName and numHits values
            prefix = @"grandma";
            _lifePoints = 7;
            break;
        case businessman:
            // Assign textureName and numHits values
            prefix = @"businessman";
            _lifePoints = 5;
            break;
        default:
            break;
    }
    // Initialize human sprite
    _humanSprite = [[CCSprite alloc] initWithImageNamed:[NSString
    stringWithFormat:@"HumanApocalypseAtlas/%@.png", prefix]];
    _humanSprite.anchorPoint = CGPointMake(0.5, 0.5);
```

```
    // Set content size
    _contentSize = CGSizeMake(_humanSprite.contentSize.width,
    _humanSprite.contentSize.height);
    // Set initial state type and decision
    _state = humanStateStill;
    _humanType = humanType;
    _decision = humanDecisionStill;

    return self;
}
@end
```

In this code, we instantiate some constants that will be useful when initializing the actions. In the `initHumanWithType` method, we take into account the type specified and we use it to initialize a string variable that we will use to initialize each type of enemy. As you can see in each `switch` case, we also initialize the life point's variable.

The following code is pretty similar to the way we initialize the zombie: we initialize the sprite, set the anchor point value, and set the content size. The only little difference is that we initialize the type and the decision variables in addition to the state.

We need to initialize the different actions so we can run them whenever needed. So in the same `initHumanWithType` method, add the following lines before `return self;`:

```
    // Initialize an array of frames
    NSMutableArray *humanWalkFrames = [NSMutableArray
    arrayWithCapacity: NUM_WALK_FRAMES];

    for (int i = 0; i < NUM_WALK_FRAMES; i++) {
        // Create a sprite frame
        CCSpriteFrame *humanWalkFrame = [[CCSpriteFrameCache
        sharedSpriteFrameCache] spriteFrameByName:[NSString
        stringWithFormat:@"HumanApocalypseAtlas/%@_walk_%i.png",
        prefix, i]];
        // Add sprite frame to the array
        [humanWalkFrames addObject:humanWalkFrame];
    }
    // Create an animation with the array of frames
    CCAnimation *humanWalkAnimation = [CCAnimation
    animationWithSpriteFrames:humanWalkFrames delay:0.2];
    // Create an animate action with the animation
    CCActionAnimate *humanWalkAction = [CCActionAnimate
    actionWithAnimation:humanWalkAnimation];
    // Create walk action
```

```
_actionWalk = [CCActionRepeatForever
actionWithAction:humanWalkAction];
// Initialize an array of frames
NSMutableArray *humanHitFrames = [NSMutableArray
arrayWithCapacity: NUM_HIT_FRAMES];

for (int i = 0; i < NUM_HIT_FRAMES; i++) {
    // Create a sprite frame
    CCSpriteFrame *humanHitFrame = [[CCSpriteFrameCache
    sharedSpriteFrameCache] spriteFrameByName:[NSString
    stringWithFormat:@"HumanApocalypseAtlas/%@_hit_%i.png",
    prefix, i]];
    // Add sprite frame to the array
    [humanHitFrames addObject:humanHitFrame];
}
// Create an animation with the array of frames
CCAnimation *humanHitAnimation = [CCAnimation
animationWithSpriteFrames:humanHitFrames delay:0.1];
// Create an animate action with the animation
_actionHit = [CCActionAnimate
actionWithAnimation:humanHitAnimation];
```

These lines initialize the walk and hit actions in a very similar way to what we saw in Zombie.m, so there is no need to duplicate the explanation.

The last action to be initialized is _actionStill, so add the following lines just after the preceding code:

```
// Initialize an array of frames
NSMutableArray *humanStillFrames = [NSMutableArray
arrayWithCapacity: 1];
// Create a sprite frame
CCSpriteFrame *humanStillFrame = [[CCSpriteFrameCache
sharedSpriteFrameCache] spriteFrameByName:[NSString
stringWithFormat:@"HumanApocalypseAtlas/%@.png", prefix]];
// Add sprite frame to the array
[humanStillFrames addObject:humanStillFrame];
// Create an animation with the array of frames
CCAnimation *humanStillAnimation = [CCAnimation
animationWithSpriteFrames:humanStillFrames delay:0.1];
// Create an animate action with the animation
_actionStill = [CCActionAnimate
actionWithAnimation:humanStillAnimation];
```

These lines don't an need explanation, so let's implement the last method, adding these lines to `Human.m`:

```
- (void) setPosition:(CGPoint)position {
    _humanSprite.position = position;
    [super setPosition:position];
}
```

This method will set the sprite position and will call its parent `setPosition` method so the node will be placed in the correct place too. This way, we will avoid unexpected behavior if the visual representation (the sprite) is placed in a different place than the node itself.

Now that the enemies' class has been created, we can modify the `createEnemies` method in `GameScene.m` to create several instances of the `Human` class along the game stage. Before it, import `Human.h` to `GameScene.h` and then replace the `createEnemies` method in `GameScene.m` with the following block of code:

```
Human *human;
    int humanType;
    int randomXPosition;
    int randomYPosition;

    for (int i = 0; i < NUM_HUMANS; i++) {
        // Create a new human sprite with a random type
        humanType = arc4random_uniform(NUM_HUMAN_TYPES);
        human = [[Human alloc] initHumanWithType:humanType];
        // Get random positions
        randomXPosition = arc4random_uniform(_screenSize.width +
        1500);
        randomYPosition = arc4random_uniform(300);
        // Set positions out of screen
        if (randomXPosition <= _screenSize.width) {
            randomXPosition = randomXPosition + _screenSize.width;
        }
        // Keep the enemies within the screen height
        if (randomYPosition <= human.contentSize.height / 2) {
            randomYPosition = randomYPosition +
            human.contentSize.height / 2;
        }
        // Set initial position
        [human setPosition:CGPointMake(randomXPosition,
        randomYPosition)];
        // Add the human to the batch and the array
        [_batchNode addChild:human.humanSprite];
        [_arrayOfHumans addObject:human];
    }
```

For each human, we calculate its type randomly before calling the initializer method. Then we want the enemies to be placed off screen but inside the space occupied by the background; that's why we modify the random values in cases where we need it after their initialization.

Then we set their initial position, add the sprites to the batch node, and add the human node to an array of humans for us to work with them easily. So declare this array by adding the following lines after `CCSpriteBatchNode *_batchNode;`:

```
// Declare array of enemies
NSMutableArray *_arrayOfHumans;
```

Initialize it by adding the following lines in the `init` method after `[self addChild:_batchNode];`:

```
// Initialize array of enemies
_arrayOfHumans = [NSMutableArray
arrayWithCapacity:NUM_HUMANS];
```

The very last thing is to declare the `NUM_HUMANS` constant, so add the following lines at the top of `GameScene.m`:

```
// Number of human types
const int NUM_HUMAN_TYPES = 2;
```

If you run the game now, you will realize that there are no visible enemies, and if you walk to the right trying to find them, the zombie will be also out of view:

So, we need a way to keep our main character visible when it walks beyond corners.

Keeping the main character in view

We will need to constantly check whether the zombies are in view, so we need to implement the `update` method that will perform the appropriate calculations. So add the following block to `GameScene.m`:

```
- (void)update:(NSTimeInterval)delta {
    // Keep the zombie on view
    [self setZombieOnView:_zombie.position];
}
```

Implement the `setZombieOnView` method with the following lines:

```
- (void)setZombieOnView:(CGPoint)position {
    // Establish the maximum positions on screen
    NSInteger positionX = MAX(position.x, _screenSize.width / 2);
    NSInteger positionY = MAX(position.y, _screenSize.height / 2);
    // Calculate the limits in both axes
    float backgroundWidth = _background0.contentSize.width +
    _background1.contentSize.width +
    _background2.contentSize.width +
    _background3.contentSize.width;
    positionX = MIN(positionX, backgroundWidth -
    (_screenSize.width / 2));
    positionY = MIN(positionY, _screenSize.height / 2);

    // Initialize current position
    CGPoint currentPosition = CGPointMake(positionX, positionY);
    // Set view point
    CGPoint cameraPosition = CGPointMake((_screenSize.width / 2) -
    currentPosition.x, (_screenSize.height / 2) -
    currentPosition.y);
    // Set the scene position
    self.position = cameraPosition;
    // Update game pad sprite's position
    _gamePad.padSprite.position =
    CGPointMake(ABS(cameraPosition.x) +
    _gamePad.padSprite.contentSize.width / 2,
    _gamePad.padSprite.position.y);
    _gamePad.buttonSprite.position =
    CGPointMake(ABS(cameraPosition.x) + _screenSize.width -
    _gamePad.buttonSprite.contentSize.width / 2,
    _gamePad.buttonSprite.position.y);
}
```

In this method, we calculate the zombie's current position, taking into account that the maximum position it will take is the center of the screen and the minimum place is the left corner of the background. We perform these minimum and maximum checks to avoid the zombie being placed beyond the background frontiers.

Once we have calculated the current position, we initialize the camera position that will be used to set the scene position. The scene will scroll along the stage, following the zombie and setting him in the center of the screen. However, the camera won't follow the main character when it's near the stage frontiers, so we can always see the background covering the screen.

In this method, we also need to update the game pad sprites' position to also keep them in view; that's why we take advantage of the camera position to calculate their new place. Note that we calculate the absolute value of the camera position because it could be negative when scrolling to the right due to how we're calculating it.

If you remember, when we initialized the content size of the game pad, we set a value bigger than the total background width. The reason is that when scrolling along the stage, the position of the pad changes, and if we don't set the appropriate content size, it won't be clickable.

We just need to make a change in GamePad to make the sprites visible outside of the class. Delete the following lines in GamePad.h:

```
// Declare a sprite to represent the pad
CCSprite *padSprite;
// Declare a sprite to represent the button
CCSprite *buttonSprite;
```

Add these two properties:

```
@property (readwrite, nonatomic) CCSprite *padSprite;
@property (readwrite, nonatomic) CCSprite *buttonSprite;
```

In GamePad.m, replace all the padSprite and buttonSprite occurrences with _padSprite and _buttonSprite respectively.

To avoid the zombie going off the screen, replace the contents of moveWithDirection with the following block of code:

```
float nextXPosition;
float nextYPosition;
// Total background width
float backgroundWidth = _background0.contentSize.width +
_background1.contentSize.width +
_background2.contentSize.width +
_background3.contentSize.width;
```

```
// Avoiding going out off screen
if ((_zombie.position.x + nextPosition.x) <
(_zombie.contentSize.width / 2) || (_zombie.position.x +
nextPosition.x) > (backgroundWidth - _zombie.contentSize.width
/ 2)) {
    nextXPosition = _zombie.position.x;
} else {
    nextXPosition = _zombie.position.x + nextPosition.x;
}
if ((_zombie.position.y + nextPosition.y) <
(_zombie.contentSize.height / 2) || (_zombie.position.y +
nextPosition.y) > (_screenSize.height / 2)) {
    nextYPosition = _zombie.position.y;
} else {
    nextYPosition = _zombie.position.y + nextPosition.y;
}
_zombie.position = CGPointMake(nextXPosition, nextYPosition);
```

We check that the next zombie's position is not out of view, and if this happens, we modify the next value to the last allowed position.

Let's go run the game and look at how the camera loves our zombie superstar! You can now walk to the right, looking for enemies.

Taking human decisions

Our enemies should have a little **Artificial Intelligence** (**AI**) for them to decide when is the best moment to walk, search for the zombie, or attack him.

We're going to implement the enemies' AI by implementing a method that will be called constantly to take decisions every frame, so we will need to add the following lines at the end of the `update` method in `GameScene.m`:

```
// Take decisions
for (Human *human in _arrayOfHumans) {
    // If the human is doing nothing
    if ((int)human.state == humanStateStill) {
        [self takeDecisionWithHuman:human];
    }
}
```

Each enemy will call to the method in which they will decide what action to take. Implement this method by adding the following code:

```
-(void) takeDecisionWithHuman:(Human *)human {
    float distance = ABS(human.humanSprite.position.x -
    _zombie.position.x);

    if ((distance > (human.contentSize.width / 2) && distance <
    _screenSize.width
        && !((int)human.state == humanStateWalking)) &&
    !((int)human.state == humanStateDamaged)) {
        [self decideWalkToPosition:_zombie.position human:human];
    } else if (distance <= human.contentSize.width / 2 &&
    !((int)human.state == humanStateHitting) && !((int)human.state
    == humanStateDamaged)) {
        [self decideAttackToZombieHuman:human];
    } else if (!((int)human.state == humanStateStill) &&
    !((int)human.state == humanStateWalking) && !((int)human.state
    == humanStateDamaged)){
        [self decideStayStillHuman:human];
    }
}
```

The human will calculate the distance between its position and the zombie's position. We want the human to walk toward the zombie when he is not close enough (half of the human width) to hit him, but not too close (half of the screen width). In this case and if the human is not already walking or has been hit, it will walk and try to find the zombie.

We give priority to the case when the zombie hits an enemy to give some advantage to our main character. If the enemy is close enough to the zombie and it's not already hitting or damaged, the human will attack the zombie. On the other hand, if the zombie is not walking, still, or has been damaged, it will remain still.

We need to implement the methods that will drive these actions. If you remember, these are the methods we declared in `HumanDelegate`.

So, first of all, in `GameScene.h`, find the following line:

```
@interface GameScene : CCScene <GamePadDelegate> {
```

Replace it with the following one:

```
@interface GameScene : CCScene <GamePadDelegate, HumanDelegate>{
```

Implement the protocol methods by adding these lines into `GameScene.m`:

```
- (void) decideWalkToPosition:(CGPoint)position human:(Human
    *)human {
    // Stop all actions
    [human.humanSprite stopAllActions];
    human.state = humanStateWalking;
    CCActionMoveTo *actionMove;
    float distance;
    float duration;

    if (human.humanSprite.position.y > position.y +
    VERTICAL_MARGIN || human.humanSprite.position.y < position.y
    - VERTICAL_MARGIN) {
        // Calculate distance
        distance = ABS(human.humanSprite.position.y - position.y);
        // Calculate duration of the movement
        duration = distance / HUMAN_SPEED;
        // Create a movement action
        actionMove = [CCActionMoveTo actionWithDuration:duration
        position:CGPointMake(human.humanSprite.position.x,
        position.y)];
    } else if (human.humanSprite.position.x > position.x +
    human.contentSize.width / 2 || human.humanSprite.position.x <
    position.x + human.contentSize.width / 2) {
        // Calculate distance
        distance = ABS(human.humanSprite.position.x - position.x)
        + human.contentSize.width / 2;
        // Calculate duration of the movement
        duration = distance / HUMAN_SPEED;
        // Create a movement action
```

```
        actionMove = [CCActionMoveTo actionWithDuration:duration
        position:CGPointMake(position.x + (human.contentSize.width
        / 2), human.humanSprite.position.y)];
    } else {
        // Calculate distance
        distance = ABS(human.humanSprite.position.x -
        human.humanSprite.position.x);
        // Calculate duration of the movement
        duration = distance / HUMAN_SPEED;
        // Create a movement action
        actionMove = [CCActionMoveTo actionWithDuration:duration
        position:CGPointMake(human.humanSprite.position.x,
        human.humanSprite.position.y)];
    }
    CCActionCallBlock *callDidMove = [CCActionCallBlock
    actionWithBlock:^{
        // Stop all actions
        [human.humanSprite stopAllActions];
        // Set new state
        human.state = humanStateStill;
        // Run still action
        [human.humanSprite runAction:human.actionStill];
    }];

    CCActionSequence *sequence = [CCActionSequence
    actionWithArray:@[actionMove, callDidMove]];
    // Run human actions
    [human.humanSprite runAction:human.actionWalk];
    [human.humanSprite runAction:sequence];
}
```

This method first stops all the running actions to avoid duplicates and initializes the state. Then we check whether the *y* axis is aligned to the zombie axis; if not, we initialize a movement action to reach the same *y* position.

Once the *y* position is the same, the human will try to be close enough to the zombie to hit him and, if the enemy is close enough, then the human will move itself in the *x* axis toward the zombie's position.

Then we initialize an action block that we will execute after the movement to recover the state of the human. This is so it can remain still and decide which other decision to take. We run the sequence with the movement and the block at the same time as the walk action is run so we simulate movement.

Add the following lines at the beginning of `GameScene.m` to create the `VERTICAL_MARGIN` and `HUMAN_SPEED` constants we have used:

```
// Vertical margin
const int VERTICAL_MARGIN = 12;
// Speed value
const float HUMAN_SPEED = 200;
```

Now add the following method:

```
- (void) decideAttackToZombieHuman:(Human *)human {
    // Stop all actions
    [human.humanSprite stopAllActions];
    human.state = humanStateHitting;

    CCActionCallBlock *callDidMove = [CCActionCallBlock
    actionWithBlock:^{
        [human.humanSprite stopAllActions];
        human.state = humanStateStill;
        _zombieCollisionDetected = FALSE;

    }];
    CCActionSequence *sequence = [CCActionSequence
    actionWithArray:@[human.actionHit, callDidMove]];
    // Run human action
    [human.humanSprite runAction:sequence];
}
```

In this case, we also stop all actions and update the human state. Then we create another action block to be executed at the end of the action to restore the variables to the state we want. Note that we're setting a new variable to `FALSE`; we will declare it soon and know what its purpose is. In this case, we create a sequence with the hitting action and the block as there is no displacement.

Let's declare the new variable by adding the following lines after `NSMutableArray *_arrayOfHumans;`:

```
    // Collision flags
    BOOL _humanCollisionDetected;
    BOOL _zombieCollisionDetected;
```

We declared two flags that we will use to control damage to the enemies and the zombie. We initialize them by adding the following lines to the `init` method just after `[self createEnemies];`:

```
    _humanCollisionDetected = FALSE;
    _zombieCollisionDetected = FALSE;
```

We just need to implement the last protocol method, so add these lines:

```
- (void) decideStayStillHuman:(Human *)human {
    // Stop all actions
    [human.humanSprite stopAllActions];
    human.state = humanStateStill;
    // Run human action
    [human.humanSprite runAction:human.actionStill];
}
```

This method just stops all actions before updating the state of the human and running its still action.

If you run the game now, you will see how the enemies try to reach the zombie and attack him furiously!

But when the enemies hit the zombie, nothing happens, so we need to implement a way to detect these collisions. Add the following lines at the end of the _arrayOfHumans loop in the update method:

```
// If some human enemy hits the zombie
if((int)human.state == humanStateHitting &&
CGRectIntersectsRect(_zombie.boundingBox,
human.humanSprite.boundingBox) &&
!_zombieCollisionDetected
```

```
        && _zombie.position.y <= (human.humanSprite.position.y
        + VERTICAL_MARGIN)
        && _zombie.position.y > (human.humanSprite.position.y
        - VERTICAL_MARGIN)) {
            _zombieCollisionDetected = TRUE;
            // Manage collisions
            [self manageCollisionForZombieWithHuman:human];
    }
```

If some human is hitting and both zombie and human texture rectangles intersect but there is no collision detected previously, we can affirm that a collision happened. Note that we let a vertical margin to hit the zombie to be less difficult to be damaged.

Then we implement the collision management method by adding the following block of code:

```
-(void) manageCollisionForZombieWithHuman:(Human *)human {
    if((int)human.state == humanStateHitting &&
    _zombieCollisionDetected) {
        _zombie.lifePoints--;
    }
}
```

This method first checks that all the required conditions are true and then we can decrease the zombie's life points.

Great, isn't it? But it would be better if we had a way to know how many life points we have before dying.

Drawing a life bar

In this section, we will implement a classic red and yellow life bar that will represent changes whenever we have been damaged.

First of all, declare two new draw nodes in GameScene.m by adding the following lines after BOOL _zombieCollisionDetected;:

```
// Draw nodes to represent life bar
CCDrawNode *_lifeBarYellow;
CCDrawNode *_lifeBarRed;
```

Initialize them with these lines at the end of the init method just before return self;:

```
_lifeBarYellow = [CCDrawNode node];
_lifeBarRed = [CCDrawNode node];
[self createLifeBars];
```

Implement the method with this block of code:

```
- (void) createLifeBars {
    float rectHeight = 70.0;
    float rectWidth = _zombie.lifePoints * 40;
    float positionX = 20;
    float positionY = [CCDirector sharedDirector].viewSize.height
    - rectHeight - 20;
    // Creating array of vertices
    CGPoint vertices[4];
    vertices[0] = CGPointMake(positionX, positionY); //bottom-left
    vertices[1] = CGPointMake(positionX, positionY + rectHeight);
    //top-left
    vertices[2] = CGPointMake(positionX + rectWidth, positionY +
    rectHeight); //top-right
    vertices[3] = CGPointMake(positionX + rectWidth, positionY);
    //bottom-right
    // Draw a polygon by specifying its vertices
    _lifeBarRed.anchorPoint = CGPointMake(0.0, 0.0);
    [_lifeBarRed drawPolyWithVerts:vertices count:4
    fillColor:[CCColor redColor] borderWidth:0.0
    borderColor:[CCColor blackColor]];
    _lifeBarYellow.anchorPoint = CGPointMake(0.0, 0.0);
    [_lifeBarYellow drawPolyWithVerts:vertices count:4
    fillColor:[CCColor yellowColor] borderWidth:0.0
    borderColor:[CCColor blackColor]];

    // Add rectangle to scene
    [self addChild:_lifeBarRed z:2];
    [self addChild:_lifeBarYellow z:2];
}
```

This method creates two rectangles in the top-left corner of the screen. The red rectangle is placed behind the yellow one for the effect to be more visual when receiving some hit.

As this bar is visual content placed on the screen, we will need to update its position when the zombie moves along the stage, so add the following lines at the end of the setZombieOnView method:

```
// Update life bar positions
_lifeBarRed.position = CGPointMake(ABS(cameraPosition.x) +
_lifeBarRed.contentSize.width / 2, _lifeBarRed.position.y);
_lifeBarYellow.position = CGPointMake(ABS(cameraPosition.x) +
_lifeBarYellow.contentSize.width / 2,
_lifeBarYellow.position.y);
```

This will update the life bar's position to keep it placed in the same top-left corner.

Now let's implement what happens when the zombie receives a hit, so add the following line to the `manageCollisionForZombieWithHuman` method just after `_zombie.lifePoints--;`:

```
[self updateLifeBarWithPoints:_zombie.lifePoints];
```

Implement the method with the following block of code:

```
- (void) updateLifeBarWithPoints:(int)lifePoints {
    if(_lifeBarYellow.parent) {
        [_lifeBarYellow removeFromParent];
    }
    float rectHeight = 70.0;
    float rectWidth = lifePoints * 40;
    float positionX = 20;
    float positionY = [CCDirector sharedDirector].viewSize.height
    - rectHeight - 20;
    // Creating array of vertices
    CGPoint vertices[4];
    vertices[0] = CGPointMake(positionX, positionY); //bottom-left
    vertices[1] = CGPointMake(positionX, positionY + rectHeight);
    //top-left
    vertices[2] = CGPointMake(positionX + rectWidth, positionY +
    rectHeight); //top-right
    vertices[3] = CGPointMake(positionX + rectWidth, positionY);
    //bottom-right
    // Draw a polygon by specifying its vertices
    _lifeBarYellow = [CCDrawNode node];
    _lifeBarYellow.anchorPoint = CGPointMake(0.0, 0.0);
    [_lifeBarYellow drawPolyWithVerts:vertices count:4
    fillColor:[CCColor yellowColor] borderWidth:0.0
    borderColor:[CCColor blackColor]];
    // Add rectangle to scene
    [self addChild:_lifeBarYellow z:2];
}
```

This method just removes the previously created yellow life bar and creates a new one with the new width that is calculated in the function of the life points.

Run the game again and look at the life bar; it's pretty similar to the classical final fight one, right?

Ok, now the enemies can attack us, but we need to defend ourselves!

Detecting collisions with enemies

In this section, we are going to implement a solution to detect collisions between our main character and the enemies to manage what happens when the zombie hits a human.

In `GameScene.m`, add the following block of code at the end of the `gamePadPushButton` method:

```
// Detect collision
for (Human *human in _arrayOfHumans){
        // Detect collision
        if (CGRectIntersectsRect(_zombie.boundingBox,
        human.humanSprite.boundingBox) && !_humanCollisionDetected
            && _zombie.position.y <= (human.humanSprite.position.y
            + 12)
            && _zombie.position.y >= (human.humanSprite.position.y
            - 12)) { // anchorpoint
            _humanCollisionDetected = TRUE;
```

```
                // Managing collisions
                [self manageCollisionForHuman:human];
                break;
        }
    }
```

In this loop, we're just checking whether the zombie bounding box intersects with some of the humans. Also, we check that the *y* value is inside a margin to make it easier to hit an enemy and take advantage of the humanCollisionDetected flag to avoid hitting more than one enemy at a time.

When all these conditions are accomplished, we can assume that a collision happened, so we update the flag value, call the new manageCollisionForHuman method, and break the loop because we don't need to iterate anymore.

Implement the new method by adding these lines:

```
-(void) manageCollisionForHuman:(Human *)human {
    // Stop actions
    [human.humanSprite stopAllActions];
    // Update human state
    human.state = humanStateDamaged;
    // Update human action
    [human.humanSprite runAction:human.actionStill];
    _zombieCollisionDetected = FALSE;
    // Create movement action
    CCActionMoveTo *actionMove = [CCActionMoveTo
    actionWithDuration:0.5
    position:CGPointMake(human.humanSprite.position.x +
    (human.humanSprite.contentSize.width / 2),
    human.humanSprite.position.y)];
    // Block to be executed at the end of the movement
    CCActionCallBlock *callDidMove = [CCActionCallBlock
    actionWithBlock:^{
        // Stop actions
        [human.humanSprite stopAllActions];
        // Update flag
        _humanCollisionDetected = FALSE;
        // Update position
        [human setPosition:human.humanSprite.position];
        // Update state
        human.state = humanStateStill;
        // Update human life points
        human.lifePoints--;
        // If human is killed
```

```
        if (human.lifePoints == 0) {
            if (_humansToDelete.count > 0) {
                [_humansToDelete replaceObjectAtIndex:0
                withObject:human];
            } else {
                [_humansToDelete addObject:human];
            }
            // Remove human from batch node
            [_batchNode removeChild:human.humanSprite];
            if (_humansToDelete.count > 0) {
                [_arrayOfHumans
                removeObjectsInArray:_humansToDelete];
            }
        }
    }
}];
// Declare and run sequence
CCActionSequence *sequence = [CCActionSequence
actionWithArray:@[actionMove, callDidMove]];
[human.humanSprite runAction:sequence];
}
```

This method stops all actions currently running on the damaged human and updates its state and running action. We update the flag to its initial value and create a move action that will place the human half its width to the right.

Then we declare a block that will be executed when the movement finishes and that stops all human running actions, updates the human collision flag, and updates its position to synchronize it with its sprite's position.

This block also updates the enemy state and life points, which we will use to check whether the human has been killed or not. The following conditional clause just adds or replaces the human with an array whether it has been initialized or not. Note that when a human has been killed, it should be removed from the batch node too; that's why we remove it from both the array of humans and the batch node.

We just need to declare the humansToDelete array. Add the following lines after NSMutableArray *_arrayOfHumans;:

```
// Declare array of killed humans
NSMutableArray *_humansToDelete;
```

Initialize it by adding the following lines to the `init` method after the initialization of `_arrayOfHumans`:

```
// Initialize array of deleted humans
_humansToDelete = [NSMutableArray
arrayWithCapacity:NUM_HUMANS];
```

Run the game now, hit some enemies, and look how they disappear!

2-star challenge – enemies' life bar

Now that we know how to create and update a life bar for the zombie, try to create a life bar for each human on the top of its sprite. This way, the zombie will know how many hits need to launch to kill its enemies!

In this case, I'm not including the solution for this challenge because I want to know whether you're capable of solving it on your own. Come on!

Game over

The last thing we need to finish this beat 'em up game is to implement a way to know whether the game is over or whether the stage has been cleared of enemies. It's pretty simple: add the following lines at the beginning of the `update` method:

```
// Check game over or stage cleared
if (_zombie.lifePoints <= 0){
    [self gameOverWithSuccess:FALSE];
} else if (_arrayOfHumans.count == 0) {
    [self gameOverWithSuccess:TRUE];
}
```

These lines check whether the zombie has been killed (life points are equal or less than zero) or whether the stage has been cleared (the number of humans is zero). Both cases call a new method with a different input value. Let's implement this method to know what it does:

```
-(void) gameOverWithSuccess:(BOOL)success{
    // Initializing the label
    CCLabelTTF *label;
    // Stop interaction and running actions
    self.paused = TRUE;
    _gamePad.userInteractionEnabled = FALSE;
    if (!success) {
        // Create the game over label
```

```
        label = [CCLabelTTF labelWithString:@"GAME OVER"
        fontName:@"Verdana-Bold" fontSize:40];
        label.color = [CCColor redColor];
    } else {
        // Create the stage cleared label
        label = [CCLabelTTF labelWithString:@"STAGE CLEARED!"
        fontName:@"Verdana-Bold" fontSize:40];
        label.color = [CCColor greenColor];
    }
    // Place and add the label to the scene
    label.position = CGPointMake(ABS(self.position.x) +
    _screenSize.width / 2, _screenSize.height / 2);
    [self addChild:label];
}
```

This method stops the user interaction to avoid touching the game pad or the button and also pauses the scene. Note that `self.paused` is the way to stop the execution of every running action. We can't use `unscheduleAllSelectors` because we haven't scheduled any selector; we're just using the `update` method to control everything.

Once everything is stopped, we initialize a label with a color and some text depending on the input and then place it at the center of the scene.

Run the game one more time and try to kill all the enemies before they kill you!

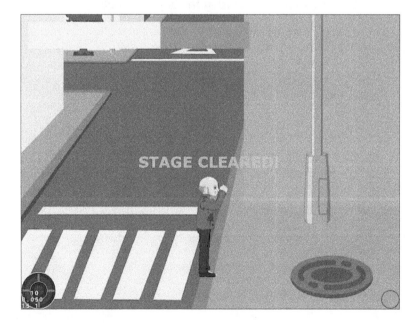

Summary

In this chapter, you learned how to develop a classic beat 'em up game that will only run on iPad devices.

To control the movements of the main character, I have shown you how to create a virtual game pad as a subclass of CCNode to take advantage of its update method. In this class, you also declared a protocol to be implemented by some delegate to define its behavior.

You learned how to reduce the number of sprite drawings with the use of batch nodes and how to create, edit, and load these batch nodes into Cocos2d texture atlases to minimize the memory used to manage images.

Once you knew how to work with a large number of images, you used some of them to animate sprites and virtualize movement.

As our main character will move along the stage, I showed you how to develop a method to move the camera to always keep the zombie in view.

You learned how to add artificial intelligence to the enemies and draw a life bar so you know how much life the main character has.

Using knowledge from previous chapters, we added collision and game over detection to know whether the game should end successfully or not.

The next chapter will cover one of the most interesting features of Cocos2d: physics.

5
Scenes at the Highest Level

Games usually consist of more than one stage, as completing levels is a key point when trying to keep players engaged. On the other hand, we all enjoy reading a book that has us looking forward to knowing what happens in the next chapter, or watching a TV series that makes us suffer when we are waiting for the next episode to be released.

In the video games industry, we also have the chance to create amazing stories that will be developed by linking stages and guiding the player through the storyline, so as developers we need a way to interweave the levels of our games.

The current chapter will teach us how to create transitions between the different scenes of a game and how to configure each of them by loading its corresponding data from external files.

Additionally, as the state of the game must be maintained as the player progresses, we will learn how to store the needed information in order to show the advances achieved.

As this chapter will also guide us through the process of developing a mathematics game, we will learn how to create a tutorial for the players to understand the mechanics of the game.

The list of topics covered in this chapter is:

- How to build a game tutorial
- How to load external data to configure levels
- How to create transitions between scenes
- How to save game data

Initializing the game

In this chapter, we are going to develop a game in which the player will advance through levels by providing the correct answer to mathematics problems.

Until now, we would think that the way to accomplish the loading and management of the different stages would be performed by having several classes derived from CCScene, but we can make it simpler and control all this behavior with just one class.

At the moment, let's initialize the first game level:

1. Open the code files of this chapter.
2. There you will find SqueezingBrains_init.zip which contains the initial project. Unzip this file.
3. Open the Xcode project SqueezingBrains.xcodeproj to get started.

The project has nothing special to mention as it's a one-scene game that shows nothing at the moment. Let's remedy that.

We're going to load the background image, but before we can do that, we need to have the corresponding file available in the project:

1. In the project navigator, select the **Resources** group.
2. Right-click and select **Add Files to "SqueezingBrains"**....
3. Look for the blackboard.png file in the Resources folder you unzipped, be sure that **Copy items into destination group's folder (if needed)** is selected, and click on **Add**.

Then add the following lines in GameScene.m at the end of the init method, just before return self;:

```
// Initialize the background
CCSprite * blackboard = [CCSprite
spriteWithImageNamed:@"SqueezingBrainsAtlas/blackboard.png"];
// Set background position
blackboard.position = CGPointMake(_screenSize.width / 2.0f,
_screenSize.height / 2.0f);
// Add background to the game scene
[self addChild:blackboard z:-1];
```

These lines create a new sprite with the image file we just added to the project and set its position right in the middle of the screen. Note how we set its z-order value to be negative, as we want it to be always in the background. Also note how we declared a local variable, because in this game the objective of the background image is just to be a static sprite that won't be involved in the game logic.

Run the project for the very first time and look at this beautiful blackboard that will transport you back to your childhood years:

Now let's load the first scene of the game, which will consist of an operation formed by two numbers or addends (one of them will be missing), the addition sign, the equals sign, and the result value. The challenge of the game is to guess which option from a list of numbers is the missing value that will fix the operation. Let's show all these objects in the scene.

First of all, add the images needed to load the different components of the level, by following these steps:

1. On the project navigator, select the **Resources** group.
2. Right-click and select **Add Files to "SqueezingBrains"…**.
3. Look for the 2.png, addition.png, equals.png, and 4.png files in the Resources folder and click on **Add**.

The next step is to declare the sprites we are going to need in order to manage the game, so add the following private variables declarations:

```
// Declare left side number
CCSprite *_leftNumber;

// Declare right side number
CCSprite *_rightNumber;
```

```
// Declare operator
CCSprite *_operator;

// Declare equals symbol
CCSprite *_equalsSymbol;

// Declare result
CCSprite *_result;
```

Nothing new here, we are just declaring five CCSprite instances. Add the call to the initializer method that will load and set all the images in their places, by pasting the following lines at the end of the init method, just after return self;:

```
// Initialize the game
[self initializeGame];
```

Implement this method with the following lines:

```
-(void) initializeGame {
    // Initialize left side number
    _leftNumber = [CCSprite spriteWithImageNamed:@"SqueezingBrainsAtl
    as/2.png"];
    // Set left number position
    _leftNumber.position = CGPointMake(_screenSize.width / 5.0f -
    _leftNumber.contentSize.width / 2.0f,
    _screenSize.height / 2.0f);
    // Add left number to the game scene
    [self addChild:_leftNumber];
}
```

This block of code initializes the left-hand number with one of the images we loaded previously, sets its position on the left side of the screen, and adds the sprite to the scene.

To complete the scene, add the following lines at the end of initializeGame, to initialize the rest of the sprites involved in the scene:

```
// Initialize operator
_operator = [CCSprite spriteWithImageNamed:@"SqueezingBrainsAtlas/
addition.png"];
// Set operator position
_operator.position = CGPointMake(2.0f * _screenSize.width /
5.0f - _operator.contentSize.width / 2.0f, _screenSize.height
/ 2.0f);
// Add operator to the game scene
[self addChild:_operator];
```

```
// Initialize equals sign
_equalsSymbol = [CCSprite spriteWithImageNamed:@"SqueezingBrainsAt
las/equals.png"];
// Set equals sign position
_equalsSymbol.position = CGPointMake(4.0f * _screenSize.width
/ 5.0f - _equalsSymbol.contentSize.width / 2.0f,
_screenSize.height / 2.0f);
// Add sign to the game scene
[self addChild:_equalsSymbol];

// Initialize result number
_result = [CCSprite spriteWithImageNamed:@"SqueezingBrainsAtlas/4.
png"];
// Set result number position
_result.position = CGPointMake(5.0f * _screenSize.width / 5.0f
- _result.contentSize.width / 2.0f, _screenSize.height /
2.0f);
// Add result number to the game scene
[self addChild:_result];
```

These lines initialize the operator, equals sign, and the result number of the scene, with their corresponding images. We place each of the components in their relative part of the view and then we add them to the scene.

Run the project and look at the initial position of the game:

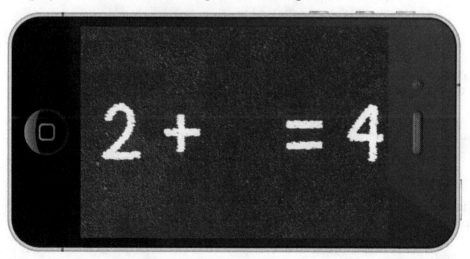

At this point, the game is showing us a problem we have to solve, an operation that needs to be completed with the missing number in order to accomplish the task. But as players, we don't know how to play this game until somebody explains how it works; that's why we are going to develop a tutorial that will be shown the first time we play the game.

Developing a tutorial for our game

A tutorial is a scene where the background of the game, the controls, and other relevant information are explained for the player to understand how to play.

There are several ways to develop the tutorial of a game, it depends on the type of game. For example, a tutorial for *Tetris* will explain that the game consists of blocks of different shapes that will drop from the top of the screen, and which we can rotate to build full rows, while a tutorial for *Grand Theft Auto* will be similar to a small mission, where we will learn to shoot guns or drive cars.

Regardless of the genre of the game, one thing is clear: a tutorial is a state machine where each state is a step of the tutorial that we need to take in order to learn how the game works.

In our case, we will manage these states by defining an enumeration type that will consist of each of the steps we need to take to solve a given level.

Go to `GameScene.h` and add the following lines at the top of the file, just after the imports section:

```
typedef enum {
    stateTutorial = 0,
    stateTutorialDragging,
    stateTutorialCheckingSolution,
    stateTutorialSuccess
} GameState;
```

As you can see, our tutorial will have four different states that define the steps of the tutorial scene.

We will need a `GameState` variable to control the state of our game, so go back to `GameScene.m` and add the following variable declaration:

```
// Declare state of the game
GameState *_gameState;
```

Initialize it by specifying the following value at the end of the `init` method, just before `return self;`:

```
// Initialize game state
_gameState = stateTutorial;
```

We are telling the game that the first state when running the game for the first time is the tutorial one. Let's check this value in order to show the tutorial steps.

First of all, replace the name of the `initializeGame` method with `initializeGameTutorial` and delete the call to the method that we did in `init`. Then add the following method:

```
-(void) onEnter {
    // When overriding onEnter we have to call [super onEnter]
    [super onEnter];

    // If tutorial state
    if(_gameState == stateTutorial) {
        [self initializeGameTutorial];
    }
}
```

The `onEnter` method is inherited from `CCNode` and it's called when the scene is loaded, so we will take advantage of it to load the tutorial. Note how we call `[super onEnter]` because this is a Cocos2d requirement, so if we don't do it, the code inside `onEnter` won't work.

Now let's initialize the different choices the user will have in order to solve the tutorial scene. For that, let's declare some variables and add some files to the project.

Declare an array which will store the different numbers the user can choose to solve each operation, by adding the following lines:

```
// Declare array of numbers
NSMutableArray *_arrayOfOptions;
```

Define a constant for the number of choices that will be available at each level:

```
Number of tutorial options
const int kNUM_TUTORIAL_OPTIONS = 4;
```

As we are going to load several images, it's better for our game's performance to use a batch, so include the following lines in the `init` method just after the initialization of `_screenSize`:

```
// Load texture atlas
[[CCSpriteFrameCache sharedSpriteFrameCache]
addSpriteFramesWithFile: @"squeezingbrains-hd.plist"];

// Load batch node with texture atlas
_batchNode = [CCSpriteBatchNode
batchNodeWithFile:@"squeezingbrains-hd.png"];
```

Declare the `batchNode` variable with the following lines:

```
// Declare global batch node
CCSpriteBatchNode *_batchNode;
```

We need to load the corresponding files, so:

1. On the project navigator, select the **Resources** group.

2. Right-click and select **Add Files to "SqueezingBrains"**....

3. Look for the `squeezingbrains-hd.plist` and `squeezingbrains-hd.png` files in the `Resources` folder and click on **Add**.

Now that all the needed files and variables have been added and initialized, we can call the method that will load the tutorial options by adding the following lines at the end of `initializeGameTutorial`:

```
// Initialize tutorial options
[self initializeTutorialOptions];
```

Implement the method with the following lines:

```
-(void) initializeTutorialOptions {
    _arrayOfOptions = [NSMutableArray arrayWithCapacity:
    kNUM_TUTORIAL_OPTIONS];

    // Declare option sprite
    CCSprite *option;

    // Initialize number 3
    option = [CCSprite
    spriteWithImageNamed:@"SqueezingBrainsAtlas/3.png"];
    [option setName:@"3"];
    // Set position
    option.position = CGPointMake(_screenSize.width /
    kNUM_TUTORIAL_OPTIONS - option.contentSize.width / 2.0f,
    option.contentSize.height / 2.0f);
    // Add number to the game scene
    [self addChild:option];
    [_arrayOfOptions addObject:option];
}
```

This method initializes the array of options with the capacity we have just defined, and declares a sprite that will be used to load each of the options.

Then we initialize the sprite with the image of the number 3 and note how we set its name property to be the same as the number the sprite represents. This is the convenience we have taken in order to identify when the chosen sprite is the correct one to pass the level (the tutorial in this case).

Once the sprite has been created, we place it in its relative position and then we add it to both the scene and the array of options.

We have loaded just one option number so let's complete this method by adding the rest of the numbers, so add the following block of code at the end of `initializeTutorialOptions`:

```
// Initialize number 2
option = [CCSprite
·spriteWithImageNamed:@"SqueezingBrainsAtlas/2.png"];
[option setName:@"2"];
// Set position
option.position = CGPointMake(2.0f * _screenSize.width /
kNUM_TUTORIAL_OPTIONS - option.contentSize.width / 2.0f,
option.contentSize.height / 2.0f);
// Add number to the game scene
[self addChild:option];
[_arrayOfOptions addObject:option];

// Initialize number 7
option = [CCSprite
spriteWithImageNamed:@"SqueezingBrainsAtlas/7.png"];
[option setName:@"7"];
// Set position
option.position = CGPointMake(3.0f * _screenSize.width /
kNUM_TUTORIAL_OPTIONS - option.contentSize.width / 2.0f,
option.contentSize.height / 2.0f);
// Add option to the game scene
[self addChild:option];
[_arrayOfOptions addObject:option];

// Initialize number 9
option = [CCSprite
spriteWithImageNamed:@"SqueezingBrainsAtlas/9.png"];
[option setName:@"9"];
// Set position
option.position = CGPointMake(4.0f * _screenSize.width /
kNUM_TUTORIAL_OPTIONS - option.contentSize.width / 2.0f,
option.contentSize.height / 2.0f);
// Add option to the game scene
[self addChild:option];
[_arrayOfOptions addObject:option];
```

These lines create the numbers 2, 7, and 9 and add them to the scene and the array of options.

Before proceeding, you can now remove the files `blackboard.png`, `2.png`, `4.png`, `addition.png`, and `equals.png`. Also, replace the lines used to initialize the corresponding sprites:

```
CCSprite * blackboard = [CCSprite
spriteWithImageNamed:@"blackboard.png"];
    .

    .

    .

_leftNumber = [CCSprite spriteWithImageNamed:@"2.png"];
    .

    .

    .

_operator = [CCSprite spriteWithImageNamed:@"addition.png"];
    .

    .

    .

_equalsSymbol = [CCSprite spriteWithImageNamed:@"equals.png"];
    .

    .

    .

_result = [CCSprite spriteWithImageNamed:@"4.png"];
```

Replace them with the following ones:

```
CCSprite * blackboard = [CCSprite
spriteWithImageNamed:@"SqueezingBrainsAtlas/blackboard.png"];
_leftNumber = [CCSprite
spriteWithImageNamed:@"SqueezingBrainsAtlas/2.png"];
_operator = [CCSprite
spriteWithImageNamed:@"SqueezingBrainsAtlas/addition.png"];
_equalsSymbol = [CCSprite
spriteWithImageNamed:@"SqueezingBrainsAtlas/equals.png"];
_result = [CCSprite
spriteWithImageNamed:@"SqueezingBrainsAtlas/4.png"];
```

If you run the project now, you will see the tutorial's initial state:

Now that the tutorial scene has been configured and loaded, we have to guide the users in order to teach them how to play. For this purpose, we will need a label that will show the instructions to follow, so declare a label with the following lines:

```
// Label to show the tutorial texts
CCLabelTTF *_tutorialLabel;
```

Initialize it by adding the following lines at the end of `initializeGameTutorial`:

```
// Initialize tutorial label
_tutorialLabel = [CCLabelTTF labelWithString:@"Choose the
correct number \nand place it in the green zone"
fontName:@"Chalkduster" fontSize:20.0f];
_tutorialLabel.color = [CCColor whiteColor];
_tutorialLabel.position = CGPointMake(_screenSize.width /
2.0f, _screenSize.height - _tutorialLabel.contentSize.height);

// Right-aligning the label
_tutorialLabel.anchorPoint = CGPointMake(0.5f, 0.5f);

[self addChild:_tutorialLabel];

// Update game state
_gameState = stateTutorialDragging;
```

We are creating a chalk-like label with a text divided into two lines to fit the view's width. It will be white and a font size big enough to read from the back of the class. Then we place it in the top center of the screen and add it to the scene.

The last line updates the game state so we can see which part of the tutorial is taking place, in order to show the corresponding labels and images.

Come on, run the game again and you will remember your childhood years, with that unforgettable smell of chalk:

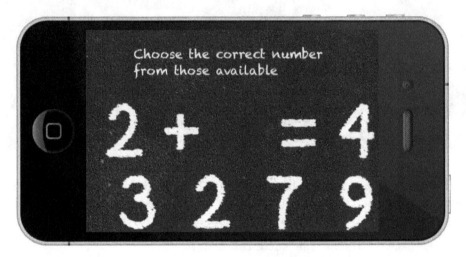

But at this moment the game has no functionality; we can't choose any number as we haven't enabled user interaction and we haven't implemented the touch methods, so add the following lines at the end of the `init` method:

```
// Enabling user interaction
self.userInteractionEnabled = TRUE;
```

We have enabled user interaction and we can now react to touches, so let's implement the protocol methods, starting by `touchBegan`:

```
- (void) touchBegan: (UITouch *) touch withEvent: (UIEvent *) event {
    if ((int)_gameState < stateTutorialCheckingSolution) {
        // Load droppable area
        [self defineDroppableArea];

        // Check what number has been touched
        CGPoint touchLocation = [touch locationInNode:self];
        [self checkNumberTouched:touchLocation];
    }
}
```

As soon as the user touches the screen, the game will check if its status is one of the tutorial's states and in this case, `if` calls the `defineDroppableArea` method. After that, it will check which number has been selected in another method.

First of all, let's implement these new methods by adding the following lines in `GameScene.m`:

```
-(void) defineDroppableArea {
    CGPoint vertices[4];

    // Set droppable area vertices
    vertices[0] = CGPointMake(3.0f * _screenSize.width / 5.0f -
    3.0f * _operator.contentSize.width / 2.0f, _screenSize.height
    / 2.0f - _equalsSymbol.contentSize.height / 2.0f); //bottom-
    left
    vertices[1] = CGPointMake(3.0f * _screenSize.width / 5.0f -
    3.0f * _operator.contentSize.width / 2.0f, _screenSize.height
    / 2.0f + _equalsSymbol.contentSize.height / 2.0f); //top-left
    vertices[2] = CGPointMake(3.0f * _screenSize.width / 5.0f +
    _operator.contentSize.width / 2.0f, _screenSize.height / 2.0f
    + _equalsSymbol.contentSize.height / 2.0f); //top-right
    vertices[3] = CGPointMake(3.0f * _screenSize.width / 5.0f +
    _operator.contentSize.width / 2.0f, _screenSize.height / 2.0f
    - _equalsSymbol.contentSize.height / 2.0f); //bottom-right

    // Initialize draw node
    _droppableArea = [CCDrawNode node];
    _droppableArea.anchorPoint = CGPointMake(0.0f, 0.0f);

    // Draw droppable area
    [_droppableArea drawPolyWithVerts:vertices count:4
    fillColor:[CCColor greenColor] borderWidth:2.0f
    borderColor:[CCColor blackColor]];

    // Add area to scene
    [self addChild:_droppableArea];
}
```

In this method, we initialize an array of four points (vertices) that will define the area of a rectangle in which the user must drop the number corresponding to the solution.

Then we create a new draw node using the array of vertices with a borderline, and we add it to the scene.

As you may have realized, we have to declare the draw node, so add the following lines after `CCLabelTTF *_tutorialLabel;`:

```
// Declare droppable area
CCDrawNode *_droppableArea;
```

Finally, we have to implement `checkNumberTouched`, so add the following lines:

```
-(void) checkNumberTouched:(CGPoint)touchLocation{
    // For each option in the array
    for (CCSprite *number in _arrayOfOptions) {
        if (CGRectContainsPoint(number.boundingBox,
        touchLocation)) {
            // The touch location belongs to the number
            _rightNumber = number;

            // Store the initial number position
            _initialNumberPosition = _rightNumber.position;

            // Place the number over the rest of options
            _rightNumber.zOrder = 1;

            break;
        }
    }
}
```

The method checks if the touch belongs to some of the numbers stored in the array of options. If this is so, we assign this number to the variable corresponding to the right-hand number, and we store its initial position, in case we need to restore it.

Finally, as we want the selected option to be placed over the rest of the sprites when moving it, we modify its z-order value to be 1.

We just need to declare `initialNumberPosition`, so add the following lines in the declaration section:

```
// Declare initial number position
CGPoint _initialNumberPosition;
```

If you run the game now, you will see the green highlighted area where you may drop the chosen number:

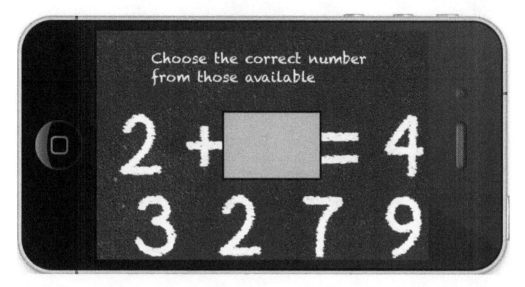

Now that touchBegan is implemented, let's implement touchMoved, so add the following block of code:

```
- (void)touchMoved:(UITouch *)touch withEvent:(UIEvent *)event
{
    if ((int)_gameState < stateTutorialCheckingSolution) {
      [_tutorialLabel setFontSize:20.0f];
        [_tutorialLabel setString:@"Drop the number in the
        highlighted area"];
    }
    // Moving the number along the screen
    CGPoint touchLocation = [touch locationInNode:self];
    _rightNumber.position = touchLocation;
}
```

As soon as we begin to move the selected number, we change the tutorial label to indicate to the user where to drop the number. Note how we only modify the text if the state is one of the tutorial ones, and we specify the font size again, because we make it bigger later when we check the solution.

Then we update the position of the selected number to be placed where the user is touching.

Now we have to define what happens when the user drops the number, so let's implement `touchEnded`:

```
- (void) touchEnded: (UITouch *) touch withEvent: (UIEvent *) event {
    // Define area to drop the number
    CGRect boardRect = CGRectMake(3.0f * _screenSize.width / 5.0f
    - 3.0f * _operator.contentSize.width / 2.0f,
    _screenSize.height / 2.0f - _equalsSymbol.contentSize.height
    / 2.0f, 2.0f * _operator.contentSize.width,
    _equalsSymbol.contentSize.height);

    // Only drop number inside the defined area
    if (CGRectContainsPoint(boardRect, [touch
    locationInNode:self])) {
        _rightNumber.position = CGPointMake(3.0f *
        _screenSize.width / 5.0f - _rightNumber.contentSize.width
        / 2.0f, _screenSize.height / 2.0f);

        // Set button visible
        _buttonCheckSolution.visible = TRUE;

        if ((int)_gameState < stateTutorialCheckingSolution) {
            // Remove droppable area from scene
            [self removeChild:_droppableArea];
            [_tutorialLabel setString:@"Now check the solution
            by\npushing the button on the right"];
            // Update game state
            _gameState = stateTutorialCheckingSolution;
        }
    }
}
```

When the user drops the number, we define a rectangle, which we compare with the position that was touched last (the current sprite's position). If this point is placed inside the rectangle defined by the droppable area, we set the correct number in a position relative to the rest of the elements of the operation.

Then we make visible a button used to check that the chosen number is the correct (which we will initialize in the next step).

If the state of the game is lower than `stateTutorialCheckingSolution`, we remove the droppable area, and update the label text and the state of the game.

There is one thing left, which is: what happens if the number is dropped in a place out of the defined rectangle? Add the following `else` block associated with the first `if` block of the `touchEnded` method:

```
else {
    // Recover initial position
    _rightNumber.position = _initialNumberPosition;
    [self removeChild:_droppableArea];
    // Update label
    [_tutorialLabel setString:@"Choose the correct number \nfrom
    those available"];
}
```

If this happens, we restore the selected number to its initial position and remove the droppable area.

Now, before we run the game to see how it works, we need to create a `buttonCheckSolution`, so first of all declare it by adding the following lines after `CGPoint _initialNumberPosition;`:

```
// Declare check solution button
CCButton *_buttonCheckSolution;
```

You will see that you are getting an **Unknown type name CCButton; did you mean UIButton?** message. It means that the `CCButton` class is not recognized, due to the fact that we haven't imported the necessary libraries, so add the following import in `GameScene.h`:

```
#import "cocos2d-ui.h"
```

We are now ready to initialize our button, so add the following call at the end of `init`:

```
// Create check button
[self createCheckButton];
```

Implement this method with the following block of code:

```
-(void)createCheckButton {
    // Initialize frame for normal state
    CCSpriteFrame *buttonFrame = [CCSpriteFrame
    frameWithImageNamed:@"SqueezingBrainsAtlas/
    check_solution.png"];
    // Initialize frame for highlighted state
    CCSpriteFrame *buttonFrameHighLight = [CCSpriteFrame
    frameWithImageNamed:@"SqueezingBrainsAtlas/
    check_solution_highlight.png"];
```

```
            // Create button
            _buttonCheckSolution = [CCButton buttonWithTitle:@""
                            spriteFrame:buttonFrame
                            highlightedSpriteFrame:buttonFrameHighLight
                            disabledSpriteFrame:buttonFrame];

            // Set button position
            _buttonCheckSolution.position = CGPointMake(_screenSize.width
            - _buttonCheckSolution.contentSize.width / 2.0f,
            _screenSize.height - 3.0f *
            _buttonCheckSolution.contentSize.height / 2.0f);
        }
```

In this method, we initialize a CCButton instance using the buttonWithTitle: spriteFrame:highlightedSpriteFrame:disabledSpriteFrame initializer, which receives a title and three sprite frames as input arguments.

In our case, we aren't specifying a title but we are creating two CCSpriteFrame instances with different images: one for the normal state of the button and another for the highlighted state.

Once the button has been created, we initialize its position to be placed on the top-right corner of the view.

We need to complement the initialization of the button by adding the following lines at the end of createCheckButton:

```
            // Specify the method called when selected
            [_buttonCheckSolution setTarget:self
            selector:@selector(checkSolution:)];

            // Make it invisible
            _buttonCheckSolution.visible = FALSE;

            // Add the button to the scene
            [self addChild:_buttonCheckSolution];
```

We specify the method that should be called when the button is selected (checkSolution), then we set it to be invisible and add it to the scene.

At this point, we need to implement the checkSolution method with these lines:

```
        - (void)checkSolution:(id)sender{
            if((int)_gameState == stateTutorialCheckingSolution) {
                if ([_rightNumber.name isEqualToString:@"2"]) {
                    [_tutorialLabel setString:@"Correct!"];
                    _gameState = stateTutorialSuccess;
```

```
    } else {
        [_tutorialLabel setString:@"Try again!"];
        _rightNumber.position = _initialNumberPosition;
        _gameState = stateTutorialDragging;
    }
    [_tutorialLabel setFontSize:25.0f];
    _buttonCheckSolution.visible = FALSE;
}
}
```

This method will take place if the state of the game is waiting to check the user's choice. If so, it checks if the name of the sprite (remember that we specified this property when initializing each option) equals the correct one that we have hardcoded.

If the value chosen is correct, we update the label text and the state so the game knows that the tutorial has ended. When the chosen value is not correct, we also update the label with a warning message, restore the number to its original position, and revert the game state to the previous one.

Finally, we make the label's font size bigger in order to emphasize it and set the button invisible again.

Time to run the game and try to solve the first operation!

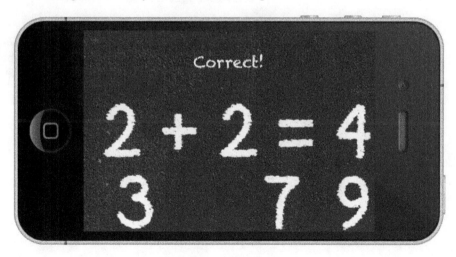

If you choose a wrong solution, the game will prompt you to try again until you succeed. When the answer is correct, we need to allow the user to move forward to the next level (**Level 1** at this point).

For this purpose, we are going to create another button that will be visible only when the operation has been solved. To get started, declare this new button by adding the following lines just after `CCButton *_buttonCheckSolution;`:

```
// Declare next level button
CCButton *_buttonNextLevel;
```

Initialize it by calling the following method in `init`:

```
// Create next level button
[self createNextLevelButton];
```

We need to implement it with this block of code:

```
- (void)createNextLevelButton {
    // Initialize frame
    CCSpriteFrame *buttonFrame = [CCSpriteFrame
    frameWithImageNamed:@"SqueezingBrainsAtlas/next_level.png"];

    // Create button
    _buttonNextLevel = [CCButton buttonWithTitle:@""
                                     spriteFrame:buttonFrame
                          highlightedSpriteFrame:buttonFrame
                             disabledSpriteFrame:buttonFrame];

    // Set button position
    _buttonNextLevel.position = CGPointMake(_screenSize.width -
    _buttonNextLevel.contentSize.width, _screenSize.height -
    _buttonNextLevel.contentSize.height);

    // Specify the method called when selected
    [_buttonNextLevel setTarget:self
    selector:@selector(goToNextLevel:)];

    // Make it invisible initially
    _buttonNextLevel.visible = FALSE;

    // Add button to the scene
    [self addChild:_buttonNextLevel];
}
```

This method is very similar to `createCheckButton`, but in this case we are creating a button with no highlighted sprite frame, as I wanted it to look like a drawing on the blackboard.

The button will be placed in the top-right corner of the view and will call the goToNextLevel method when selected.

To conclude this method, we set the button to be initially invisible and then we add it to the scene.

This button will call a method that will store the current user's progress, but as we want it to persist after different game launches, we will take advantage of the NSUserDefault class available in iOS.

Storing data using NSUserDefault

The NSUserDefault class provides an easy way to store user preferences in the default system. It can be used to save some user configurations such as preferred filters in a hotel booking application, sound activation in a game, and it can even be used to keep progress in games.

This class offers methods to store several data types (bool, float, double, integer, URL, and even custom objects) to save whatever the game needs.

Therefore we can implement the goToNextLevel method, but first of all, we must declare a pair of keys we will use to store the needed data. Add the following lines at the top of GameScene.m:

```
#define kTutorialSucceded @"Tutorial_Succeded"

#define kCurrentLevel @"Current_Level"
```

Now add the following lines to implement the method:

```
- (void)goToNextLevel:(id)sender{
    // If we had succeeded the tutorial
    if((int)_gameState == stateTutorialSuccess) {
        // Store tutorial success in user default
        [[NSUserDefaults standardUserDefaults] setBool:TRUE
        forKey:kTutorialSucceded];
    }

    // Get level information
    int currentLevel = [[NSUserDefaults standardUserDefaults]
    integerForKey:kCurrentLevel];
    // Increase level number
    currentLevel++;
    // Update level information
```

```
[[NSUserDefaults standardUserDefaults]
setInteger:currentLevel++ forKey:kCurrentLevel];
// Force to update defaults
[[NSUserDefaults standardUserDefaults] synchronize];
// Initialize scene
GameScene *nextLevelScene = [GameScene scene];
// Load new level
[[CCDirector sharedDirector] pushScene:nextLevelScene];
}
```

This method will be used no matter what the state of the game, but when it is the last step of the tutorial, we set the kTutorialSucceded key we've just created to TRUE so we can know in later runs that we don't need to load the tutorial again.

Then the method gets the current level information from the kCurrentLevel key, increments it, and updates the user default value. This way we will know which level we should load next. Note how we force the update of the user defaults by calling synchronize as it makes sure that we won't lose information if the game crashes suddenly.

Finally, we instantiate a new scene and push it to the top of the scenes stack.

There is one thing left to check in this new functionality, which is to make the next level button visible. Add the following lines in checkSolution, just after _gameState = stateTutorialSuccess;:

```
_buttonNextLevel.visible = TRUE;
```

Now you can run the project and play with this behavior:

As you will realize, at this moment the game is a never-ending tutorial, but don't worry, it's due to the fact that we haven't taken into account the user's default values when loading the scene. We are going to solve this in the next steps.

Loading data from external files

When loading the new scene, we are going to create the level using the information stored in an external file, in order to make our game independent.

The files used for this purpose are `.plist` files (also known as property list files) and they are commonly used to contain information to configure applications and games. Its contents have an XML structure and the root node is a dictionary where the children nodes are formed by a key-value sequence.

If we want to store custom objects in our `.plist` files, we just need to implement `encodeWithCoder` and `initWithCoder`, as we did in *Chapter 3, Your First Online Game*, to serialize the match data.

Xcode offers an easy way to create a new `.plist` file, which we are going to take advantage of to contain the information of our game.

Follow the next steps:

1. Right-click on the **Resources** group in the project navigator and select **New File...**.
2. Click on **iOS | Resource | Property List** and click on **Next**.
3. Call it `levelsInfo.plist` and click on **Create**.

Open the file and create a tree structure of level information similar to the one shown in the following screenshot, or you can just use the `levelsInfo.plist` file included in the `Resources` folder:

Key	Type	Value
▼ Information Property List	Dictionary	(4 items)
▼ Level1	Dictionary	(5 items)
left number	String	1
operation	String	sum
result	String	5
solution	String	4
▼ options	Dictionary	(4 items)
option1	String	7
option2	String	3
option3	String	4
option4	String	5
▶ Level2	Dictionary	(5 items)
▶ Level3	Dictionary	(5 items)
▶ Level4	Dictionary	(5 items)

Once our game information file is created, it's time to read it from our game and load the contents of each level properly. In `onEnter`, replace the following line:

```
if(_gameState == stateTutorial) {
```

Instead, add the following:

```
if(_gameState == stateTutorial && [[NSUserDefaults
standardUserDefaults] integerForKey:kCurrentLevel] == 0) {
```

We have changed the condition to initialize the game tutorial, so we can now take the `kCurrentLevel` key into account to double-check the state.

Then add the following lines of code at the end of the method:

```
else {
        // Load plist file into a dictionary
        NSDictionary *dictionary = [NSDictionary
        dictionaryWithContentsOfFile:[[NSBundle mainBundle]
        pathForResource:@"levelsInfo" ofType:@"plist"]];

        // Load current level data
        NSDictionary *levelDictionary = [dictionary
        valueForKey:[NSString stringWithFormat:@"Level%d",
         [[NSUserDefaults standardUserDefaults]
        integerForKey:kCurrentLevel]]];

        // Read left number information
        _leftNumber = [CCSprite spriteWithImageNamed:[NSString
        stringWithFormat:@"SqueezingBrainsAtlas/%@.png",
         [levelDictionary valueForKey:@"left number"]]];
        // Set sprite position
        _leftNumber.position = CGPointMake(_screenSize.width /
        5.0f - _leftNumber.contentSize.width / 2.0f,
        _screenSize.height / 2.0f);
        // Add number to the game scene
        [self addChild:_leftNumber];
}
```

When the scene initializes, we load `levelsInfo.plist` into `NSDictionary` that will keep all the information stored in the file. Note how we use the `NSBundle` singleton to read our `.plist` file.

Then we take the contents of the current level by retrieving the values for the key associated with **Level 1** (the level at this very moment).

Once we have the contents of the level in the dictionary, we can read each key to get the number for the option associated with `leftNumber`. Then we set its position, as we did when loading the tutorial, and add the sprite to the scene.

To load the rest of the possible options to solve the operation, add these lines at the end of `else`:

```
// Read operator information
_operator = [CCSprite spriteWithImageNamed:[NSString
stringWithFormat:@"SqueezingBrainsAtlas/%@.png",
 [levelDictionary valueForKey:@"operation"]]];
// Set sprite position
_operator.position = CGPointMake(2.0f * _screenSize.width
/ 5.0f - _operator.contentSize.width /
2.0f, _screenSize.height / 2.0f);
// Add operator to the game scene
[self addChild:_operator];

// Read equals symbol information
_equalsSymbol = [CCSprite
spriteWithImageNamed:@"SqueezingBrainsAtlas/equals.png"];
// Set symbol position
_equalsSymbol.position = CGPointMake(4.0f *
_screenSize.width / 5.0f - _equalsSymbol.contentSize.width
/ 2.0f, _screenSize.height / 2.0f);
// Add symbol to the game scene
[self addChild:_equalsSymbol];

// Read result information
_result = [CCSprite spriteWithImageNamed:[NSString
stringWithFormat:@"SqueezingBrainsAtlas/%@.png",
 [levelDictionary valueForKey:@"result"]]];
// Set result position
_result.position = CGPointMake(5.0f * _screenSize.width /
5.0f - _result.contentSize.width / 2.0f,
_screenSize.height / 2.0f);
// Add result to the game scene
[self addChild:_result];
```

These lines load the values to initialize, position, and add to the scene the operator, the equals symbol, and the results sprite.

Before performing the next step, declare the following variable:

```
// Declare solution variable
NSString *_solution;
```

We are going to use this string to store the solution for the level, so we can compare it with the name of the option selected, and check whether it's the correct answer or not.

Go back to `onEnter` and add the following lines at the end of the `else` clause:

```
// Store solution value
_solution = [levelDictionary valueForKey:@"solution"];

// Load options data
NSDictionary * levelOptionsDictionary = [levelDictionary
objectForKey:@"options"];

// Load options in an array
NSArray *options = [levelOptionsDictionary allKeys];

// Initialize the array of choices
_arrayOfOptions = [NSMutableArray
arrayWithCapacity:kNUM_TUTORIAL_OPTIONS];
```

We initialize the solution string with the value stored in the external file, and then we initialize another dictionary with the values of the options for the level. Note how we get the values inside options thanks to the `allKeys` method.

We also initialize the array of options to be ready for the next step. Add the following lines after the initialization of the options array:

```
CCSprite *optionNumber;
// Iterate array
for(int i = 0; i < [options count]; i++) {
    NSString *name = [levelOptionsDictionary
    valueForKey:[options objectAtIndex:i]];
    // Initialize number
    optionNumber = [CCSprite
    spriteWithImageNamed:[NSString
    stringWithFormat:@"SqueezingBrainsAtlas/%@.png",
    name]];
    // Set option name
    [optionNumber setName:name];
```

```
// Set number position
optionNumber.position = CGPointMake((i + 1) *
_screenSize.width / [options count] -
optionNumber.contentSize.width / 2.0f,
optionNumber.contentSize.height / 2.0f);
// Add number to the game scene
[self addChild:optionNumber];
// Add number to array
[_arrayOfOptions addObject:optionNumber];
}
```

We declare a sprite variable, which we are going to use to load all the options of the level.

Then we iterate the array of options, to get the value of each option that we use to initialize the choice number and set its name property. Once we have initialized the sprite, we set its position and then we add it to the array and the scene.

There is one thing left to do, which is to update the text label with the value of the level, so add the following block of code at the end of the else instruction:

```
// Initialize tutorial label
_tutorialLabel = [CCLabelTTF labelWithString:[NSString
stringWithFormat:@"Level %d", [[NSUserDefaults
standardUserDefaults] integerForKey:kCurrentLevel]]
fontName:@"Chalkduster" fontSize:22.0f];
_tutorialLabel.color = [CCColor whiteColor];
_tutorialLabel.position = CGPointMake(_screenSize.width /
2.0f, _screenSize.height - 2.0f *
_tutorialLabel.contentSize.height);

// Right-aligning the label
_tutorialLabel.anchorPoint = CGPointMake(0.5f, 0.5f);

[self addChild:_tutorialLabel];
```

We set the value of the current level for the label and initialize it when loading the tutorial, setting its color, position, and anchor point, then we add it to the scene.

Load the game now and take a look at **Level 1**:

If you try to solve this level, you will experience strange behavior due to the fact that we haven't updated some conditions and methods. In touchMoved, replace the if condition:

```
if ((int)_gameState < stateTutorialCheckingSolution) {
```

Instead, use these lines:

```
if ((int)_gameState < stateTutorialCheckingSolution &&
[[NSUserDefaults standardUserDefaults]
integerForKey:kCurrentLevel] == 0) {
```

This way we are using the level value to check the game's state.

Then add the else clause:

```
else {
        [_tutorialLabel setFontSize:22.0f];
        [_tutorialLabel setString:[NSString
        stringWithFormat:@"Level %d", [[NSUserDefaults
        standardUserDefaults] integerForKey:kCurrentLevel]]];
}
```

These lines load the level information at the top of the scene.

In `touchEnded`, replace the next line:

```
if ((int)_gameState < stateTutorialCheckingSolution) {
```

Replace it with the following one, to take the level information into account:

```
if ((int)_gameState < stateTutorialCheckingSolution &&
[[NSUserDefaults standardUserDefaults]
integerForKey:kCurrentLevel] == 0) {
```

Also, add its `else` clause:

```
else {
        // Remove droppable area from scene
        [self removeChild:_droppableArea];
}
```

That will force the removal of the green area if we are not playing the tutorial.

Then replace the contents of the last `else` block of the `touchEnded` method with these lines:

```
        // Recover initial position
        _rightNumber.position = _initialNumberPosition;
        // Remove droppable area from scene
        [self removeChild:_droppableArea];
        if ((int)_gameState < stateTutorialCheckingSolution &&
        [[NSUserDefaults standardUserDefaults]
        integerForKey:kCurrentLevel] == 0) {
        //Update label
        [_tutorialLabel setString:@"Choose the correct number
        \nfrom those available"];
        }
```

We have just wrapped the label string to be updated during the tutorial.

In the method `checkSolution`, replace the following line:

```
if((int)_gameState == stateTutorialCheckingSolution) {
```

Instead, use the following one to take the level into account:

```
if((int)_gameState == stateTutorialCheckingSolution &&
[[NSUserDefaults standardUserDefaults]
integerForKey:kCurrentLevel] == 0) {
```

Complement this `if` block with the following `else` block:

```
else {
    if ([_rightNumber.name isEqualToString:_solution]) {
        [_tutorialLabel setString:@"Correct!"];
        _buttonNextLevel.visible = TRUE;
    } else {
        [_tutorialLabel setString:@"Try again!"];
        _rightNumber.position = _initialNumberPosition;
    }
    [_tutorialLabel setFontSize:25.0f];
    _buttonCheckSolution.visible = FALSE;
}
```

These lines are executed to check the solution of a non-tutorial level, and they check if the selected option's name matches the solution loaded from the `.plist` file. If so, it updates the label and buttons to show success, but if not, it will recover the number position and show a different message.

If you run the game now, you will be able to complete the tutorial and the levels from 1 to 4 (as they are specified in the external file).

Transitions

In Cocos2d, we can create transitions between scenes, in order to replace the current scene with the following one. You can think of transitions in games as transitions between slides in a presentation, so we can animate them.

We can create six types of animations thanks to the class methods available: `transitionCrossFadeWithDuration`, `transitionFadeWithColor:duration`, `transitionFadeWithDuration`, `transitionMoveInWithDirection:duration`, `transitionPushWithDirection:duration`, and `transitionRevealWithDirection:duration`.

You can play with these methods, but we are going to use `transitionMoveInWithDirection` for this game, so you need to replace the following lines in `goToNextLevel`:

```
[[CCDirector sharedDirector] pushScene:nextLevelScene];
```

Instead, use the following lines:

```
// Create transition
CCTransition *transition = [CCTransition
transitionMoveInWithDirection:CCTransitionDirectionLeft
duration:0.5f];
// Push scene with transition
[[CCDirector sharedDirector] pushScene:nextLevelScene
withTransition:transition];
```

It will create a lateral movement transition and replace the current scene with the next one.

Come on, run the game and look at the amazing effect you just created!

3-star challenge – create a map scene

Now that you know how to load new scenes and navigate between them, create a map scene where the player will be able to select the level to play. This kind of scene is very common in video games, as it allows users to play the next scene in the story or to replay a previous level.

Summary

In this chapter, we learned how to develop a state machine in order to define a tutorial which will teach the user the mechanics of the mathematics game that we developed throughout the chapter.

By doing this, we defined the steps needed to take in order to solve a level's arithmetic operation.

Then we learned how to store the progress of the player in the user defaults so we can load the correct level, and how to force the synchronization of these values in order to prevent unexpected crashes.

The chapter also teaches us how to create .plist files to store the data that will define the different levels, and how to create these files by using Xcode.

Finally, we have seen how to load transitions between scenes and how to push scenes in two different ways.

In the next chapter, we are going to create a platforms game in which we will define custom collision logic, and we will learn how to create a varied terrain. So read on and learn the basics of one of the most popular game genres.

6
Physics Behavior

One of the features that makes the difference and converts games into successful products of entertainment is simulating reality accurately. It helps players feel like part of the game by being immersed in the world represented and augmenting their involvement.

Building a realistic game has been key to video game development since its origins, and as the technology evolved, it has been easier to simulate behaviors such as gravitational forces or collisions thanks to the rise of physics engines.

This chapter introduces you to Chipmunk, the physics engine included in Cocos2d, and shows you how to create the game's space thanks to the `CCPhysicsNode` class and configure its properties.

Also, this chapter will teach you how to define a physics world, create bodies and shapes and configure their properties, and give physical behavior to sprites. With this knowledge, you will develop a snooker game (a kind of pool game) where you can implement all you have learned.

The topics covered in this chapter are:

- How to create the game's space with `CCPhysicsNode`
- How to create bodies and shapes
- How to give physical behavior to sprites
- How to configure physics objects
- How to manage collisions

Physics engines

If you have played games such as *Pong*, *Air Hockey*, or *Angry Birds*, you may have noticed that there are some physical rules applied to the objects in the scene. Thanks to these rules, we can see how balls and pucks rebound against blocks and how birds demolish the pigs' constructions.

You might think that all these rules were implemented one by one, defining the exit angles when rebounding, the gain of velocity when hitting the puck, or the arc traced by launched birds. *Pong* was implemented by hand as it was first released in 1972 and the first physics engines date from the 80s. There are no complex behaviors in the game, but you can imagine the number of lines of code needed to simulate gravity, collision, and bouncing in a game similar to *Angry Birds*.

Physics engines were developed to ease tasks when simulating physical systems in games, films, and computer graphics, so we can specify the parameters of our "world" and the engine will do the rest.

In physics, we can talk about three types of objects/bodies:

- **Static**: These are bodies that always remain immobile, which means that they don't respond to gravity and impulses nor lose their position on their own. You can think of a wall on the street as a static body.

- **Dynamic**: These bodies can move and collide with other dynamic objects as well as with static bodies. A bouncing ball is a good representation of a dynamic body.

- **Kinematic**: These bodies do not respond to forces and they are usually moved by setting its velocity. They also only collide with dynamic bodies. A good example is a moving platform in a platform game, as it should always keep its movement no matter how the moving platform is collided into.

If we think of a scene with static (walls) and dynamic bodies (balls), you can understand their behavior. If you throw a ball against a wall, it will rebound, and it would also rebound against other balls in the scene in the case of colliding. But walls will never respond to collisions as they remain immobile.

To define this dynamic behavior, there is a concept in physics called **elasticity**. A collision in which the sum of bodies' energy is conserved is an elastic collision, for example, when two snooker balls impact each other. An inelastic collision is a collision in which energy is not conserved, for example, when two play dough balls impact and the energy is applied to deform the balls' shape.

Another key concept is **force**, which is a push or pull acting upon one body as the consequence of its interaction with another body. One important force is **friction**, which is a force that acts between objects in contact, reducing their energy. Friction is what, for example, makes a ball stop after making it roll on the floor. Without friction, the ball would move at the same velocity infinitely as happened to the character played by Sandra Bullock in *Gravity*.

In addition, bodies have a mass and density values to measure its weight that will affect the behavior of the body when colliding.

Objects are also defined by their shape (or shapes if it's a complex body) because the way they collide with other bodies depends on this property. Shapes can be rectangles, circles, or any kind of polygon, and depending on this, the contact points between colliding objects may vary.

Finally, bodies can also be connected by joints to represent complex objects such as hinge pins or elbow joints.

As you can imagine, video game physics engines simulate behaviors in a limited way because they depend on the capacity of computational calculation and the complexity of the real world. Who hasn't got stuck between boxes with no way to go, and who hasn't seen impossible gestures on characters' bodies?

Despite this, physics engines are powerful tools to add realistic behavior to objects in our games easily.

Game physics in Cocos2d

Earlier versions of Cocos2d were distributed with two physics engines: Box2D and Chipmunk, but after the release of Cocos2d v3, Box2D has been excluded and Chipmunk is now fully integrated.

During these previous versions, developers used to choose one of the engines depending on their preferred programming language (Box2D was written in C++, while Chipmunk was written in C), the framework syntax, or the implementation of the physics engine.

Until Cocos2d-Swift v3.x, Box2D was the most popular library, and it was even distributed with Cocos2d. However, the sponsorship of Chipmunk by Apportable has now set it in a privileged position.

Introducing Chipmunk

Chipmunk (`http://chipmunk-physics.net`) is an easy-to-use physics engine and has been fully integrated in Cocos2d-Swift since version 3.0 of the framework. Now, including physics in Cocos2d games is as easy as creating instances of the `CCPhysics*` family of classes. In addition, the Objective-C wrapper for Chipmunk physics, Objective-Chipmunk, is now free so there is no need to write C or C++ code anymore.

The `CCNode` class now has a `physicsBody` property that allows us to add gravity behavior, manage collisions, and combine nodes with joints easily, and in case you need more powerful physics, we can take advantage of the Objective-Chipmunk library.

In this last release of Chipmunk, a debug rendering has been included that draws a debug overlay and collision shapes, as well as new collision detection modes that we will see in detail throughout the chapter.

Now we'll describe the main classes that take part in game physics and take a look at their properties.

CCPhysicsNode

CCPhysicsNode (`http://www.cocos2d-swift.org/docs/api/Classes/CCPhysicsNode.html`) is a class derived from `CCNode` that will act as the space or world of the project. For those of you who have worked with Box2D previously, in Chipmunk a space is the equivalent to the Box2D concept of the world.

A physics node is responsible for containing the children bodies of the scene and giving them physical behavior. As this class is a subclass of `CCNode`, to add a body to the space we will need to create an instance of `CCPhysicsBody` that will need to be attached to another node, which, in turn, will be added to the space. Don't worry if it looks a little confusing, it's easier than it seems and you will understand it as soon as we create our first body in the next section.

A physics node has the following specific properties:

- `collisionDelegate`: The delegate class that will be in charge of managing collisions between bodies.
- `debugDraw`: This property activates the debug mode on the node, drawing debug overlays and shapes. By default, it's disabled.
- `gravity`: This defines a gravity force on both the x and y axes. By default, its value is (`0.0`, `0.0`).

- `iterations`: This is the number of iterations the physics engine will run when simulating physics. The higher its value, the stronger the simulation and the bigger the use of CPU too. It defaults to `10`.

- `sleepTimeThreshold`: This is a threshold value shown in seconds to determine whether a body should fall asleep to free up CPU resources. The default value is `0.5`.

- `space`: This property links to Objective-Chipmunk's `space` property, which represents the universe where physics simulation will take place.

CCPhysicsBody

CCPhysicsBody (`http://www.cocos2d-swift.org/docs/api/Classes/CCPhysicsBody.html`) is a class that inherits from `NSObject` and represents a body in a physics space. In fact, a physics body is linked to the `CCNode` class to describe its physical properties. Some of the most interesting body properties are:

- `affectedByGravity`: This flags describes whether a body is affected by gravity or not. By default, its value is `TRUE`.

- `absolutePosition`: The body's position relative to the space.

- `body`: This property links to Objective-Chipmunk's `body` property.

- `collisionType`: This is a string that identifies the collision pair delegate method that should be called. This property will help identify the method implemented by the delegate that will manage the event.

- `density`: This is the mass of the object divided by its area. The default value is `1.0`.

- `elasticity`: This makes reference to the restitution property used in physics and other engines such as Box2D. It describes how the energy is conserved in a collision. By default, its value is `0.2`.

- `friction`: This represents the absorption of energy when two bodies collide. By default, its value is `0.7`.

- `sensor`: A sensor is affected by collisions by calling the corresponding delegate method, but it won't have a physical effect on it. Basically, it's a space that will register collisions but won't interact physically with them. Its default value is `FALSE`.

- sleeping: If a body is sleeping, it will use minimal CPU until another body collides with it. A sleeping body will only be woken by a collision so, for example, this property should not be used when we want objects to fall after the platform under them disappears, as these objects will remain frozen until another body collides with them.

- type: This shows whether the body is static (for example, a wall) or dynamic (for example, a ball). By default, bodies are dynamic.

Creating your first physics

Now that you know the main actors that can intervene in a physics simulation, let's create our first space. Before getting down to work with physics, open the code files of this chapter from the code bundle where you'll find SnookerMunk_init.zip, which contains the initial project, and open it.

If you take a look at the project, you will realize that it just has one thing to highlight. Specifically, in AppDelegate.m, you will find this line:

```
CCSetupScreenOrientation: CCScreenOrientationPortrait,
```

We are just setting the portrait orientation of the project as this way the device will be more comfortable to hold.

Now let's add some physics. In GameScene.m, declare some private variables by adding the following lines:

```
// Declare global variable for screen size
CGSize _screenSize;

// Declare the physics space
CCPhysicsNode *_space;

// Declare physics body
CCPhysicsBody *_ball;
// Declare ball node
CCNode *_ballNode;

// Declare physics body
CCPhysicsBody *_rect;
// Declare rectangle node
CCNode *_rectNode;
```

We declare a screen size variable as always to know the screen width and height at every moment.

We are going to add two bodies to the space, which is why we declare two
`CCPhysicsBody` instances and two `CCNodes` instances.

Now in the `init` method, add the following lines just before `return self;`:

```
// Initialize screen size variable
_screenSize = [CCDirector sharedDirector].viewSize;

// Initialize the physics node
_space = [CCPhysicsNode node];

// Set the node gravity
_space.gravity = CGPointMake(0.0f, -200.0f);

// Draw debug shapes and overlays
_space.debugDraw = TRUE;

// Add the physics node to the scene
[self addChild:_space];
```

We first initialize the screen size variable as we did in previous chapters, and then
initialize the physics node by calling its `node` method, which will initialize it in
autorelease mode.

Once the node is initialized, we can set the desired attributes. For this first test, we
want to simulate the gravitational force; that's why we pass a point to the `gravity`
attribute that gives the direction and strength desired. Then we tell the space to draw
debug shapes so we can see what is happening.

Now let's include the first body by adding the following lines of code in the `init`
method before `return self;`:

```
// Initialize ball
_ball = [CCPhysicsBody bodyWithCircleOfRadius:60.0f
andCenter:CGPointMake(0.0f, 0.0f)];

// Initialize the ball node
_ballNode = [CCNode node];
// Link physics body to the node
_ballNode.physicsBody = _ball;
// Set node's position
_ballNode.position = CGPointMake(_screenSize.width/2.0f +
60.0f, _screenSize.height/2.0f);
// Add ball to the space
[_space addChild:_ballNode];
```

We first initialize the ball by specifying the circle radius and its center point. We are going to set its center point at (0.0, 0.0), but that's not the bottom-left point of the screen, it's the bottom-left point of the node. Each physics body needs to be attached to CCNode instances to be part of the space, so we need to take this into account when specifying its anchor point value or it will be placed in an undesired place.

After initializing the physics body, we initialize the node that will contain the ball and then we link the node's physicsBody attribute to the ball. This way, we can then add the node with the ball to the space after setting its desired position.

To initialize the rectangle, add the following lines in the init method before return self;:

```
// Initialize rectangle
_rect = [CCPhysicsBody bodyWithRect:CGRectMake(0.0f, 0.0f,
60.0f, 100.0f) cornerRadius:10.0f];

// Initialize the rect node
_rectNode = [CCNode node];
// Link physic body to the node
_rectNode.physicsBody = _rect;
// Set node's position
_rectNode.position = CGPointMake(_screenSize.width/2.0f -
80.0f, _screenSize.height/2.0f);
// Add rect to the space
[_space addChild:_rectNode];
```

In this case, we create the rectangle by specifying its initial x and y values to (0.0f, 0.0f) for the same reason explained previously. The corner radius is a property relative to the center of the node to make the corners of the rectangle smoother.

 In Cocos2d-Swift v3.0 and v3.1, cornerRadius doesn't work properly and modifying its value has no effect on the body's visual representation.

Once the rectangle has been created, we create the node that will be linked to it, specify its position, and then we can add it to the space.

If you now run the project, you will see a rectangle and a circle falling down and disappearing from view as seen in the following image:

What we are seeing in this image is the center of gravity of the nodes (the yellow dot) and the debug overlays of the bodies we have created. These overlays allow us to visualize collision points and tunneling shapes, so we can check whether the bodies react as we expect. Now let's make our bodies collide to see how their shapes interact between them. For that, find the following lines:

```
_ballNode.position = CGPointMake(_screenSize.width/2.0f + 60.0f,
_screenSize.height/2.0f);
_rectNode.position = CGPointMake(_screenSize.width/2.0f - 80.0f,
_screenSize.height/2.0f);
```

Replace them with the following ones:

```
_ballNode.position = CGPointMake(_screenSize.width/2.0f + 10.0f,
_screenSize.height/2.0f);
_rectNode.position = CGPointMake(_screenSize.width/2.0f - 10.0f, _
screenSize.height/2.0f);
```

Run the project again and you will see how they overlap:

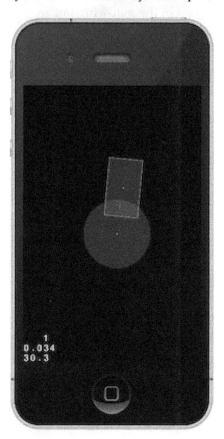

For now, the circle and rectangle fall down unlimitedly, but how can we represent a ground to stop their fall? If we stop to consider it, it's easier than it seems. We should create some static body that lies at the bottom of the scene covering the full width and see what happens.

Add the following declarations:

```
// Declare physics body
CCPhysicsBody *_ground;
// Declare ground node
CCNode *_groundNode;
```

As we saw in the previous example, we need to declare a physics body and a node to add a new child to the space. Then we need to add the following lines to the `init` method, just before `return self;`:

```
// Declare an array of shapes
NSMutableArray* shapes = [NSMutableArray array];

// Create shape for the ground
CCPhysicsShape *shape0 = [CCPhysicsShape
pillShapeFrom:CGPointMake(0.0f, 0.0f)
to:CGPointMake(_screenSize.width, 0.0f) cornerRadius:10.0f];
// Add shape to the array
[shapes addObject:shape0];
// Initialize ground body
_ground = [CCPhysicsBody bodyWithShapes:shapes];
// Set static type to body
_ground.type = CCPhysicsBodyTypeStatic;

// Initialize the ground node
_groundNode = [CCNode node];
// Link physics body to the node
_groundNode.physicsBody = _ground;
// Add ground to the space
[_space addChild:_groundNode];
```

We are going to create a pill shape that will work as a floor and for this purpose, we need to create an array of shapes.

For the moment, we just create a pill physics shape that will cover the entire width of the screen and will be placed at the bottom of the view. We specify its `cornerRadius` value and then we add it to the array.

The next step creates the ground body from the array of shapes to define it and we specify that the body is static so the dynamic bodies in the scene can collide with it.

The last lines are similar to the rectangle and ball cases: we initialize the ground node and link the physics body to it before adding the body to the space.

Run the project again and you will see how the dynamic bodies (the ball and the rectangle are dynamic by default) interact with the ground:

Now that we have introduced shapes, let's take a deeper look at their class.

CCPhysicsShape

CCPhysicsShape (http://www.cocos2d-swift.org/docs/api/Classes/ CCPhysicsShape.html) is a class that inherits from NSObject. Shapes are linked to bodies as soon as we create one of them and represent that shape's geometry. In our previous examples, we created three kinds of shapes (circle, rectangle, and pill) when initializing the bodies. You can create shapes by using one of the four initializers available:

- circleShapeWithRadius:center: Creates a circle with a specified radius and is centered at a position relative to the node that contains it

- rectShape:cornerRadius: Creates a rectangle with a CGRect instance and rounded corners

- `pillShapeFrom:to:cornerRadius`: Creates a pill with start and end points and specifies its corner radius value similar to its width
- `polygonShapeWithPoints:count:cornerRadius`: Creates a convex polygon specifying an array of points and the corner radius

Besides these four ways, you can also create complex bodies by joining shapes.

The most important purpose of shapes is their role in collision detection as these tasks are responsible for shapes not bodies or nodes.

Some of the most interesting properties of shapes are:

- `area`: This represents the area of the shape in square points and it's relative to the `CCPhysicsNode` class that is linked to the shape
- `body`: This is the body linked to the shape
- `elasticity`: This is similar to the bodies' property
- `density`: You can set this property, which means that we don't have to assign an area or mass as it will use the bodies' shape to calculate those values
- `mass`: This is the mass of the shape
- `next`: This is the next shape linked in the list of shapes (for complex bodies)
- `node`: This represents the node linked to the shape
- `sensor`: This is similar to the bodies' property
- `shape`: This property links to Objective-Chipmunk's `shape` property

Creating sprites with physics

If you thought that the only way to view bodies was using the debug draw mode, you were wrong. In the current version of Cocos2d, `CCNode` has a property called `physicsBody` where we can link a physical body to the node.

This feature makes it as easy to create a sprite that responds to physical stimulations as declaring a common sprite and setting the `CCPhysicalBody` instance to it. Let's prove this with an example.

We are going to create a star, so paste the following lines in the variables declaration section in `GameScene.m`:

```
// Declare a sprite
CCSprite *_star;
```

We want the star to have an image so:

1. In the project navigator, select the `Resources` group.
2. Right-click and select **Add Files to "SnookerMunk"**....
3. Look for the `star.png` file in the `Resources` folder you unzipped.
4. Be sure that **Copy items into destination group's folder (if needed)** is selected and click on **Add**.

Now add the following lines at the end of the `init` method just before `return self;`:

```
// Initialize the sprite with an image
_star = [CCSprite spriteWithImageNamed:@"star.png"];

// Set the initial position of the star
_star.position = CGPointMake(_screenSize.width/2,
_screenSize.height/2.0f + 40.0f);

// Create physics body
CCPhysicsBody *starBody = [CCPhysicsBody
bodyWithCircleOfRadius:30.0f
andCenter:ccp(_star.contentSize.width/2.0f,
_star.contentSize.height/2.0f)];

// Link a circle body to the sprite
_star.physicsBody = starBody;

// Add the sprite to the space
[_space addChild:_star];
```

We initialize the sprite as always, using the image added previously, and initialize its position in the space. Then we create a physics body for the star that is a circle. In this case, the center has to be set in the center of the sprite in contrast to what we did with the ball. Then we link the physics body to the sprite and add it to the space.

If you run the game now, what do you think you will see?

Nice, isn't it? We have created a sprite that collides with other objects and responds to these events in an expected way for a physical object. The only weird thing is that we see the debug shapes at the same time as we see the sprite's image.

If you set the value of _space.debugDraw to FALSE and run the project again, you will see how the circle and rectangle shapes have disappeared and we just see the sprites.

If you look at the draw calls value, you will realize that there is two draws whereas they were three with active debug draws. This happens because these draws corresponds to the action of drawing the star sprite and the space. If you look at the previous images, you will realize that drawing shapes doesn't affects to the number of debug draws.

Before proceeding, revert the value of space.debugDraw as we will perform some tests before being serious.

As you might be wondering, linking a star sprite to a circle shape could cause problems when managing collisions. Fortunately, there are several tools to help us define the correct shape of a physical body.

Defining shapes

There are several tools that can help us define the shapes of our objects so we can manage collisions in an accurate way. Some of them are paid and some of them are free.

Between the most important editors, we find Physics Body Editor (former box2d-Editor, `http://www.aurelienribon.com/blog/projects/physics-body-editor/`) and R.U.B.E (`https://www.iforce2d.net/rube/`), which are compatible with Chipmunk and PhysicsEditor (`https://www.codeandweb.com/physicseditor`).

In this chapter, we are going to cover PhysicsEditor as it's the most popular of the previous editors and it has both a trial and paid version.

PhysicsEditor

As mentioned in the preceding section, PhysicsEditor is a popular and powerful tool to define collision shapes, especially when working with concave polygons or shapes.

We saw when talking about `CCPhysicsShape` that it can create convex polygons by an array of points, but what's the difference between convex and concave polygons?

A convex polygon is a simple polygon defined by a convex set, in other words, an area where every pair of points can be joined by a line that is within the polygon. In the following image taken from Wikipedia (`http://en.wikipedia.org/wiki/Convex_set`), you can see what a convex set looks like:

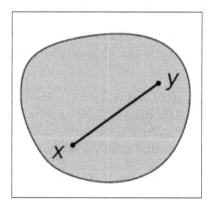

There is another property that we can check to know whether it's a convex polygon or not: every internal angle is equal to or lower than 180 degrees.

Of course, there are more than these two properties that define a convex polygon, but we don't need to go into greater detail.

On the other hand, a concave polygon is a polygon defined by a non-convex set, which means that we can find a pair of points where part of their joining line lies out of the area. The following image (taken from Wikipedia too: `http://en.wikipedia.org/wiki/Convex_set`) represents a non-convex set:

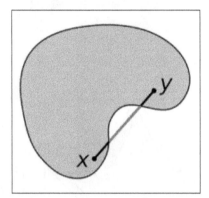

In opposition to convex polygons, concave ones will also have at least one angle greater than 180 degrees.

There is another interesting property of these kinds of polygons: we will always be able to partition a concave polygon into several convex polygons.

Due to the nature of concave polygons, it's very difficult to define their shapes and collision points and that is where PhysicsEditor plays an important role.

Defining shapes

This editor allows us to define collisions settings and physical parameters as well. Let's define our star's shape, so open the PhysicsEditor, look for the **Add new image** button placed in the bottom-left corner of the screen, and choose the `star.png` image placed in the `Resources` folder (or drag and drop the image in the left-side section). I recommend you choose the biggest resolution image and reuse it on all the devices to avoid different behaviors depending on the display.

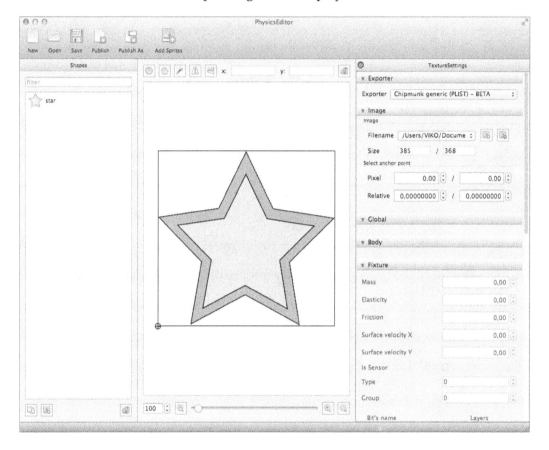

As you can see in the preceding screenshot, there are three main sections on the screen:

- The **Shapes** section on the left where we can see the shapes we are working with.
- The main view in the center that displays the shape and the configurations we are setting up. In the image, the violet circle in the bottom-left corner references the anchor point.

- The **TextureSettings** section on the right side allows us to modify the **Exporter** format, size, anchor point, or even some physics attributes.

At this very moment, we can't edit the physics properties as we need to define our image's shape, so before proceeding, choose the **Shape** tracer tool available in the top of the center section. It will show the following screen:

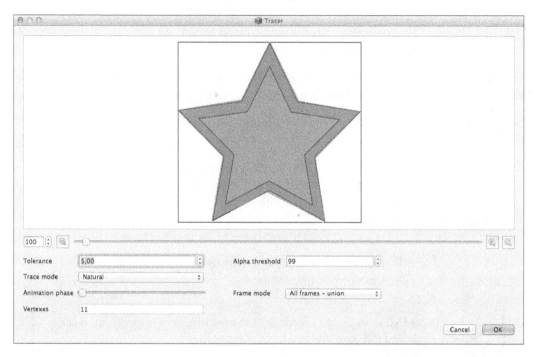

The tracer tool is an automatic way to detect the shape of our object and is the perfect option when working with concave bodies. We can specify the **Tolerance** field so the approach is the most accurate possible. We can also specify the **Trace mode** and **Frame mode** fields or even know (not edit) the number of vertexes used to trace the shape (it will depend on the tolerance value and the trace mode).

You may take into account that the larger the number of vertexes, the more accurate the shape, but also the harder it is to detect collisions.

Choose **Natural** for the **Trace mode** field and **Tolerance** of **5,00**; it will result in an amount of **11** vertexes, which is pretty accurate, so click on **OK**.

Back in the main screen, we can now see the resulting shape and we are able to modify its settings, but before that we need to update the available exporters as Cocos2d-Swift v3 is not available in this version (1.0.11). If you unzip the `physicseditor-cocos2d-v3.zip` file included in the `Resources` folder, you will see two directories:

- `exporters`: This is the updated exporter for Cocos2d v.3x
- `loaders`: This contains the classes required to import the files exported by PhysicsEditor into your Xcode project

In PhysicsEditor, click on the **Preferences** menu and specify the route to the `exporters` directory in the **Custom exporter directory** field and click on **OK**.

Now, in the **Exporter** settings drop-down menu, you will see the new **Cocos2D (V3)** option, so choose it.

You may have realized that the settings section has changed to show the Cocos2d v3-specific properties. For the star set, the anchor point needs to be relative **0,5 / 0,5** (you can set these values in the **Relative** field or by dragging the violet circle), an **Elasticity** value of **0,2**, **Friction** of **0,7**, and a **Mass** value of **1,0** so the star has a little bounciness. You can leave the rest of the settings as their default values.

Once you have set the desired values, click on **Publish** and save it as `star_shape.plist` in the `Resources` folder of our project.

Note that if we need to work with convex objects, PhysicsEditor has a circle and polygon tool to edit the shapes too.

Now we can load this new shape into our project, but first we need to make some changes.

Loading PhysicsEditor shapes in Xcode

First of all in Xcode, set the value of `_space.debugDraw` to `TRUE` again so we can see the shapes we've just created.

Then follow these steps:

1. Drag and drop the files GCCShapeCache.h and GCCShapeCache.m that you will find in the Resources/physicseditor-cocos2d-v3/loaders/cocos2d-v3 folder into the **Classes** group.

2. Ensure the **Copy items into destination group's folder (if needed)** option is selected and click on **Finish**.

In GameScene.m, add the following import so we can use the loader classes:

```
#import "GCCShapeCache.h"
```

Add the following lines in the init method, just after if (!self) return(nil);:

```
// Load the star shape
[[GCCShapeCache sharedShapeCache]
addShapesWithFile:@"star_shape.plist"];
```

This way, we load the shape we have created in PhysicsEditor and it will be available in the project.

Then find the following block of code:

```
// Create physic body
CCPhysicsBody *starBody = [CCPhysicsBody
bodyWithCircleOfRadius:30.0f
andCenter:ccp(_star.contentSize.width/2.0f,
_star.contentSize.height/2.0f)];
// Link a circle body to the sprite
_star.physicsBody = starBody;
```

Replace it with the following lines:

```
// Link the new shape to the star
[[GCCShapeCache sharedShapeCache] setBodyWithName:@"star"
onNode:_star];
```

Here we are telling Xcode that we want to set the shape with the name @"star" into the _star sprite. It will internally create a body with the attributes defined in the .plist file.

It's time to run the project and check the result of creating a shape from an external editor:

You may have realized that our customized star doesn't collide anymore; this is due to the fact that it's a concave object and we have to configure its collision properties or it won't know how to behave.

Advanced collision detection with Chipmunk

Chipmunk provides powerful tools to detect and manage collisions between physics bodies, taking advantage of CCPhysicsBody and CCPhysicsShape properties and implementing the CCPhysicsCollisionDelegate protocol.

CCPhysicsBody and CCPhysicsShape properties

Chipmunk's bodies and shapes have three properties we can take advantage of to define the collision relationship between them:

- `collisionCategory`: This is the collision category that defines an object.
- `collisionMask`: This is the property that defines the objects that can collide with it. This property is an array that contains the collision categories that will collide with the object.
- `collisionGroup`: Thanks to this property, we can define a group of objects that won't collide with each other.

These properties allow us to define the collision relationships to achieve the effect desired. For example, let's make the star collide with all the bodies and vice versa.

In `GameScene.m`, add the following lines at the end of the `init` method before the `return` statement:

```
// Define the star collision category
_star.physicsBody.collisionCategories = @[@"star"];
// Define the mask for the star
_star.physicsBody.collisionMask = @[@"body"];

// Define the ball collision category
_ball.collisionCategories = @[@"body"];
// Define the mask for the ball
_ball.collisionMask = @[@"star", @"body"];

// Define the rectangle collision category
_rect.collisionCategories = @[@"body"];
// Define the mask for the rectangle
_rect.collisionMask = @[@"star", @"body"];
```

In this block, we are making the star register to the `@"star"` category and specifying the collision category it will collide with by configuring its collision mask.

Then we set up the ball and the rectangle in the same way. They are registered to the `@"body"` category and both will collide with the `@"star"` and `@"body"` categories.

Can you imagine what will happen when we run the project? Let's check it out:

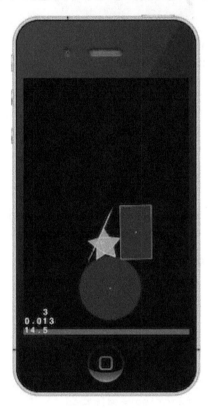

As expected, all the physics objects collide with each other. Note how the star has a more accurate shape than when it was first created with a circle shape.

We have just used the collision mask and categories, so let's make some changes to understand how collision groups work.

Add the following block of code in the `init` method, just before `return self;`:

```
// Create an array
NSMutableArray *collisionGroup = [[NSMutableArray alloc]
init];
// Add the objects we want
[collisionGroup addObject:_star];
[collisionGroup addObject:_ball];

// Set the collision group to each body
_star.physicsBody.collisionGroup = collisionGroup;
_ball.collisionGroup = collisionGroup;
```

The `collisionGroup` property expects an object that will contain the objects that form the group; that's why we create an array and add the star and ball.

Run the project again and see how the star and ball don't collide with each other, while the rectangle and the ground do.

In addition to this collision detection handling, there is another way to detect bodies and shapes' intersections that consists of implementing the `CCPhysicsCollisionDelegate` (`http://www.cocos2d-swift.org/docs/api/Protocols/CCPhysicsCollisionDelegate.html`) protocol.

CCPhysicsCollisionDelegate

This delegate is called when two physics bodies or shapes intersect between them. It provides four methods that can be implemented to define the interaction of the bodies in the collision:

- `ccPhysicsCollisionBegin:(CCPhysicsCollisionPair *)pair typeA:(CCNode *)nodeA typeB:(CCNode *)nodeB`: This method is called as soon as two physics bodies collide. If this method returns FALSE, the collision between `CCPhysicsCollisionPair` bodies won't happen.

- `ccPhysicsCollisionPreSolve:(CCPhysicsCollisionPair *)pair typeA:(CCNode *)nodeA typeB:(CCNode *)nodeB`: This method is called as soon as two physics bodies collide but before the physics solver takes place. This way, we can customize the result of the collision by modifying the friction, elasticity, or surface velocity properties. If this method returns FALSE, the collision solver will not work.

- `ccPhysicsCollisionPostSolve:(CCPhysicsCollisionPair *)pair typeA:(CCNode *)nodeA typeB:(CCNode *)nodeB`: This method is called as soon as two physics bodies collide but after the physics solver takes place. In this case, we can customize the collision resultant by modifying the `totalKineticEnergy` and `totalImpulse` properties of `CCPhysicsCollisionPair`.

- `ccPhysicsCollisionSeparate:(CCPhysicsCollisionPair *)pair typeA:(CCNode *)nodeA typeB:(CCNode *)nodeB`: This method is called as soon as two physics bodies stop colliding.

It's important to note that the sequence of methods called when a collision happens will be:

- `ccPhysicsCollisionBegin`
- `ccPhysicsCollisionPreSolve`
- `ccPhysicsCollisionPostSolve`
- `ccPhysicsCollisionSeparate`

There is another important thing in these methods and that is the `typeA` and `typeB` nodes. These types make reference to the `collisionType` property of the `CCPhysicsBody` or `CCPhysicsShape` object.

If we want the `typeA` object to collide with whatever body or shape we have, we can replace `typeB` with a wildcard. This way, there would be three different methods for two objects of types `typeA` and `typeB`: `typeA` collides with `typeB`, `typeA` collides with the wildcard, and `typeB` collides with the wildcard.

The first method raised will be that `typeA` collides with `typeB` and then the wildcards will be called randomly.

Let's see a practical example of this approach.

The first thing is to define the delegate of `CCPhysicsCollisionDelegate`, so find the following line in `GameScene.h`:

```
@interface GameScene : CCScene {
```

Replace it with the following one:

```
@interface GameScene : CCScene <CCPhysicsCollisionDelegate> {
```

This way, we have set `GameScene` as the implementer of the protocol. Now find the block of code we implemented for the collision category, group, and mask:

```
// Define the star collision category
_star.physicsBody.collisionCategories = @[@"star"];
// Define the mask for the star
_star.physicsBody.collisionMask = @[@"body"];

// Define the ball collision category
_ball.collisionCategories = @[@"body"];
// Define the mask for the ball
_ball.collisionMask = @[@"star", @"body"];
```

```
// Define the rectangle collision category
_rect.collisionCategories = @[@"body"];
// Define the mask for the rectangle
_rect.collisionMask = @[@"star", @"body"];
// Create an array
NSMutableArray *collisionGroup = [[NSMutableArray alloc]
init];
// Add the objects we want
[collisionGroup addObject:_star];
[collisionGroup addObject:_ball];

// Set the collision group to each body
_star.physicsBody.collisionGroup = collisionGroup;
_ball.collisionGroup = collisionGroup;
```

Replace it with the following block of code:

```
// Set collision delegate of space
_space.collisionDelegate = self;

// Define the star collision category
_star.physicsBody.collisionCategories = @[@"star"];
// Define a blank mask for the star
_star.physicsBody.collisionMask = @[@""];

// Define collision type for the star
_star.physicsBody.collisionType = @"star";
// Define collision type for the ball
_ball.collisionType = @"body";
// Define collision type for the rectangle
_rect.collisionType = @"body";
// Define collision type for the ground
_ground.collisionType = @"ground";
```

We first define GameSpace as the delegate for the CCPhysicsCollisionDelegate protocol.

Then we set the collision categories and mask for the star object. We have to do this to give physical behavior to an object created through PhysicsEditor or it will cross every shape and body. Note how we just create a blank mask as we don't need to specify any one, we just need to provide this property.

Now we set the `collisionType` property of the star, ball, rectangle, and ground. Then we just need to implement the desired methods, so add the following lines to `GameScene.m`:

```
- (BOOL) ccPhysicsCollisionBegin:(CCPhysicsCollisionPair *)pair
body:(CCNode *)body ground:(CCNode *)ground{
    CCLOG(@"BODY - GROUND - COLLISION");
    return TRUE;
}


- (BOOL) ccPhysicsCollisionBegin:(CCPhysicsCollisionPair *)pair
star:(CCNode *)star ground:(CCNode *)ground{
    CCLOG(@"STAR - GROUND - COLLISION");
    return TRUE;
}


- (BOOL) ccPhysicsCollisionBegin:(CCPhysicsCollisionPair *)pair
star:(CCNode *)star body:(CCNode *)body{
    CCLOG(@"STAR - BODY - COLLISION");
    return TRUE;
}
```

We have implemented the methods to manage the collisions between `body` – `ground`, `star` – `ground`, and `star` – `body` and set a log just to know when they are called. Note how we have replaced `typeA` and `typeB` arguments of the methods by the corresponding collision type (star, body, and ground).

 You can define as many pair methods as collision pairs that exist.

Run the game and take a look at the logs to understand what is happening; they show that several collisions happened:

```
2014-08-16 22:31:35.123 SnookerMunk[17087:907] STAR - BODY - COLLISION
2014-08-16 22:31:35.766 SnookerMunk[17087:907] BODY - GROUND -
COLLISION
2014-08-16 22:31:36.065 SnookerMunk[17087:907] STAR - BODY - COLLISION
2014-08-16 22:31:36.066 SnookerMunk[17087:907] STAR - BODY - COLLISION
2014-08-16 22:31:36.215 SnookerMunk[17087:907] BODY - GROUND -
COLLISION
2014-08-16 22:31:36.290 SnookerMunk[17087:907] STAR - BODY - COLLISION
2014-08-16 22:31:36.291 SnookerMunk[17087:907] STAR - BODY - COLLISION
2014-08-16 22:31:36.818 SnookerMunk[17087:907] STAR - GROUND -
COLLISION
2014-08-16 22:31:36.819 SnookerMunk[17087:907] STAR - GROUND -
COLLISION
2014-08-16 22:31:36.820 SnookerMunk[17087:907] STAR - GROUND -
COLLISION
```

At this point, there is no news compared with the previous execution when we set the collision mask, group, and category, but we can take advantage of this protocol for several things.

For example, let's imagine that we don't want the star to collide with the ground if some condition is accomplished. So find the following line in the `ccPhysicsCollisionBegin:(CCPhysicsCollisionPair *)pair star:(CCNode *)star ground:(CCNode *)ground` method:

```
return TRUE;
```

Replace it with these lines:

```
BOOL result = TRUE;
if (TRUE) {
    result = FALSE;
}
return result;
```

We are saying to this method that it has to register the collision (you will see the same logs) but it may ignore it (the condition is always TRUE). So if you run the project now, you will see how the star collides with the rectangle and the ball but then it will cross the ground and fall infinitely:

This technique is very useful to have total control over the collisions happening in our space. In addition, we can combine the returned value of the ccPhysicsCollisionBegin and ccPhysicsCollisionPreSolve methods with a logical AND function.

Let's see another example of what we can do in these physics collision methods, but before proceeding, restore the return TRUE; instruction in the ccPhysicsCollisionBegin:(CCPhysicsCollisionPair *)pair star: (CCNode *)star ground:(CCNode *)ground method.

Add the following method to GameScene.m:

```
- (BOOL) ccPhysicsCollisionPreSolve:(CCPhysicsCollisionPair *)pair
ground:(CCNode *)ground wildcard:(CCNode *)body{
    CCLOG(@"PRESOLVE GROUND - BODY - COLLISION");
    // Apply vertical impulse
    [body.physicsBody applyImpulse:ccp(0.0f, 1000.0f)];
    return TRUE;
}
```

Note the use of the wildcard type to specify that we want this method to be called when the ground collides with the rest of the bodies in the scene. It will apply a vertical impulse to whichever object that collides with the ground.

Run the game and look how our bodies bounce!

Creating a snooker game with Chipmunk

Now that we know how to create bodies and manage collisions, let's implement a snooker game.

Let's start at the beginning, so replace the contents of GameScene.h with the following lines:

```
#import <Foundation/Foundation.h>
#import "cocos2d.h"

@interface GameScene : CCScene <CCPhysicsCollisionDelegate> {
}

+ (GameScene *)scene;
- (id)init;

@end
```

This is the default content of a header file, but in addition we are declaring `GameScene` as the delegate of the `CCPhysicsCollisionDelegate` protocol in the same way we did in previous sections.

Then we replace the contents of `GameScene.m` with the following lines:

```
#import "GameScene.h"

@implementation GameScene {
    // Declare global variable for screen size
    CGSize _screenSize;

    // Declare the physics space
    CCPhysicsNode *_space;
}

+ (GameScene *)scene
{
    return [[self alloc] init];
}
```

To get started, we declare the screen size variable and the space of the physics world. The `scene` method will call `init`, so implement it by adding these lines at the end of the file:

```
- (id)init
{
    // Apple recommends assigning self with supers return value
    self = [super init];
    if (!self) return(nil);

    // Initialize screen size variable
    _screenSize = [CCDirector sharedDirector].viewSize;

    // Initialize the physics node
    _space = [CCPhysicsNode node];

    // Add the physics node to the scene
    [self addChild:_space];

    return self;
}
```

In this method, we initialize the screen size variable as well as the physics node. Note that in this case, we are not specifying the gravity so it will be 0.0 on both the *x* and *y* axes. This means that the objects placed in this space will remain still until some force is applied to them.

If you run the project now, you will see only a blank screen, so let's add a table to play on. First of all, you will need to add the texture atlas so:

1. In the project navigator, select the **Resources** group.
2. Right-click and select **Add Files to "SnookerMunk"**....
3. Look for the snookerMunk-hd.plist and snookerMunk-hd.png files in the Resources folder.
4. Be sure that **Copy items into destination group's folder (if needed)** is selected and click on **Add**.

Now that the required files are included in the project, add the following variable declaration:

```
// Declare global batch node
CCSpriteBatchNode *_batchNode;
```

This is the batch we will take advantage of to improve the rendering performance of our game due to the amount of images we need to load.

Then we add the texture atlas and the batch node with the following lines at the end of the init method before return self;:

```
// Load texture atlas
[[CCSpriteFrameCache sharedSpriteFrameCache]
addSpriteFramesWithFile: @"snookerMunk-hd.plist"];

// Load batch node with texture atlas
_batchNode = [CCSpriteBatchNode
batchNodeWithFile:@"snookerMunk-hd.png"];

// Add the batch node to the scene
[self addChild:_batchNode];

// Create a background for the table
CCSprite *background = [CCSprite
spriteWithImageNamed:@"SnookerMunkAtlas/snooker_table.png"];
background.position = CGPointMake(_screenSize.width / 2.0f,
_screenSize.height / 2.0f);
[self addChild:background z:-1];
```

We load the texture atlas files as we saw in the previous chapter using CCSpriteFrameCache and take advantage of the batch node.

Then we create a new sprite for the background placing it in the center of the screen. Note how we are adding the background to the scene in spite of the space, as we don't need the background to be more than a static image. To simulate the pockets and the edges, we will create physics bodies, but for now run the project and look at the marvelous snooker table:

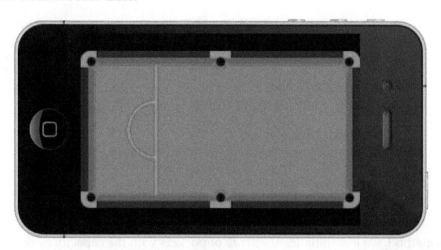

Setting the snooker table

In this section, we are going to create some physics bodies to simulate the edges of the table and the pocket to keep the balls inside the field and detect when a ball has been pocketed.

To get started, declare an array to keep control of the pockets:

```
// Array of pockets
NSMutableArray *_pockets;
```

Before initializing them, add the following lines to the init method:

```
// Initialize debug mode
_space.debugDraw = YES;

// Initialize pockets bodies
[self initializePockets];
```

We activate the debug mode so we can see the shapes and bodies we will create for the pockets and edges. Then we call the `initializePockets` method that we will implement with the following lines:

```
- (void)initializePockets {

    // Initialize the pockets array
    _pockets = [NSMutableArray arrayWithCapacity: NUM_POCKETS];

    // Initialize sprite to get content size
    CCSprite *pocket = [[CCSprite alloc]
    initWithImageNamed:@"SnookerMunkAtlas/pocket.png"];

    // Declare physics body
    CCPhysicsBody *pocketBody;

    // Initial pocket position
    CGPoint initialPocketPosition = CGPointMake(5.0f *
    pocket.contentSize.width / 2.0f, pocket.contentSize.height);
    // Current pocket position
    CGPoint currentPocketPosition;
}
```

In this method, we just initialize the array of pockets with the capacity desired and create a new sprite with the pocket image to know its size. This sprite's content size is used to initialize a `CGPoint` variable that we will use to recursively update to set the different pockets' positions.

We also declare a physics body variable and another point variable to keep the following pocket's position.

Define some constants that we are using in this method by adding the following lines at the beginning of `GameScene.m` just after the imports section:

```
// Define ball width
const float BALL_WIDTH = 7.0f;
// Define number of pockets
const int NUM_POCKETS = 6;
// Define pocket width
const float POCKET_WIDTH = 10.0f;
```

These are constants for the balls and pockets' widths and the number of pockets.

Now we can implement the loop to initialize the pockets by adding the following lines at the end of `initializePockets`:

```
for (int i = 0; i < 3; i++) {
        // Update current pocket position
        currentPocketPosition = initialPocketPosition;
        currentPocketPosition.y += i * (_screenSize.height / 2.0f
        - 2.0f * POCKET_WIDTH);
        for (int j = 0; j < 2; j++) {

                // Initialize pocket
                pocket = [[CCSprite alloc]
                initWithImageNamed:@"SnookerMunkAtlas/pocket.png"];
                // Set pocket position
                pocket.position = currentPocketPosition;
                // Initialize body as a circle
                pocketBody = [CCPhysicsBody
                bodyWithCircleOfRadius:BALL_WIDTH/2.0f
                andCenter:CGPointMake(pocket.contentSize.width/2.0f,
                pocket.contentSize.height/2.0f)];
                // Define pocket as a sensor
                pocketBody.sensor = TRUE;
                // Set collision type for the pocket
                pocketBody.collisionType = @"pocket";
                // Set type as static
                pocketBody.type = CCPhysicsBodyTypeStatic;
                // Link sprite with its physics body
                pocket.physicsBody = pocketBody;

                // Add pocket to the array
                [_pockets addObject:pocket];
                // Add pocket to the space
                [_space addChild:pocket];

                // Update current pocket position
                currentPocketPosition.x = _screenSize.width - 5.0f *
                pocket.contentSize.width / 2.0f;
        }
}
```

In this loop, we create six pockets, updating their position to be placed on the four squares of the table and in the middle of both sides. To achieve that, we modify the current position along the nested `for` instances.

The most important thing here is how we configure each pocket's physics body. We create a circle two times smaller than its width, as we will use it to detect collisions, or in other words, when a ball has been pocketed.

We define each pocket's body as a sensor, which means that it will register collisions but it won't interact physically with them. This way, the balls won't rebound when a ball passes through it and we will be able to make the necessary checks such as detecting faults or valid pocketed balls.

Then we set the pocket's collision type to manage collisions and set its body type to be static as we want them to stay still.

Finally, we link the pocket with its physics body and then we add the object to the array and the space.

If you run the game now, you will see the six pocket images in their correct places with a little blue dot in the center that represents its physics body:

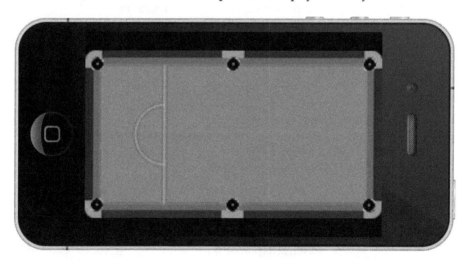

As you can observe, the pockets are a little bigger than the balls to make it easier to pocket them.

Now it's time for the edges, but first of all, add the following constants declarations in GameScene.m:

```
// Define edges width
const float EDGE_WIDTH = 3.0f;
// Define number of edges
const int NUM_EDGES = 6;
// Define distance between pocket and edge
const float DISTANCE_POCKET_EDGE = 15.0f;
```

These are constants for the edge width, the number of edges, and the distance between edges and pockets that we will use when placing them.

Then we declare an array to store the edges:

```
// Array of edges
NSMutableArray *_edges;
```

At the end of the `init` method, we add the call to the method in charge of initializing the edges:

```
// Initialize edges bodies
[self initializeEdges];
```

We implement this last method by adding the following lines of code:

```
- (void)initializeEdges {

    // Initialize the edges array
    _edges = [NSMutableArray arrayWithCapacity: NUM_EDGES];

    // Declare physics body
    CCPhysicsBody *edge;
    // Declare node to link body
    CCNode *edgeNode;

    // Initial edge position
    CGPoint initialEdgePosition = CGPointMake(5.0f * POCKET_WIDTH,
    2.0f * POCKET_WIDTH + DISTANCE_POCKET_EDGE);
    // Current edge position
    CGPoint currentEdgePosition;

    CGFloat edgeHeight = _screenSize.height/2.0f - (3.0f *
    POCKET_WIDTH + DISTANCE_POCKET_EDGE);
}
```

With these lines, we are declaring the array of edges with the constant we declared previously. We also initialize the `edge` variable, a physics body, and a node that will be linked to the `edge` body so it can be added to the space.

We also set the initial edge position and define the edge height; both variables will be very useful in the next step.

We add the following nested `for` loops at the end of the method:

```
for (int i = 0; i < 2; i++) {
        // Update current pocket position
        currentEdgePosition = initialEdgePosition;
        currentEdgePosition.y += i * (edgeHeight + 2.0f *
        POCKET_WIDTH);
        for (int j = 0; j < 2; j++) {
            // Initialize edge
            edge = [CCPhysicsBody
            bodyWithRect:CGRectMake(currentEdgePosition.x,
            currentEdgePosition.y, EDGE_WIDTH, edgeHeight)
            cornerRadius:0.0f];

            // Set collision type for the edge
            edge.collisionType = @"edge";
            // Set type as static
            edge.type = CCPhysicsBodyTypeStatic;
            // Configure physics properties
            edge.elasticity = 0.5f;
            edge.friction = 0.5f;

            // Initialize the rect node
            edgeNode = [CCNode node];
            // Link physic body to the node
            edgeNode.physicsBody = edge;

            // Add edge to the array
            [_edges addObject:edgeNode];
            // Add edge to the space
            [_space addChild:edgeNode];

            // Update current pocket position
            currentEdgePosition.x = _screenSize.width - 5.0f *
            POCKET_WIDTH;
        }
}
```

With this block of code, we are creating the four edges on the left and right sides of the table. We won't pay attention to the positions, but let's take a look at the lines concerning the physical body.

We create a rectangle for each of the four edges and set their collision types. We configure the rectangle as a static body in order to remain immobile when a ball hits them, and then we configure the rectangle's elasticity and friction in a way that the collisions and movements feel as realistic as possible.

The lower the value for the elasticity, the more inelastic the collision.

Once the physics body has been set up, we link it to the node, which we add to the array of edges and to the space.

We don't currently have top and bottom edges. To create them, add the following lines at the end of `initializeEdges`:

```
// Initialize bottom edge
edge = [CCPhysicsBody bodyWithRect:CGRectMake(5 * POCKET_WIDTH
+ DISTANCE_POCKET_EDGE, 2.0f * POCKET_WIDTH, _screenSize.width
- (10.0f * POCKET_WIDTH + 2.0f * DISTANCE_POCKET_EDGE),
EDGE_WIDTH) cornerRadius:0.0f];
// Set collision type for the edge
edge.collisionType = @"edge";
// Set type as static
edge.type = CCPhysicsBodyTypeStatic;
// Configure physics properties
edge.elasticity = 0.5f;
edge.friction = 0.5f;
// Initialize the rect node
edgeNode = [CCNode node];
// Link physic body to the node
edgeNode.physicsBody = edge;
// Add edge to the array
[_edges addObject:edgeNode];
// Add edge to the space
[_space addChild:edgeNode];

// Initialize top edge
edge = [CCPhysicsBody bodyWithRect:CGRectMake(5.0f *
POCKET_WIDTH + DISTANCE_POCKET_EDGE, _screenSize.height - 2.0f
* POCKET_WIDTH, _screenSize.width - (10.0f * POCKET_WIDTH +
2.0f * DISTANCE_POCKET_EDGE), EDGE_WIDTH) cornerRadius:0.0f];
// Set collision type for the edge
edge.collisionType = @"edge";
// Set type as static
edge.type = CCPhysicsBodyTypeStatic;
// Configure physics properties
edge.elasticity = 0.5f;
edge.friction = 0.5f;
```

```
// Initialize the rect node
edgeNode = [CCNode node];
// Link physics body to the node
edgeNode.physicsBody = edge;
// Add edge to the array
[_edges addObject:edgeNode];
// Add edge to the space
[_space addChild:edgeNode];
```

The creation of these edges is pretty similar to the previous four but we create them separately because they don't fit properly in the loop. If you pay attention, you will see the only difference is the position of the bodies.

Run the game now and you will see a kind of skeleton over the background:

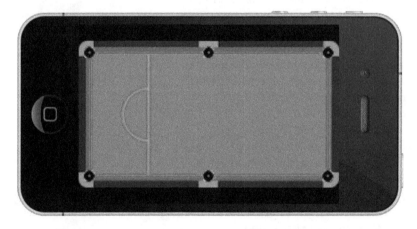

These edges and pockets will intervene as soon as the balls start colliding with them, so now that we have the table set, let's create the balls.

Configuring the snooker balls

We are going to create a class to initialize and control the behavior of the balls, so follow these steps:

1. Right-click on the **Classes** group in the project navigator and select **New File…**.
2. Click on **iOS | cocos2d v3.x | CCNode class**.
3. Make this class a subclass of CCSprite, call it Ball, and click on **Create**.

Note that we will create each ball as a subclass of CCSprite because we just need a sprite with some extended properties and there is no need to extend CCNode in this case.

Open Ball.h and replace its contents with the following lines:

```
#import <Foundation/Foundation.h>
#import "cocos2d.h"

typedef enum {
    white = 0,
    red,
    yellow,
    green,
    brown,
    blue,
    pink,
    black
} BallColors;
@interface Ball : CCSprite {

}
// Property for ball color
@property (readwrite, nonatomic) BallColors *ballColor;
// Property for number of points
@property (readonly, nonatomic) unsigned int points;

// Declare init method
- (Ball *) initBallWithColor:(BallColors)color;
@end
```

This class contains an enumerator to define the different colors the balls can be, and that's why we declare a property to keep the color. In addition, each ball has different values in points, so we declare a property that will store these values to make the corresponding calculations during the game.

This class has a custom initializer method that will receive a color input argument to create a new ball.

Open Ball.m and replace its contents with the following lines:

```
#import "Ball.h"

@implementation Ball

// Define ball width
const float BALL_WIDTH = 7.0f;
```

```objc
- (Ball *) initBallWithColor:(BallColors)color {
    self = [super init];
    if (!self) return(nil);

    NSString *fileName;
    NSString *collisionType;
    switch (color) {
        case white:
            // Assign image name, points, and color
            fileName = @"SnookerMunkAtlas/ballWhite.png";
            _points = 0;
            _ballColor = white;
            collisionType = @"white";
            break;
        case red:
            // Assign image name, points, and color
            fileName = @"SnookerMunkAtlas/ballRed.png";
            _points = 1;
            _ballColor = red;
            collisionType = @"red";
            break;
        case yellow:
            // Assign image name, points, and color
            fileName = @"SnookerMunkAtlas/ballYellow.png";
            _points = 2;
            _ballColor = yellow;
            collisionType = @"yellow";
            break;
        case green:
            // Assign image name, points, and color
            fileName = @"SnookerMunkAtlas/ballGreen.png";
            _points = 3;
            _ballColor = green;
            collisionType = @"green";
            break;
        default:
            break;
    }
    return self;
}
@end
```

This file contains the initializer method that calls the parent `init` method and initializes the points and color properties.

We also declare a `fileName` variable and collision type to initialize the balls, as well as the properties, in a `switch` instruction. Each collision type will be different because we want to perform different checks in the case of a red, white, or other color ball being pocketed.

There are some colors that are not present in this `switch` sentence, so add the following block of code before `default` to complete them:

```
case brown:
    // Assign image name, points, and color
    fileName = @"SnookerMunkAtlas/ballBrown.png";
    _points = 4;
    _ballColor = brown;
    collisionType = @"brown";
    break;
case blue:
    // Assign image name, points, and color
    fileName = @"SnookerMunkAtlas/ballBlue.png";
    _points = 5;
    _ballColor = blue;
    collisionType = @"blue";
    break;
case pink:
    // Assign image name, points, and color
    fileName = @"SnookerMunkAtlas/ballPink.png";
    _points = 6;
    _ballColor = pink;
    collisionType = @"pink";
    break;
case black:
    // Assign image name, points and color
    fileName = @"SnookerMunkAtlas/ballBlack.png";
    _points = 7;
    _ballColor = black;
    collisionType = @"black";
    break;
```

There is nothing to comment in this block as it's similar to the previous one. We just need to complete the method by adding the following lines before `return self;`:

```
// Initialize sprite with the file name
self = (Ball *)[[CCSprite alloc] initWithImageNamed:fileName];

// Initialize the ball's physics body
CCPhysicsBody *ballBody = [CCPhysicsBody
bodyWithCircleOfRadius:BALL_WIDTH
andCenter:CGPointMake(self.contentSize.width/2.0f,
self.contentSize.height/2.0f)];
// Set collision type
ballBody.collisionType = collisionType;
// Configure physics properties
ballBody.friction = 0.8f;
ballBody.density = 0.8f;
ballBody.elasticity = 0.5f;
// Set to sleep
ballBody.sleeping = TRUE;
// Link sprite with body
self.physicsBody = ballBody;
```

As we are creating a class derived from `CCSprite`, the first thing is to create the sprite from the image we have initialized in `switch`.

Then we create a circle as a physics body and set its collision type. We configure the body's properties by setting its friction, density, and elasticity to simulate realistic behavior of the balls.

We set each ball to be sleeping to consume the minimum processor capacity while no body collides with it. This is important due to the number of objects that will coexist at the same time.

Now that the `Ball` class exists, add the following import to `GameScene.h`:

```
#import "Ball.h"
```

We declare the following variables in `GameScene.m`:

```
// Declare cue ball
Ball *_cueBall;

// Declare color balls
Ball *_yellowBall;
Ball *_greenBall;
Ball *_brownBall;
Ball *_blueBall;
```

```
Ball *_pinkBall;
Ball *_blackBall;

// Declare array for red balls
NSMutableArray *_redBalls;

// Declare properties for default balls position
CGPoint _positionWhite;
CGPoint _positionRed;
CGPoint _positionYellow;
CGPoint _positionGreen;
CGPoint _positionBrown;
CGPoint _positionBlue;
CGPoint _positionPink;
CGPoint _positionBlack;
```

We declare a `Ball` variable for each different color except the red one, and as there will be 15 red balls, we declare an array that will store all of them. We also declare a position variable for each color to know their default place in the table when some of them have been pocketed.

We are going to initialize the balls using three different methods (cue ball, red balls, and color balls), so add the following lines at the end of the `init` method just after `[self initializeEdges];`:

```
// Initialize balls
[self initializeCueBall];
[self initializeRedBalls];
[self initializeColorBalls];
```

Let's start implementing the first of these methods, so add the following block of code:

```
- (void)initializeCueBall {

    // Initialize cue ball
    _cueBall = [[Ball alloc] initBallWithColor:white];
    _positionWhite = CGPointMake(_screenSize.width / 2.0f,
    _screenSize.height / 5.0f);
    _cueBall.position = _positionWhite;
    // Add ball to space
    [_space addChild:_cueBall];
}
```

This method just initializes the cue ball (white ball) by calling the `initBallWithColor` method and setting its initial position.

For the red balls initializer method, first add this constant declaration:

```
// Define number of red balls
const int NUM_RED_BALLS = 15;

// Define number of red balls rows
const int NUM_RED_ROWS = 5;
```

Implement the method with the following lines:

```
- (void)initializeRedBalls {

    // Initialize array of red balls
    _redBalls = [NSMutableArray arrayWithCapacity: NUM_RED_BALLS];

    // Set initial position for the red ball
    _positionRed = CGPointMake(_screenSize.width/2.0f, 3.0f *
    _screenSize.height/4.0f);

    CGPoint redBallCurrentPosition;
    Ball *redBall;

    for (int i = 0; i < NUM_RED_ROWS; i++) {
        // Update positions
        redBallCurrentPosition = _positionRed;
        redBallCurrentPosition.x -= i * BALL_WIDTH/2.0f;
        redBallCurrentPosition.y += i * BALL_WIDTH;

        for (int j = 0; j < i + 1; j++) {
            // Initialize red ball
            redBall = [[Ball alloc] initBallWithColor:red];
            // Set position
            redBall.position =
            CGPointMake(redBallCurrentPosition.x,
            redBallCurrentPosition.y);
            // Add ball to space and array
            [_space addChild:redBall];
            [_redBalls addObject:redBall];

            // Update position
            redBallCurrentPosition.x += BALL_WIDTH;

        }
    }
}
```

This method has no mystery; we create 15 red balls, placing them in an inverse triangle shape. Note how we don't need to specify its body's properties as this task is performed in the initializer method of the `Ball` class.

Finally, implement the last balls initializer with these lines:

```
-  (void)initializeColorBalls {

    // Initialize yellow ball
    _yellowBall = [[Ball alloc] initBallWithColor:yellow];
    _positionYellow = CGPointMake(2.0f * _screenSize.width / 3.0f
    - BALL_WIDTH, _screenSize.height / 4.0f + 3.0f * BALL_WIDTH /
    2.0f);
    _yellowBall.position = _positionYellow;
    [_space addChild:_yellowBall];

    // Initialize green ball
    _greenBall = [[Ball alloc] initBallWithColor:green];
    _positionGreen = CGPointMake(_screenSize.width / 3.0f +
    BALL_WIDTH, _screenSize.height / 4.0f + 3.0f * BALL_WIDTH /
    2.0f);
    _greenBall.position = _positionGreen;
    [_space addChild:_greenBall];

    // Initialize brown ball
    _brownBall = [[Ball alloc] initBallWithColor:brown];
    _positionBrown = CGPointMake(_screenSize.width / 2.0f,
    _screenSize.height / 4.0f + 3.0f * BALL_WIDTH / 2.0f);
    _brownBall.position = _positionBrown;
    [_space addChild:_brownBall];

    // Initialize blue ball
    _blueBall = [[Ball alloc] initBallWithColor:blue];
    _positionBlue = CGPointMake(_screenSize.width / 2.0f,
    _screenSize.height / 2.0f);
    _blueBall.position = _positionBlue;
    [_space addChild:_blueBall];

    // Initialize pink ball
    _pinkBall = [[Ball alloc] initBallWithColor:pink];
    _positionPink = CGPointMake(_screenSize.width/2.0f,
    _positionRed.y - BALL_WIDTH);
    _pinkBall.position = _positionPink;
    [_space addChild:_pinkBall];
```

```
                // Initialize black ball
                _blackBall = [[Ball alloc] initBallWithColor:black];
                _positionBlack = CGPointMake(_screenSize.width / 2.0f, 9.0f *
                screenSize.height / 10.0f - BALL_WIDTH);
                _blackBall.position = _positionBlack;
                [_space addChild:_blackBall];
        }
```

This just creates a new ball for each color, sets their default position, and adds them to the space. Come on, run the game and look at the beautiful colored balls!

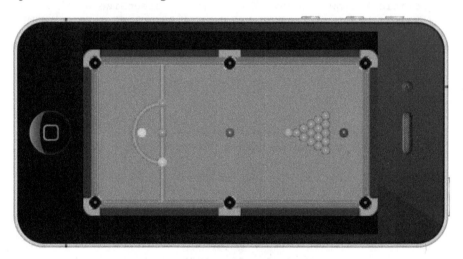

Hitting the cue ball

It's time to hit the white ball, but we are not going to use a cue, we will use just the touch events. In this section, we need to enable touch management, so add the following line to the init method:

```
                // Enable touches management
                self.userInteractionEnabled = TRUE;
                // Initialize flag
                _cueBallTouched = FALSE;
```

Then declare the new BOOL variable:

```
                // Declare flag
                BOOL _cueBallTouched;
```

We will use this variable to control whether the cue ball has been touched or not because this information is necessary in order to hit it. Let's implement the protocol methods starting with `touchBegan`:

```
- (void) touchBegan: (UITouch *) touch withEvent: (UIEvent *) event
{
    // Check if the touch is placed inside the cue ball
    [_cueBall.physicsNode pointQueryAt:touch.locationInWorld
    within:0.1f block:^(CCPhysicsShape *shape, CGPoint point,
    CGFloat distance)
        {
            CCLOG(@"CUE BALL TOUCHED");
            _cueBallTouched = TRUE;
        }];
}
```

In this method, we take the touch point and see whether it's placed inside the shape defined by the cue ball. Note how we take advantage of the `pointQueryAt` method for this purpose. The `within` argument is the radius used to check whether we are touching the cue ball. If so, the block defined is executed; in this case, we just show a log message and update the flag variable.

Now let's implement the `touchMoved` method, but before that, declare the following variable:

```
// Declare vector force
CCDrawNode *_forceVector;
```

Add the following lines:

```
- (void) touchMoved: (UITouch *) touch withEvent: (UIEvent *) event{
    // Get the touch location
    CGPoint newTouchLocation = [touch locationInNode:self];
    if (_cueBallTouched) {
        // Remove existing vector
        if(_forceVector.parent) {
            [_forceVector removeFromParent];
        }
        // Create node
        _forceVector = [CCDrawNode node];
        // Draw a vector from touch position to cue ball
        [_forceVector drawSegmentFrom:_cueBall.position
        to:newTouchLocation radius:2.0f color:[CCColor
        whiteColor]];
        [_space addChild:_forceVector];
    }
}
```

This code will be executed only if the flag indicates that the cue ball has been touched. If so, we get the touch point located in the scene and remove the vector if it has been previously added to the scene.

The next lines create a 2 pixels radius line between the touch position and the ball, and we add the line to the space. This line will represent the force that will be applied to the cue ball when the touch ends.

If you run the game, you will see the white line representing the force vector, but it won't do anything until we implement the following method:

```
- (void)touchEnded:(UITouch *)touch withEvent:(UIEvent *)event {
    CGPoint touchLocation = [touch locationInNode:self];

    // Calculate the vector
    CGPoint vector = CGPointMake(_cueBall.position.x -
    touchLocation.x, _cueBall.position.y - touchLocation.y);
    // Apply physic impulse to the cue ball
    [_cueBall.physicsBody applyImpulse:ccp(vector.x, vector.y)];
    // Remove existing vector
    if (_forceVector.parent) {
        [_forceVector removeFromParent];
    }
}
```

We calculate the vector between the cue ball and the touch position and use it to apply an impulse to the ball. The `applyImpulse` method does just this: it applies an impulse to the body of the ball with a force defined by the vector specified. Finally, we remove the line to clean the view. Run the game now and hit some balls with the cue ball!

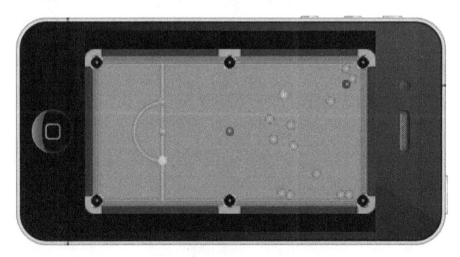

But there is a problem here: the balls can pass over the pockets with no interaction, so it's time to manage the collisions between the objects. Before proceeding, if you want, you can set the debug draw to NO.

Managing collisions between snooker bodies

Now that we know how to apply a force to the cue ball, collisions start to happen between the balls and the pockets, edges, and other balls.

We will take advantage of the collision types we defined to control some of the rules of the game (we are not covering all them because of the complexity of the game, and it's not the purpose of this chapter).

Remember that we declared GameScene as the collision protocol's implementer, so the next step is to set our scene as the delegate by adding the following line at the end of the init method:

```
// Set collision delegate of space
_space.collisionDelegate = self;
```

Now let's implement the collision between the pockets and the cue ball with the following lines:

```
- (BOOL) ccPhysicsCollisionBegin:(CCPhysicsCollisionPair *)pair
white:(CCNode *)ballWhite pocket:(CCNode *)pocket{
    // Set velocities to 0
    _cueBall.physicsBody.velocity = CGPointZero;
    _cueBall.physicsBody.angularVelocity = 0.0f;
    // Set body to sleep
    _cueBall.physicsBody.sleeping = TRUE;
    // Set the original position
    _cueBall.position = _positionWhite;

    //Change turn
    if(_turn == player1Turn) {
        _turn = player2Turn;
    } else {
        _turn = player1Turn;
    }
    // State fault
    _gameState = fault;

    return TRUE;
}
```

If you remember, we defined the pockets as sensors so they will trigger their corresponding method but won't generate any physical response. Note how we set the types as white and pocket so the method would just be called when the cue ball hits the pocket sensor (the blue circle we created).

When this collision takes place, we stop the white ball by setting its velocity property to zero and we set it to sleep so it consumes the minimum CPU possible. We also position the cue ball in its original place.

If the cue ball is pocketed, this means that a fault has happened and the turn changes to the next player, so we update the turn and the game state.

To control these states, we need to define some enumerations, so add the following lines to GameScene.h:

```
typedef enum {
    notStarted = 0,
    cueBall,
    redBallInPocket,
    fault
} GameState;

typedef enum {
    player1Turn = 0,
    player2Turn
} PlayerTurn;
```

We define a state for the game when it hasn't yet started: one to control when the cue ball has to be hit, another to know when a red ball has been pocked, and the last one to control whether a foul happened. We also declare two turn types so we can know which player has to play.

Back in GameScene.m, add the following constant definition:

```
// Define red ball value
const int RED_BALL_POINTS = 1;
```

Declare the following variables:

```
// Declare game state
GameState *_gameState;

// Declare player turn
PlayerTurn *_turn;
```

```
// Declare points counter
int _player1Points;
int _player2Points;
```

We declare a variable to keep the state of the game and the player turn, and also we declare two counters for each of the player points. Initialize them by adding the following lines at the end of the `init` method:

```
// Initialize game state
_gameState = notStarted;

// Set initial turn
_turn = player1Turn;

// Initialize counters
_player1Points = 0;
_player2Points = 0;
```

There's no need to mention anything here as we are just initializing the variables.

Finally, let's implement the collision method between the pocket and the red balls, so add the following block of code:

```
- (BOOL) ccPhysicsCollisionBegin:(CCPhysicsCollisionPair *)pair
red:(CCNode *)ballRed pocket:(CCNode *)pocket{
    // If there hasn't been a fault
    if ((int)_gameState != fault) {
        // Add points to the corresponding player
        if(_turn == player1Turn) {
            _player1Points += RED_BALL_POINTS;
        } else {
            _player2Points += RED_BALL_POINTS;
        }
        // Update the game state
        _gameState = redBallInPocket;

        // Remove the red ball from the array and the space
        [_redBalls removeObject:ballRed];
        [_space removeChild:ballRed];
    }

    return TRUE;
}
```

This method will check whether the game is in a non-fault state, so everything happening is allowed. In this case, we just increment the corresponding player point's counter and update the state to know that a red ball has been pocketed (in snooker, the system to gain points is pocketing a red ball (1 point) before another color ball).

Then, we remove the red ball from the array of balls and from the space.

Before running the game, we should add a pair of labels to show the scores of each player, so add the following lines into the declarations section:

```
// Label to show the player1 score
CCLabelTTF *_scoreLabelP1;

// Label to show the player2 score
CCLabelTTF *_scoreLabelP2;
```

Then, initialize them with the following lines in `init`:

```
// Initialize score label
_scoreLabelP1 = [CCLabelTTF labelWithString:[NSString
stringWithFormat:@"P1: %i", _player1Points] fontName:@"Arial"
fontSize:15];
_scoreLabelP1.color = [CCColor whiteColor];
_scoreLabelP1.position = CGPointMake(_screenSize.width / 4.0f,
_screenSize.height);

// Left-aligning the label
_scoreLabelP1.anchorPoint = CGPointMake(0.0f, 1.0f);

// Initialize score label
_scoreLabelP2 = [CCLabelTTF labelWithString:[NSString
stringWithFormat:@"P2: %i", _player2Points] fontName:@"Arial"
fontSize:15.0f];
_scoreLabelP2.color = [CCColor whiteColor];
_scoreLabelP2.position = CGPointMake(3.0f * _screenSize.width
/ 4.0f, _screenSize.height);

// Right-aligning the label
_scoreLabelP2.anchorPoint = CGPointMake(1.0f, 1.0f);

// Add the score labels to the scene
[self addChild:_scoreLabelP1];
[self addChild:_scoreLabelP2];
```

These lines just create two labels with the initial point counters values for both players and set with left and right anchor points to be centered while their width changes.

Then we need to implement a method to update these labels with the current points value, so add the following lines:

```
-(void) updateScores{
    // Update scores
    [_scoreLabelP1 setString:[NSString stringWithFormat:@"P1: %i",
    _player1Points]];
    [_scoreLabelP2 setString:[NSString stringWithFormat:@"P2: %i",
    _player2Points]];
}
```

This method will be called from the red ball's `ccPhysicsCollisionBegin` method, so add the following call at the end of this method, before the `return TRUE;` line:

```
// Update scores
[self updateScores];
```

Come on, run the game and gain some points!

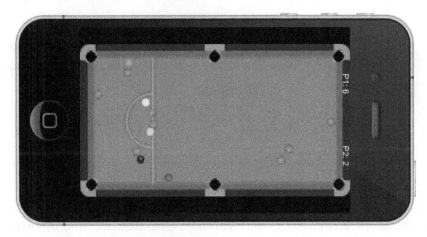

Let's make a couple of changes to some methods. To get started, add the following block of code to `touchMoved`, just before the `if` condition:

```
if (_gameState == notStarted || _gameState == fault) {
    if (CGRectContainsPoint(_cueBall.boundingBox,
    newTouchLocation)) {
        _cueBall.position = newTouchLocation;
    }
} else
```

This will allow us to move the white ball at the beginning of the match or after a fault.

Add the following lines to `touchEnded` before initializing the vector point:

```
if (_gameState == notStarted || _gameState == fault) {
    // Get the difference between the touched location and the
    pad center
    CGPoint point = CGPointMake(touchLocation.x -
    _positionBrown.x, touchLocation.y - _positionBrown.y);
    // Convert point to radians
    CGFloat radians = ccpToAngle(point);
    // Calculate degrees
    CGFloat degrees = CC_RADIANS_TO_DEGREES(radians);
    // Calculate direction
    if (degrees <= 0 && degrees >= -180.0f &&
    ccpDistance(touchLocation, _positionBrown) < D_RADIUS) {
        _cueBall.position = touchLocation;
        _gameState = cueBall;
    } else {
        _cueBall.position = _positionWhite;
    }
} else if (_cueBallTouched) {
```

Add the } character at the end of the method. This code calculates where we are placing the white ball, so its position belongs to the field delimited by a D shape.

Finally, add the `D_RADIUS` constant declaration:

```
// Define D area radius
const float D_RADIUS = 50.0f;
```

Execute the game and try to move the cue ball to the desired start position before the game starts.

That's it; now the game looks more realistic, but we are going to leave the game as is because you have learned how to deal with physics in Cocos2d, and there is no need to learn the rules of snooker as it's a pretty complex game.

Summary

In this chapter, you learned the uniqueness of physical behaviors in video games and how to make the best use of the physics engine included in Cocos2d, that is, Chipmunk.

We configured the Chipmunk space thanks to the `CCPhysicsNode` class and its properties such as gravity. Then we added some bodies and convex shapes and saw the attributes we can modify on the `CCPhysicsBody` and `CCPhysicsShape` classes to get the desired result.

You also learned that we can provide physics behavior to objects beyond bodies and shapes by creating a sprite and linking a physics body to it. Then you learned to create concave shapes and configure their physics properties thanks to physics editors such as PhysicsEditor and how to load this shape in our Xcode project.

To define the interaction between objects in the same space, you saw how to detect and manage collisions with the different approaches Chipmunk offers. Thanks to the knowledge acquired in the chapter, we implemented a kind of snooker game in which we applied other methods to move bodies in a space where there is no gravity.

In the next chapter, you are going to learn how to keep the game state and how to load it thanks to the use of external files so we can create different levels. Thanks to this, we will be able to define the scenes that will be part of a game.

7
Jump and Run

The first video games were full of platforms and this genre continued to be one of the most popular until the emergence of smartphones. They were so popular that I'm sure all of you can enumerate a list of at least 10 popular platform games that will include some of the following: *Sonic* (yes, I was a Sega fanboy), *Super Mario Bros*, *Mega Man*, *LittleBigPlanet*, *Ghosts 'n Goblins*, *Prince of Persia*, *Tomb Raider*, *Crash Bandicoot*, *Caveman Ninja*, or *Rayman*.

With the current generation of cell phones, this genre has evolved to adapt itself to new interfaces by removing the classic directional pad and reacting to the different ways of touching the screen.

In this chapter, we are going to learn how to develop a platform game for iOS devices in which we will use custom physics and code specific collision logic. As we want the game to be unpredictable, we will develop a solution to design a varied scene by creating platforms randomly so the player can't memorize their appearance.

Similar to the platforms, we will texture the terrain using different sprites and create cliffs that will kill our main character, and we will also add a menu to our game so we can choose some basic configurations.

List of topics covered in this chapter:

- How to code custom physics and specific collision logic
- How to create a varied scene
- How to texture the terrain with multiple sprites
- How to add a menu to the game

Initializing the game

In the code files of this chapter, you will find `JumpAndRun_init.zip`, which includes an initial project that we will use as the basis for the rest of the chapter.

We are not going to see the classes in depth, but let's take a look at the most important things so you understand the rest of the development process.

The game that we are going to develop is a platform game starring our old Yeti friend, who after escaping from the killer snowballs must climb some snow platforms to avoid falling into the abyss. That's why there are three different classes besides `GameScene`: `Yeti`, `Floor`, and `Platform`.

If you open `Yeti.h`, you will see that it derives from `CCNode` and that we have defined the following enumeration:

```
typedef enum {
    yetiStill = 0,
    yetiRunning,
    yetiJumping,
    yetiFalling
} YetiStates;
```

We will use this to keep control of the different states the Yeti could adopt. As you can see, our character will have run and jump actions and will be still or falling into the abyss (whether he falls or not depends on you).

In this file, we also declare properties for the state, a sprite that will be the visual representation of the Yeti, and three different actions that will be run depending on the state. In addition, in `Yeti.h`, we declare the initializer method and a custom method to set the position to the node and the sprite.

In `Yeti.m`, you will see the definition of three constants, `NUM_RUN_FRAMES`, `NUM_JUMP_FRAMES`, and `NUM_STILL_FRAMES`, that we will use to create the animations.

In the following couple of lines, you will see the implementation of the `initYeti` method where we initialize the state of the Yeti to be still, as well as the sprite, the anchor point, and its content size so we can check collisions and set positions easily.

Inside this method, we also implement the three actions that will cover the movements of our friend: be still, jump, and run. These implementations are pretty similar to the previous action definitions we have already covered in this book so we don't need to look at this in depth; here is a piece of code which we use:

```
// Initialize an array of frames
NSMutableArray *yetiJumpFrames = [NSMutableArray
arrayWithCapacity: NUM_JUMP_FRAMES];
```

```
for (int i = 0; i < NUM_JUMP_FRAMES; i++) {
    // Create a sprite frame
    CCSpriteFrame *yetiJumpFrame = [[CCSpriteFrameCache
    sharedSpriteFrameCache]
    spriteFrameByName:@"JumpAndRunAtlas/yeti_jump.png"];

    // Add sprite frame to the array
    [yetiJumpFrames addObject:yetiJumpFrame];
}

// Create an animation with the array of frames
CCAnimation *yetiJumpAnimation = [CCAnimation
animationWithSpriteFrames:yetiJumpFrames delay:0.1f];

// Create an animate action with the animation
_actionJump = [CCActionAnimate
actionWithAnimation:yetiJumpAnimation];
```

We initialize an array that will store the frames of the action and we initialize them with the different images that confirm the movement, in this case, just one. Then we create an animation with these frames that we use to initialize the jump action.

At the bottom of the file, we implement the setPosition method so we update both the node's and the sprite's position at the same time:

```
- (void) setPosition:(CGPoint)position {
    _yetiSprite.position = position;
    [super setPosition:position];
}
```

Now open Floor.h where you will see the following enumeration definition:

```
typedef enum {
    MediumTerrain = 0,
    LargeTerrain,
    SmallAbyss,
    BigAbyss
} TerrainSize;
```

In this case, we are declaring two different floor sizes and two abyss sizes so the terrain of our game has different difficulties to overcome. Later in GameScene.m, we will understand the purpose of this enumeration.

You should have realized that this class also extends CCNode, as we want it to consist of more than just a sprite.

In this file, we also declare a property for the sprite and the floor size and two methods: the initializer and the custom position setter.

You will see that `Floor.m` is less complex than `Yeti.m`. The initializer creates the sprite with a different file depending on the size of the floor and assigns it to the `_floorSize` property. There, we also set the anchor point for both node and sprite and initialize the content size.

The custom position value setter doesn't need explanation as it is similar to the one in `Yeti.m`.

Finally, `Platform` is almost equivalent to `Floor` with the only particularity that it handles different sizes thanks to the following enumeration:

```
typedef enum {
    Platform_M_Up = 0,
    Platform_L_Up,
    Platform_XL_Up,
    Platform_M_Down,
    Platform_L_Down,
    Platform_XL_Down
} PlatformSize;
```

The game will have three different platforms differentiated by the size and they will have two heights. This means there will be six different platforms that we will join so they can set up a kind of staircase.

Now let's take a deeper look at `GameScene.m` (`GameScene.h` has nothing worth highlighting). In the declaration section, you will find the following variables:

```
// Declaring a private CCSprite instance variable
Yeti *_yeti;

// Declare initial floor
Floor *_floor;

// Declare initial platform
Platform *_platform;

// Declare global variable for screen size
CGSize _screenSize;

// Declare global batch node
CCSpriteBatchNode *_batchNode;

// Declare background scrolling node
CCParallaxNode *_backGroundScrollingNode;
```

We are declaring a variable for the Yeti so we can control its behavior, and we declare two more variables for the initial floor and platform. In addition, we declare common variables to keep the screen's size value and the batch node to improve our game's performance. As you will realize, we have a parallax node that we will use to scroll the background.

We also have the following variables:

```
// Array of floors
NSMutableArray *_arrayOfFloors;

// Array of platforms
NSMutableArray *_arrayOfPlatforms;

// Declare top platform's position
float _platformPositionUp;

// Declare bottom platform's position
float _platformPositionDown;

// Declare gravity acceleration
float _gravity;

// Declare background scroll loop
CCActionRepeatForever *_loop;
```

We declare two arrays to keep all the floors and platforms that will take part in the scene. We also have two `float` variables to store the positions for the top and bottom platforms that will be instantiated programmatically depending on the screen and Yeti sizes.

To simulate gravity, we will have a `float` variable whose value we can update dynamically to make the game easier or harder, and we declare an action to control the continuous scrolling of the background.

In the `init` method, we don't need to pay attention to the usual initializations, but let's look at the following method call:

```
// Configure initial scene
[self configureInitialScene];
```

This method call's implementation is the following:

```
-(void) configureInitialScene{
    // Initialize floors array with capacity
    _arrayOfFloors = [NSMutableArray
    arrayWithCapacity:NUM_FLOORS];

    // Initialize platform array with capacity
    _arrayOfPlatforms = [NSMutableArray
    arrayWithCapacity:NUM_PLATFORMS];

    // Init floor
    _floor = [[Floor alloc] initFloorWithSize:
    (TerrainSize)LargeTerrain];

    // Set floor's initial position
    [_floor setPosition:CGPointMake(0.0f, 0.0f)];

    // Add floor to the scene
    [_batchNode addChild:_floor.floorSprite];

    // Add floor to array
    [_arrayOfFloors addObject:_floor];
}
```

In this method, we initialize both arrays of floors and platforms, making use of the constants defined at the top of the file. In addition, we create an initial floor object with the L size and we set its position on the bottom-left corner of the screen. Once the floor has been created, we add it to both the scene and the array of floors.

The next step in the `init` method is to initialize the Yeti by calling the following method:

```
        // Add main character
        [self configureYeti];
```

Here, we perform these actions:

```
-(void) configureYeti{
    // Init yeti variable
    _yeti = [[Yeti alloc] initYeti];

    // Set yeti's initial position
    [_yeti setPosition:CGPointMake(_screenSize.width/8.0f,
    _screenSize.height/2.0f)];
```

```
    // Run initial action
    [_yeti.yetiSprite runAction:_yeti.actionStill];

    // Add yeti to the scene
    [_batchNode addChild:_yeti.yetiSprite z:1];
}
```

In this method, we initialize the Yeti and its actions by calling the initializer method. We place it on the left side of the screen and at half of the screen's height; this way we will realize the effect of the custom gravity from the beginning of the game.

Then we run the still action and add the character to the scene.

Once the Yeti and the floor have been initialized, we can initialize the platforms' positions and the gravity value:

```
    // Set platform's default position
    _platformPositionUp = _floor.floorSprite.contentSize.height +
    2.0f * _yeti.yetiSprite.contentSize.height;
    _platformPositionDown = _floor.floorSprite.contentSize.height
    + _yeti.yetiSprite.contentSize.height;
    // Set gravity acceleration
    _gravity = -20.0f;
```

We initialize the top and bottom platform positions taking into account the floor's content and the Yeti's content sizes so they don't collide while the Yeti is running on the floor or on some platform. We also set the gravity's value that will represent our custom physics.

Finally, in the `init` method, we initialize the background scrolling by calling the following method:

```
    // Configure background scrolling
    [self configureBackgroundScrolling];
```

This performs the following initializations:

```
- (void) configureBackgroundScrolling{

    // Create the layers that will take part in the background
    scrolling
    CCSprite *background1 = [CCSprite
    spriteWithImageNamed:@"JumpAndRunAtlas/background.png"];
    CCSprite *background2 = [CCSprite
    spriteWithImageNamed:@"JumpAndRunAtlas/background.png"];
    CCSprite *background3 = [CCSprite
    spriteWithImageNamed:@"JumpAndRunAtlas/background.png"];
```

```
// Define start positions
CGPoint backgroundOffset1 = CGPointZero;
CGPoint backgroundOffset2 =
CGPointMake(background1.contentSize.width - 1.0f, 0.0f);
CGPoint backgroundOffset3 =
CGPointMake(background1.contentSize.width +
background2.contentSize.width - 2.0f, 0.0f);

// Initialize background scrolling node
_backGroundScrollingNode = [CCParallaxNode node];
```

In this method, we are defining a parallax effect with just one layer (the background one) as we just want it to scroll horizontally to simulate that the Yeti is running.

To achieve this, we create a parallax node with the same background image repeated three times so they concatenate and represent the movement properly.

The last block of code of this method is the following one:

```
// Add parallax children defining z-order, ratio and offset
[_backGroundScrollingNode addChild:background1 z:0
parallaxRatio:CGPointMake(1.0f, 0.0f)
positionOffset:backgroundOffset1];
[_backGroundScrollingNode addChild:background2 z:0
parallaxRatio:CGPointMake(1.0f, 0.0f)
positionOffset:backgroundOffset2];
[_backGroundScrollingNode addChild:background3 z:0
parallaxRatio:CGPointMake(1.0f, 0.0f)
positionOffset:backgroundOffset3];

// Add the node to the scene
[_batchNode addChild:_backGroundScrollingNode z:-1];

// Create the move actions
CCActionMoveBy *move1 = [CCActionMoveBy
actionWithDuration:BACKGROUND_DURATION position:CGPointMake(-
(background1.contentSize.width +
background2.contentSize.width), 0)];
CCActionMoveBy *move2 = [CCActionMoveBy actionWithDuration:0
position:CGPointMake(background1.contentSize.width +
background2.contentSize.width, 0.0f)];

// Create a sequence with both movements
CCActionSequence *sequence = [CCActionSequence
actionWithArray:@[move1, move2]];

// Create an infinite loop for the movement action
_loop = [CCActionRepeatForever actionWithAction:sequence];
}
```

In this block, we define the scrolling properties such as ratio and position offset, and we create two movement actions that will move the backgrounds from right to left and then recover them to their initial position. This way, we have a loop action that we will be able to activate whenever we want.

Let's run the project so we can view how our game looks at this point:

Configuring a varied scene

Once the initial scene and the basic components have been initialized, we are going to create the rest of the blocks that will form our game. The purpose of this section is to learn how to configure a varied terrain based on a few restrictions, so the game is playable and not impossible to win.

We'll start by declaring the variables that will support this configuration, so add the following constants definition:

```
// Number of different platforms
const int kPLATFORM_TYPES = 6;

// Number of different floors
const int kFLOOR_TYPES = 4;
```

This will help us to create the floors and platforms randomly later. Next, add the following variable declarations:

```
// Declare small abyss' width
float _smallAbyss;

// Declare big abyss' width
float _bigAbyss;

// Declare next platform's position
float _nextPlatformPosition;

// Declare next floor's position
float _nextFloorPosition;
```

The small and big abyss variables will be constants that will be initialized programmatically to create the holes between floors depending on the screen width.

The last two variables will store the position of the next platform and the floor so we know at every moment where the next block will be placed.

Then add the following method call at the end of the `init` method, just before `return self;`:

```
// Configure whole scene
[self configureWholeScene];
```

Implement this method with these lines:

```
-(void) configureWholeScene{
    int floorType;
    int platformType;

    // Initialize abyss widths
    _smallAbyss = _screenSize.width / 5.0f;
    _bigAbyss = _screenSize.width / 3.0f;

    for (int i = 0; i < NUM_FLOORS; i++) {
        for (int j = 0; j < NUM_PLATFORMS; j++) {
            // Create uniformly random floor type
            floorType = arc4random_uniform(kFLOOR_TYPES);
            // Create uniformly random platform type
            platformType = arc4random_uniform(kPLATFORM_TYPES);
        }
    }
}
```

In this method, we declare two integer variables that will be used to store the types of both the floor and platform being created each time. Then we initialize the widths for the small and big abyss, which we will use to create the threats in the game.

Once we have initialized these variables, we set a loop with the number of iterations we want (in our case, the number of floors multiplied by the number of platforms) and on each iteration, we create a random number for the floor type and the platform type.

Note how the random values are chosen from the number of block types using `arc4random_uniform` so they are uniformly distributed.

Now that we have a random type for the floor, we can define the positions of the blocks and the type of the platform. Add the following lines at the end of the second `for` statement:

```
switch (floorType) {
    case SmallAbyss:
        _nextFloorPosition = _floor.floorSprite.position.x +
        _floor.floorSprite.contentSize.width + _smallAbyss;
        _nextPlatformPosition = _floor.floorSprite.position.x +
        _floor.floorSprite.contentSize.width;
        floorType = floorType - 2;
                break;
    case BigAbyss:
        _nextFloorPosition = _floor.floorSprite.position.x +
        _floor.floorSprite.contentSize.width + _bigAbyss;
        _nextPlatformPosition = _floor.floorSprite.position.x +
        _floor.floorSprite.contentSize.width;
        floorType = floorType - 2;
                break;

    default:
        _nextFloorPosition +=
        _floor.floorSprite.contentSize.width;
        _nextPlatformPosition +=
        _platform.platformSprite.contentSize.width +
        arc4random_uniform(_screenSize.width/5.0f);
                break;
}
```

If the floor type corresponds to a small abyss, we set the position for the next floor with a distance of _smallAbyss as the width. The platform will be placed on the edge of the abyss so the Yeti has the opportunity to avoid it. At the end of this case, we update the floor type value to be an M block.

If the floor type is a big abyss, we perform the same changes with the only difference being that we add the width of _bigAbyss and update the floor type to be an L block.

If the floor is of any other type, then the floor will be placed just after the previous one and the next platform will be placed in a random position over the floor.

Now add the following lines after the previous switch statement:

```
// Init platform
_platform = [[Platform alloc]
initPlatformWithSize:(PlatformSize)platformType];
    switch (platformType) {
        case Platform_M_Up:
        case Platform_L_Up:
        case Platform_XL_Up:
            [_platform
            setPosition:CGPointMake(_nextPlatformPosition,
            _platformPositionUp)];
                break;
        case Platform_M_Down:
        case Platform_L_Down:
        case Platform_XL_Down:
            [_platform
            setPosition:CGPointMake(_nextPlatformPosition,
            _platformPositionDown)];
                break;
        default:
                break;
    }
// Add platform to array and scene
[_batchNode addChild:_platform.platformSprite];
[_arrayOfPlatforms addObject: _platform];
```

This block of code initializes the platform with the type randomly selected and depending on this, we set its position in the top or bottom platform by using another switch statement.

Once the platform has been created, we add it to the scene and the array of platforms.

Finally, we add the last block of code after the preceding lines:

```
// Init floor
_floor = [[Floor alloc]
initFloorWithSize:(TerrainSize)floorType];
 [_floor setPosition:CGPointMake(_nextFloorPosition,
0.0f)];
```

```
// Add floor to the scene
[_batchNode addChild:_floor.floorSprite z:0];
// Add floor to array
[_arrayOfFloors addObject: _floor];
```

With these lines, we initialize the floor with the type we have manipulated and we place it at the position calculated, then we add it to the scene and the array of floors.

It's time to view what we have done so far:

At the moment, we can't enjoy our creation further than looking at a couple of floors and platforms, but don't worry, we are going to fix this soon.

Scrolling the background and blocks

To simulate that the Yeti is running for its life, we will scroll the background, the floors, and the platforms independently.

To do this, let's start by defining a constant that we will use to control the speed of the blocks:

```
// Value for the blocks speed
const float kBLOCKS_SPEED = 220.0f;
```

Now we call the method that will start everything by adding the following lines at the end of the `init` method just before `return self;`:

```
// Make the yeti run
[self makeYetiRun];
```

We implement it by adding the following block of code:

```
-(void) makeYetiRun{
    // Run action
    [_yeti.yetiSprite runAction:_yeti.actionRun];
    // Update state
    _yeti.yetiState = yetiRunning;

    // Move platforms
    [self movePlatforms];
    // Move floors
    [self moveFloors];

    // Run the scrolling action
    if ([_backGroundScrollingNode numberOfRunningActions] == 0) {
        [_backGroundScrollingNode runAction:_loop];
    }
}
```

In this method, we start the previously defined running action and we update the Yeti's state to reflect this situation.

Then we call two methods that will make the floors and platforms move. Finally, we start running the parallax effect if it hasn't been started previously.

Now let's implement the `movePlatforms` method; add the following lines:

```
-(void) movePlatforms{
    CCActionMoveTo *actionMovePlatform;
    float durationPlatform;
    for (Platform *platform in _arrayOfPlatforms) {
        if ([platform numberOfRunningActions] == 0) {
            // Set platform's last position
            CGPoint nextPosition = CGPointMake((-1) *
            platform.contentSize.width, platform.position.y);
            // Set movement's duration
            durationPlatform = ccpDistance(nextPosition,
            platform.position) / kBLOCKS_SPEED;
            // Define movement
```

```
            actionMovePlatform = [CCActionMoveTo
            actionWithDuration:durationPlatform
            position:nextPosition];
            // Run movement
            [platform.platformSprite
            runAction:actionMovePlatform];
        }
    }
}
```

For each platform in the array of platforms, we define its final position to be at the left side of the screen, out of view. We set the duration of this movement, taking into account the distance between the initial and final position and the speed of the blocks, so all of them move at the same speed.

With this data, we define the movement action and start running it.

Now we just need to implement the moveFloors method:

```
-(void) moveFloors{
    CCActionMoveTo *actionMoveFloor;
    float durationFloor;
    for (Floor *floor in _arrayOfFloors) {
        if ([floor numberOfRunningActions] == 0) {
            // Set floor's last position
            CGPoint nextPosition = CGPointMake((-1.0f) *
            floor.contentSize.width, floor.position.y);
            // Set movement's duration
            durationFloor = ccpDistance(nextPosition,
            floor.position) / kBLOCKS_SPEED;
            // Define movement
            actionMoveFloor = [CCActionMoveTo
            actionWithDuration:durationFloor
            position:nextPosition];
            // Run movement
            [floor.floorSprite runAction:actionMoveFloor];
        }
    }
}
```

This method is pretty similar to the platform's one so we won't take a deeper look. It just calculates the distance and the duration of the movement, and creates and runs a movement action for each floor in the floors array.

If you run the game now, you will be able to see how the Yeti and all the blocks created in the previous section move.

You should notice that the position of the Yeti creates a strange effect as it seems to be floating, so let's solve this problem by letting it appear to land on the floor blocks.

Coding custom physics

In this section, you will learn how to code the custom physics that will be involved in the game, such as gravity and collisions.

As we all know, gravity is a force that pushes the objects (in this case, the Yeti) down until they collide with the floor or another object stops their fall.

To represent this programmatically, we need to decrease our main character's height position until it collides with some floor block or falls into an abyss.

Remember that we have set the gravity force value to be -5.0, so let's make this force influence the Yeti's position. To do this, we need to implement the update method in the following way:

```
- (void)update:(NSTimeInterval)delta {
    // Make the yeti fall
    [_yeti setPosition:CGPointMake(_yeti.yetiSprite.position.x,
    _yeti.yetiSprite.position.y + _gravity)];
}
```

As you can see, this method is pretty simple as we are just adding the gravity's value to the Yeti's height. If you want to check how this will affect the game, run the project and look at the sprite falling infinitely.

To avoid this happening, we need a way to detect when the Yeti collides with the floor so it stops falling. Add the following lines at the end of the `update` method:

```
// Check collisions
[self checkBlockCollisionWithYeti];
```

Add the implementation of this new method:

```
- (void) checkBlockCollisionWithYeti {
    for (Floor *currentFloor in _arrayOfFloors) {
        if (_yeti.yetiSprite.position.x +
        _yeti.yetiSprite.contentSize.width >
        currentFloor.floorSprite.position.x &&
        _yeti.yetiSprite.position.x <
        currentFloor.floorSprite.position.x +
        currentFloor.floorSprite.contentSize.width &&
        _yeti.yetiSprite.position.y <=
        currentFloor.floorSprite.contentSize.height - _yetiOffset)
        {
            // If the yeti collides with some floor
            [_yeti
            setPosition:CGPointMake(_yeti.yetiSprite.position.x,
            currentFloor.floorSprite.contentSize.height -
            _yetiOffset)];
        }
    }
}
```

In this method, we iterate the array of floors (remember that currently it has just one element) and we check whether the Yeti's x position is inside the floor's width and the Yeti's y position is less than or equal to the floor's y position. If this is the case, then the Yeti's fall will be stopped by floor block.

Note how we set the new position, taking into account the floor height's and an offset that we use to keep the character inside the floor sprite and make it more attractive visually.

Declare this variable by adding the following lines:

```
// Declare yeti's offset
double _yetiOffset;
```

Initialize its value by adding the following lines at the end of the `configureYeti` method:

```
// Initialize offset's value
_yetiOffset = _yeti.yetiSprite.contentSize.height/5;
```

Run the project and you will see how our friend's life is no longer in danger:

Jumping over the platforms

Now that the Yeti is running along the scene, we need a way to avoid the dangerous and mortal abysses, something like the ability to jump.

For this purpose, we need to declare a new action, so add the following lines:

```
// Declare jump
CCActionJumpBy *_yetiJump;
```

Initialize it by adding the following lines at the end of the `configureInitialScene` method:

```
// Define yeti's jump
_yetiJump = [CCActionJumpBy actionWithDuration:0.75f
position:CGPointMake(0.0f, 0.0f) height: _screenSize.height -
_yeti.yetiSprite.contentSize.height jumps:1];
```

The action receives the duration we want the jump to take as an input parameter as well as the delta position, which represents the offset from the original position that will be applied to the action.

The jump will follow a negative parabolic path, so the height specified represents the top height the sprite will achieve. We set the screen height minus the Yeti height as we don't want the character to jump out of view.

Finally, we can specify the number of jumps that will be executed during the action; in our case, we just want one.

After these lines, let's enable user interaction so we can make the Yeti jump by pushing the screen:

```
// Enable touches management
self.userInteractionEnabled = TRUE;
```

We implement the `touchBegan` method:

```
- (void)touchBegan:(UITouch *)touch withEvent:(UIEvent *)event
{
    // Make the yeti jump
    [self jumpYeti];
}
```

When the screen is touched, we will just execute the following method:

```
- (void) jumpYeti{
    // Jump if the yeti is not already jumping
    if ([_yeti.yetiSprite numberOfRunningActions] > &&
    (int)_yeti.yetiState != yetiJumping) {
        _yeti.yetiState = yetiJumping;
        [_yeti.yetiSprite stopAllActions];
        [_yeti.yetiSprite runAction:_yeti.actionJump];
        [_yeti.yetiSprite runAction:_yetiJump];
    }
}
```

In this method, we avoid performing a new jump action while a jump is currently being executed.

If the preceding condition matches, then we update the Yeti's state and we stop all running actions on the Yeti sprite to prevent unexpected behavior. Finally, we run the Yeti's jump action and the previously defined `yetiJump` variable.

The last thing left to do is add the following block of code in
`checkBlockCollisionWithYeti` at the end of the `if` statement:

```
if ([_yeti.yetiSprite numberOfRunningActions] == 0 &&
(int)_yeti.yetiState == yetiJumping) {
            // Run action
            [_yeti.yetiSprite runAction:_yeti.actionRun];
            // Update state
            _yeti.yetiState = yetiRunning;
} else if ([_yeti.yetiSprite numberOfRunningActions] == 0 &&
(int)_yeti.yetiState == yetiStill) {
            [self makeYetiRun];
}
```

If the Yeti's state is jumping but there are no running actions, this means that the
Yeti's jump has finished so we can update the state of the Yeti to running and run
`actionRun` again.

If the state is still and there is no running action, then we make the Yeti run properly.
You can remove the call to `makeYetiRun` from the `init` method.

It's time to run the game again and check how our Yeti friend jumps along the scene:

At this time, we can avoid the floor obstacles that are not so wide, but we will need to jump over the platforms to avoid the big abysses. That's why we should improve the checkBlockCollisionWithYeti method to recognize platforms too.

In the same checkBlockCollisionWithYeti method, add the following lines at the end:

```
// Check collisions with platforms
for (Platform *currentPlatform in _arrayOfPlatforms) {
    if (_yeti.yetiSprite.position.x +
    _yeti.yetiSprite.contentSize.width >=
    currentPlatform.platformSprite.position.x
    && _yeti.yetiSprite.position.x <=
    currentPlatform.platformSprite.position.x +
    currentPlatform.platformSprite.contentSize.width
    && _yeti.yetiSprite.position.y <=
    currentPlatform.platformSprite.position.y +
    currentPlatform.platformSprite.contentSize.height) {
    }
}
```

In the preceding block of code, we are iterating the array of platforms and for each one, we check whether the Yeti is placed between the edges of the block. If this happens, we also need to check whether the Yeti is over the platform and if so, we can consider that the Yeti has jumped on a block.

Now add the following lines inside the if statement:

```
// Top-platform-bottom-yeti collision
[_yeti
setPosition:CGPointMake(_yeti.yetiSprite.position.x,
currentPlatform.platformSprite.position.y +
currentPlatform.platformSprite.contentSize.height -
_yetiOffset/2)];

if ([_yeti.yetiSprite numberOfRunningActions] == 0 &&
(int)_yeti.yetiState == yetiJumping) {
    // Run action
    [_yeti.yetiSprite runAction:_yeti.actionRun];
    // Update state
    _yeti.yetiState = yetiRunning;
}
```

Once we know the Yeti matches all the conditions, we set its position over the platform (with a little offset to make it more natural) and then we update the running actions as we did with the floor collision.

Let's go! Run the game and jump over the platforms; you will realize how these conditions work.

Adding a menu to the game

Usually, games show an initial menu where players can, for instance, access the configuration screen or choose to start the game, so in this section, we are going to develop an initial menu where the user will be able to select the difficulty level of the game.

We're going to create a separate scene class for this purpose, so follow these steps:

1. Right-click on the **Classes** group in the project navigator and select **New File...**.
2. Click on **iOS | cocos2d v3.x | CCNode class** and make this class a subclass of CCScene.
3. Call it MenuScene and click on **Create**.

In MenuScene.h, add the following imports:

```
#import "cocos2d-ui.h"
#import "GameScene.h"
```

The first import corresponds to the library that contains the buttons class, and the second one is needed as we will use it to initialize the game scene from the menu.

So, we now add the following constant definition:

```
#define kGameDifficulty @"Game_Difficulty"
```

We will take advantage of this constant to store the difficulty level selected by the user in the memory.

Finally, we replace the rest of the class with these lines:

```
@interface MenuScene : CCScene {

}

+ (MenuScene *)scene;
- (id)init;

@end
```

Here, we are just declaring the common class and instance methods to initialize the scene properly.

Then in MenuScene.m, we add the following lines after @implementation MenuScene:

```
{
    // Declare a layout for the menu
    CCLayoutBox *_menuLayout;

    // Declare global variable for screen size
    CGSize _screenSize;

    // Declare global batch node
    CCSpriteBatchNode *_batchNode;

}
```

We declare the global variables we will need for this scene. Note how we declared a layout box, which is a class that allows us to organize nodes in a vertical or horizontal way and specify a distance between them.

Implement the scene method as always:

```
+ (MenuScene *)scene
{
    return [[self alloc] init];
}
```

We initialize the scene, implementing the `init` method in the following way:

```
- (id)init
{
    // Apple recommends assigning self with supers return value
    self = [super init];
    if (!self) return(nil);

    // Initialize screen size variable
    _screenSize = [CCDirector sharedDirector].viewSize;

    // Load texture atlas
    [[CCSpriteFrameCache sharedSpriteFrameCache]
    addSpriteFramesWithFile: @"jumpandrun-hd.plist"];

    // Load batch node with texture atlas
    _batchNode = [CCSpriteBatchNode
    batchNodeWithFile:@"jumpandrun-hd.png"];

    // Add the batch node to the scene
    [self addChild:_batchNode];

    return self;
}
```

There is nothing to highlight in the preceding lines, as we just did the usual initializations. To complete the method, add the following lines at the end of the `init` method, just before `return self;`:

```
    // Initialize the background
    CCSprite *background = [CCSprite
    spriteWithImageNamed:@"JumpAndRunAtlas/menu_background.png"];
    // Set background position
    background.position = CGPointMake(0.0f, 0.0f);
    // Add background to the game scene
    [self addChild:background z:-1];

    // Create menu
    [self createMenuButtons];
```

The last initializations are a call to the `createMenuButtons` method, which we need to implement with the following lines:

```
-(void) createMenuButtons {
    // Create button
    CCButton *buttonEasyDifficulty = [CCButton
    buttonWithTitle:@"Easy" fontName:@"Chalkduster"
    fontSize:20.0f];
```

```
// Set button selector
[buttonEasyDifficulty setTarget:self
selector:@selector(easySelected:)];

// Create button
CCButton *buttonMediumDifficulty = [CCButton
buttonWithTitle:@"Medium" fontName:@"Chalkduster"
fontSize:20.0f];
// Set button selector
[buttonMediumDifficulty setTarget:self
selector:@selector(mediumSelected:)];

// Create button
CCButton *buttonHardDifficulty = [CCButton
buttonWithTitle:@"Hard" fontName:@"Chalkduster"
fontSize:20.0f];
// Set button selector
[buttonHardDifficulty setTarget:self
selector:@selector(hardSelected:)];
}
```

We are creating three buttons in a similar way as we did in the previous chapter, with the difference that we aren't specifying a frame, just a title, font, and size. As you can see, each of these buttons calls a different method that will specify a different difficulty for the game.

Finally, add the following lines at the end of `createMenuButtons`:

```
// Create menu
_menuLayout = [[CCLayoutBox alloc] init];
_menuLayout.direction = CCLayoutBoxDirectionVertical;
_menuLayout.spacing = 20.0f;

// Set menu position
_menuLayout.anchorPoint = CGPointMake(0.5f, 0.5f);
_menuLayout.position = CGPointMake(_screenSize.width/2.0f,
_screenSize.height/2.0f);

// Add buttons to the menu
[_menuLayout addChild:buttonHardDifficulty];
[_menuLayout addChild:buttonMediumDifficulty];
[_menuLayout addChild:buttonEasyDifficulty];

// Add menu to the scene
[_batchNode addChild:_menuLayout];
```

We are initializing the menu. Note how we set its direction to vertical so the menu buttons appear in a stacked way and we separate `20.0f` points with the other elements.

Then we place the menu in the center of the screen and add the buttons in the inverse order, as we want the last button added to be on the top of the stack. The last thing left to do in the method is add the menu layout to the scene, but we still have to implement each button's selectors.

Add these lines for the easy difficulty button:

```
- (void) easySelected: (id) sender {
    // Create transition
    CCTransition *transition = [CCTransition
    transitionCrossFadeWithDuration:0.15f];

    // Create new game scene
    GameScene *gameScene = [GameScene scene];

    // Store difficulty
    [[NSUserDefaults standardUserDefaults] setInteger:1
    forKey:kGameDifficulty];
    [[NSUserDefaults standardUserDefaults] synchronize];

    // Push scene with transition
    [[CCDirector sharedDirector] pushScene:gameScene
    withTransition:transition];
}
```

We will show a transition after one of the buttons has been selected, so we declare a cross-fade one. Then we initialize a `GameScene` instance and store a value of 1 in the user defaults. Finally, we push the scene with the previously created transition.

We add the following lines for the medium difficulty level:

```
- (void) mediumSelected: (id) sender {
    // Create transition
    CCTransition *transition = [CCTransition
    transitionCrossFadeWithDuration:0.15f];

    // Create new game scene
    GameScene *gameScene = [GameScene scene];

    // Store difficulty
    [[NSUserDefaults standardUserDefaults] setInteger:2
    forKey:kGameDifficulty];
```

```
    [[NSUserDefaults standardUserDefaults] synchronize];

    // Push scene with transition
    [[CCDirector sharedDirector] pushScene:gameScene
    withTransition:transition];
}
```

We add the following ones for the hard difficulty level:

```
-(void) hardSelected:(id)sender {
    // Create transition
    CCTransition *transition = [CCTransition
    transitionCrossFadeWithDuration:0.15f];

    // Create new game scene
    GameScene *gameScene = [GameScene scene];

    // Store difficulty
    [[NSUserDefaults standardUserDefaults] setInteger:3
    forKey:kGameDifficulty];
    [[NSUserDefaults standardUserDefaults] synchronize];

    // Push scene with transition
    [[CCDirector sharedDirector] pushScene:gameScene
    withTransition:transition];
}
```

Now that the menu scene has been configured, we just need to link it to the rest of the game, so let's start by importing the MenuScene class in AppDelegate.m:

```
#import "MenuScene.h"
```

Replace the contents of startScene with the following line:

```
return [MenuScene scene];
```

In GameScene.h, add the same import:

```
#import "MenuScene.h"
```

Then, going back to GameScene.m, declare the next variable:

```
    // Declare difficulty
    NSInteger _difficulty;
```

This variable will store the difficulty level in the user defaults and we will use this to increase the speed of the game. So initialize the _difficulty value by adding the following lines at the end of configureInitialScene:

```
// Initialize difficulty with user defaults
_difficulty = [[NSUserDefaults standardUserDefaults]
integerForKey:kGameDifficulty];
```

Finally, replace the instances of kBLOCKS_SPEED in movePlatforms and moveFloors with this:

```
(kBLOCKS_SPEED * _difficulty)
```

If you run the game now, you will see the following start menu:

2-star challenge – adding pinecones to the scene

Now that we know how to create a varied (not random) terrain, I propose you use the knowledge acquired in this chapter to add pinecones to the game so they appear in a varied way in the scene.

For this purpose, you will find the JumpAndRunAtlas/pinecone.png image in the atlas to load these objects.

The solution

To accomplish this challenge, we will need to make a few changes to `GameScene.m`. First of all, declare an array of pinecones so we can handle them easily:

```
// Declare array of pinecones
NSMutableArray *_arrayOfPinecones;
```

Initialize this array by adding the following lines at the end of `configureInitialScene`:

```
// Initialize pinecones' array with capacity
_arrayOfPinecones = [NSMutableArray
arrayWithCapacity:NUM_FLOORS * NUM_PLATFORMS];
```

We have initialized the array with the capacity of the maximum number of platforms that will be in the scene.

The next step is loading pinecones when a condition (that will be specified later) is met, so add the following lines at the end of the second `for` statement of `configureWholeScene`:

```
// Init pinecone's flag
int loadPinecone = arc4random_uniform(2);

// Declare pinecone sprite
CCSprite *pineconeSprite;

if (loadPinecone == 1) {
    // Create pinecone
    pineconeSprite = [[CCSprite alloc]
    initWithImageNamed:@"JumpAndRunAtlas/pinecone.png"];
    // Set pinecone position
    [pineconeSprite
    setPosition:CGPointMake(_nextPlatformPosition +
    _platform.platformSprite.contentSize.width / 2.0f,
    _platform.platformSprite.position.y +
    _platform.platformSprite.contentSize.height)];
    // Add pinecone to the scene and the array
    [_batchNode addChild:pineconeSprite];
    [_arrayOfPinecones addObject: pineconeSprite];
}
```

We have decided to load the pinecones when a random number between 0 and 1 has a value of 1, so first of all we initialize an integer variable with a random number.

If the condition is met, then we initialize the pinecone sprite with the previously mentioned image and place it at the center of the current platform.

Finally, we add this new sprite to the scene and the array of pinecones.

Once we have configured the position of these objects, we will move them in the same way we did with the floors and platforms. So add the following lines to `makeYetiRun`:

```
// Move pinecones
[self movePinecones];
```

Then implement this method with the following block of code:

```
- (void) movePinecones{
    CCActionMoveTo *actionMovePinecone;
    float durationPinecone;
    for (CCSprite *pinecone in _arrayOfPinecones) {
        if ([pinecone numberOfRunningActions] == 0) {
            // Set pinecone's last position
            CGPoint nextPosition = CGPointMake((-1.0f) *
            pinecone.contentSize.width, pinecone.position.y);
            // Set movement's duration
            durationPinecone = ccpDistance(nextPosition,
            pinecone.position) / (kBLOCKS_SPEED * _difficulty);
            // Define movement
            actionMovePinecone = [CCActionMoveTo
            actionWithDuration:durationPinecone
            position:nextPosition];
            // Run movement
            [pinecone runAction:actionMovePinecone];
        }
    }
}
```

This method is pretty similar to the floors and platforms methods, with the only difference that we are displacing the sprites that represent the pinecones.

Come on! Run the game and look at these tempting and exclusive items!

1-star challenge – adding a score label

The goal of platform games is usually overcoming challenges to rescue someone at the end of the game, or picking up coins or another kind of object to beat some record. This will be the purpose of our game: earning as many points as possible.

In this challenge, I want you to add a label in the top-right corner of the screen that will show the points our Yeti has earned so far.

The solution

To implement this challenge, we will basically perform the same changes that we made in *Chapter 1, Sprites, Sounds, and Collisions,* for the same purpose.

I created a Text (.fnt) bitmap font called font that you will find in the Resources folder. First of all, you need to add some font files to the project, so follow these steps:

1. In the navigator project, on the left, right-click on the **Resources** group and select **Add Files to "JumpAndRun"**....

2. Look up the font.fnt and font.png files in the Resources folder and select **Add**.

Then add the following declarations to `GameScene.m`:

```
// Score count
int _gameScore;

// Label to show the score
CCLabelBMFont *_scoreLabel;
```

We have declared an integer variable that will store the count of points earned and a label that will show this count.

Then in the `init` method, we initialize these variables by adding the following lines at the end:

```
// Initialize score count
_gameScore = 0;

// Initialize and place score label
_scoreLabel = [CCLabelBMFont labelWithString:[NSString
stringWithFormat:@"SCORE: %i", _gameScore]
fntFile:@"font.fnt"];
_scoreLabel.position = CGPointMake(_screenSize.width - 40.0f,
_screenSize.height - 40.0f);
_scoreLabel.anchorPoint = CGPointMake(1.0f, 0.5f);

// Add score label to scene
[self addChild:_scoreLabel];
```

We set the score counter to `0` and initialize the label with some text and our preferred font. Finally, we set the score label's position to be placed in the top-right corner and add it to the scene. Note how we modify its anchor point to allow the label to grow to the left as its width increases.

As we want to constantly check whether the Yeti has collided with a pinecone, we need to check the `update` method, so add the following lines after `[self checkBlockCollisionWithYeti];`:

```
// Check pinecone collision
[self checkPineconeCollected];
```

This will call the following method:

```
-(void) checkPineconeCollected {
    for (CCSprite *pinecone in _arrayOfPinecones) {
        if (CGRectIntersectsRect(pinecone.boundingBox,
        _yeti.yetiSprite.boundingBox)) {
            // Increase score
```

```
        [self increaseScore];
        // Make it disappear
        [pinecone setVisible:FALSE];
      }
    }
  }
```

This method iterates the array of pinecones and detects when the Yeti collides with one of them. If this happens, we will call a method that will increase the counter and make the object disappear from view.

To end the challenge, we implement the `increaseScore` method:

```
- (void) increaseScore{
    _gameScore += 10;
    [_scoreLabel setString:[NSString stringWithFormat:@"SCORE:
    %i", _gameScore]];
}
```

In this method, we increase the counter value and also update the score label. If you run the game now, you will see what we have just done:

Summary

In this chapter, we addressed platform games, one of the most popular genres of all time, and how to build one of these games on iOS devices.

We covered how to create a scene where the terrain is loaded depending on some rules we set previously. Thanks to the variety of blocks available, we were able to texture a kind of random ground that is playable at the same time.

Then you learned how to deal with horizontal scrolling so all the blocks travel at the same speed and everything in the scene works together to simulate that the Yeti is running.

As we wanted to control how nodes interact with each other, we developed our own collision system in order to detect when the Yeti was touching the floor or a platform block. This way, we can be more accurate when defining physics interactions.

This chapter also showed you how to create an initial menu in the game for the player to choose the difficulty level. You also learned how to continue this selection in the scene.

Keep reading if you want to learn how to develop a tower defense game and how to provide actors with artificial intelligence, among other topics.

8
Defend the Tower

War has existed almost since the dawn of humanity, and because of that most civilizations have raised castles and fortresses to defend themselves from their enemies.

Of course, we don't like wars but what about playing at war? Or simulating that we are being besieged? In this chapter, we are going to develop a game similar to *Plants versus Zombies* in which we defend our fortress, a tower, from the enemies' attacks and try to defeat them before our fort is destroyed.

Sprites have no intelligence, that's why throughout this chapter we are going to develop a way to make the non-playable characters (the enemies) recognize and follow a path to reach the fortress, and we will also control their attacks by developing a way to load waves of enemies.

As we need to protect ourselves from these attacks, we will learn how to set up the different places where we can build our defenses. We will also provide them with a specific artificial intelligence so they know when enemies are approaching or moving out of their sight.

The enemies, defenses, and the scene itself will need to be aware of the existence and situations of each other, so we will develop a way to keep this information distributed between the interested nodes.

The list of topics covered in this chapter is:

- How to develop a pathfinding algorithm
- How to load waves of enemies
- How to set up predefined defense positions
- How to provide defenses with AI
- How to share information between nodes

Initializing the game

In the code files of this chapter, you will find `DefenseTheTower_init.zip`, which includes an initial project that we will use as the basis for the rest of the chapter.

If you open the project in Xcode, you will find the following classes in the **Classes** group: `AppDelegate`, `Defense`, and `GameScene`.

The first one is similar to the delegates we used in our previous games, so we don't need to go into deeper detail.

Open `Defense.h` and you will see the definition of the `DefenseLevel` enumeration:

```
typedef enum {
    levelOne = 0,
    levelTwo,
    levelThree
} DefenseLevel;
```

It contains the three different levels a defense object can be.

This header class also declares a property for the defense level, the sprite that will give it a visual representation, and the damage it deals to enemies:

```
// Property for defense level
@property (readwrite, nonatomic) DefenseLevel *defenseLevel;
// Property for the sprite
@property (readwrite, nonatomic) CCSprite *defenseSprite;
// Property for the attack points
@property (readwrite, nonatomic) int attackPoints;
```

The file also declares an initializer method that receives a level and a position value:

```
// Declare init method
-(Defense *) initDefenseWithLevel:(DefenseLevel)level
andPosition:(CGPoint)position;
```

In `Defense.m`, we can see the implementation of this `init` method:

```
NSString *fileName;
    switch (level) {
        case levelOne:
            // Assign image
            fileName = @"DefenseTheTower/defense_level_1.png";
            // Set attack points
            _attackPoints = 1;
            break;
```

```
        case levelTwo:
            // Assign image
            fileName = @"DefenseTheTower/defense_level_2.png";
            // Set attack points
            _attackPoints = 2;
            break;
        default:
            break;
}
```

In this file, we set its filename, attack points, and energy cost depending on the `DefenseLevel` received as input. The rest of the method initializes the sprite, the content size, anchor point, and position of the new defense.

Finally, open `GameScene.m` (the header file has nothing to highlight) where you will see the following variable declarations:

```
// Declare global variable for screen size
CGSize _screenSize;

// Declare global batch node
CCSpriteBatchNode *_batchNode;
```

We declare the screen size variable so we can use its value for relative positions and sizes, and we also declare a batch node to improve the performance of our game.

The `init` method initializes the preceding variables:

```
// Initialize screen size variable
_screenSize = [CCDirector sharedDirector].viewSize;

// Load texture atlas
[[CCSpriteFrameCache sharedSpriteFrameCache]
addSpriteFramesWithFile: @"defensethetower-hd.plist"];

// Load batch node with texture atlas
_batchNode = [CCSpriteBatchNode
batchNodeWithFile:@"defensethetower-hd.png"];
// Add the batch node to the scene
[self addChild:_batchNode];
```

It creates the background sprite that will show a road in the middle of the countryside to our beloved fortress.

Run the initial project and you will see the following screen:

Developing a pathfinding algorithm

One way to provide nodes with intelligence is to predefine their behavior in response to external stimuli, or to give them a goal to reach.

In this case, we are going to make our enemies follow a path, which we will subdivide into steps. For this purpose, let's create a new class by following these steps:

1. Right-click on the **Classes** group in the project navigator and select **New File...**.

2. Click on **iOS | cocos2d v3.x | CCNode** class and make this class a subclass of CCNode.

3. Call it PathStep and click on **Create**.

Replace the contents of PathStep.h with the following lines:

```
#import <Foundation/Foundation.h>
#import "cocos2d.h"

@interface PathStep : CCNode {

}
```

```
// Property for the next step
@property (nonatomic, assign) PathStep *nextPathStep;
// Property for the sprite
@property (readwrite, nonatomic) CCSprite *pathStepSprite;

// Init method
- (PathStep *) initWithPosition:(CGPoint)position;

@end
```

We are extending the class from CCNode because we need it to have more potential than a mere sprite. This node will keep the information needed for the next step; this way the enemies will always know what their next move is. On the other hand, we define a sprite to visualize for debug tasks, as the purpose of the path is to be invisible. In this file, we also declare an initializer method to create each path's step.

Open PathStep.m and implement the initWithPosition method:

```
- (PathStep *) initWithPosition:(CGPoint)position {
    self = [super init];
    if (!self) return(nil);

    // Initialize sprite
    _pathStepSprite = [[CCSprite alloc]
    initWithImageNamed:@"DefenseTheTower/path_step.png"];

    // Set path step's anchor point
    self.anchorPoint = CGPointMake(0.5f, 0.5f);
    _pathStepSprite.anchorPoint = CGPointMake(0.5f, 0.5f);

    //Set path step position
    [self setPosition:position];

    return self;
}
```

This method initializes the sprite that is a blue circle and sets its anchor point to be located in the center of the node, so we can place it on the position provided as an input argument.

The position provided to the initWithPosition method will be defined in GameScene, but before it, add the following method to PathStep.m:

```
- (void) setPosition:(CGPoint)position {
    _pathStepSprite.position = position;
    [super setPosition:position];
}
```

The preceding method will set the correct position for the node and its sprite.

Now that we have a way to create a single step, let's create several steps to generate the desired path the enemies should follow. Add the following import and constant declarations in GameScene.m:

```
#import "PathStep.h"

// Number of path steps
const int kNUM_PATH_STEPS = 10;
// Define number of cells that fit in height
const int kNUM_CELLS = 6;
// Define increment in X
const float kINCREMENT_X = 2.0f;
```

This will allow us to create the needed path steps, as we are taking into account the initial and the final steps. We also set the number of cells that fit in the screen's height and the step increment in the *x* axis.

Declare the following variables at the top of GameScene.m:

```
// Declare array of path steps
NSMutableArray *_pathSteps;

// Declare variable to keep square size
float _squareSize;
```

The first one is an array to keep the steps on the screen so we can handle them at every moment. We also declare a float for the size of a cell on the screen so we can place all the nodes in a relative position.

Add the following lines at the end of the init method:

```
// Initialize square size
_squareSize = _screenSize.height / kNUM_CELLS;

// Load path steps
[self loadPathSteps];
```

We initialize the square size and call the following method:

```
- (void)loadPathSteps {
    // Initialize array of path steps
    _pathSteps = [[NSMutableArray alloc]
    initWithCapacity:kNUM_PATH_STEPS];
```

```
// Create path step
PathStep *pathStep9 = [[PathStep alloc]
initWithPosition:CGPointMake(_squareSize * kINCREMENT_X *
5.0f, _squareSize * 4.5f)];
[_pathSteps addObject:pathStep9];
[_batchNode addChild:pathStep9.pathStepSprite];

// Create path step
PathStep *pathStep8 = [[PathStep alloc]
initWithPosition:CGPointMake(_squareSize * kINCREMENT_X *
4.0f, _squareSize * 4.5f)];
[_pathSteps addObject:pathStep8];
[_batchNode addChild:pathStep8.pathStepSprite];
pathStep8.nextPathStep = pathStep9;

// Connect path steps with a line
CCDrawNode *line8 = [CCDrawNode node];
[line8 drawSegmentFrom:pathStep8.position
to:pathStep9.position radius:1 color:[CCColor blueColor]];
[_batchNode addChild:line8];
}
```

In this method, we are going to create the path that the enemies will follow until they reach the tower.

We first initialize the array of steps with the constant we defined previously, and then we create a path step placed just at the same location as the fortress will be (the final step). We also add this object to the array of steps and to the scene. Note how we are placing each step using values relative to both _squareSize and kINCREMENT.

To follow a path, we need to create another path step, but in this case we also set its nextPathStep property to be the previously created step; this way when an enemy reaches this point, it will know where the following target is.

Just as a visual representation, we create a line that will join both steps.

Add the following block of code at the end of loadPathSteps:

```
// Create path step
PathStep *pathStep7 = [[PathStep alloc]
initWithPosition:CGPointMake(_squareSize * kINCREMENT_X *
4.0f, _squareSize * 2.5f)];
[_pathSteps addObject:pathStep7];
[_batchNode addChild:pathStep7.pathStepSprite];
pathStep7.nextPathStep = pathStep8;
```

```
// Connect path steps with a line
CCDrawNode *line7 = [CCDrawNode node];
[line7 drawSegmentFrom:pathStep7.position
to:pathStep8.position radius:1.0f color:[CCColor blueColor]];
[_batchNode addChild:line7];

// Create path step
PathStep *pathStep6 = [[PathStep alloc]
initWithPosition:CGPointMake(_squareSize * kINCREMENT_X *
3.0f, _squareSize * 2.5f)];
[_pathSteps addObject:pathStep6];
[_batchNode addChild:pathStep6.pathStepSprite];
pathStep6.nextPathStep = pathStep7;

// Connect path steps with a line
CCDrawNode *line6 = [CCDrawNode node];
[line6 drawSegmentFrom:pathStep6.position
to:pathStep7.position radius:1.0f color:[CCColor blueColor]];
[_batchNode addChild:line6];
```

These lines create two more points and their corresponding line. We need to add
some similar blocks of code:

```
// Create path step
PathStep *pathStep5 = [[PathStep alloc]
initWithPosition:CGPointMake(_squareSize * kINCREMENT_X *
3.0f, _squareSize * 4.5f)];
[_pathSteps addObject:pathStep5];
[_batchNode addChild:pathStep5.pathStepSprite];
pathStep5.nextPathStep = pathStep6;

// Connect path steps with a line
CCDrawNode *line5 = [CCDrawNode node];
[line5 drawSegmentFrom:pathStep5.position
to:pathStep6.position radius:1.0f color:[CCColor blueColor]];
[_batchNode addChild:line5];

// Create path step
PathStep *pathStep4 = [[PathStep alloc]
initWithPosition:CGPointMake(_squareSize * kINCREMENT_X *
2.0f, _squareSize * 4.5f)];
[_pathSteps addObject:pathStep4];
[_batchNode addChild:pathStep4.pathStepSprite];
pathStep4.nextPathStep = pathStep5;
```

```
// Connect path steps with a line
CCDrawNode *line4 = [CCDrawNode node];
[line4 drawSegmentFrom:pathStep4.position
to:pathStep5.position radius:1.0f color:[CCColor blueColor]];
[_batchNode addChild:line4];
```

This block creates the horizontal line at the top center of the screen, so add the following lines:

```
// Create path step
PathStep *pathStep3 = [[PathStep alloc]
initWithPosition:CGPointMake(_squareSize * kINCREMENT_X *
2.0f, _squareSize * 1.5f)];
[_pathSteps addObject:pathStep3];
[_batchNode addChild:pathStep3.pathStepSprite];
pathStep3.nextPathStep = pathStep4;

// Connect path steps with a line
CCDrawNode *line3 = [CCDrawNode node];
[line3 drawSegmentFrom:pathStep3.position
to:pathStep4.position radius:1.0f color:[CCColor blueColor]];
[_batchNode addChild:line3];

// Create path step
PathStep *pathStep2 = [[PathStep alloc]
initWithPosition:CGPointMake(_squareSize * kINCREMENT_X,
_squareSize * 1.5f)];
[_pathSteps addObject:pathStep2];
[_batchNode addChild:pathStep2.pathStepSprite];
pathStep2.nextPathStep = pathStep3;

// Connect path steps with a line
CCDrawNode *line2 = [CCDrawNode node];
[line2 drawSegmentFrom:pathStep2.position
to:pathStep3.position radius:1 color:[CCColor blueColor]];
[_batchNode addChild:line2];
```

It creates the path steps and the line at the bottom left of the screen. Finally, add the last points and lines:

```
// Create path step
PathStep *pathStep1 = [[PathStep alloc]
initWithPosition:CGPointMake(_squareSize * kINCREMENT_X,
_squareSize * 3.5f)];
[_pathSteps addObject:pathStep1];
[_batchNode addChild:pathStep1.pathStepSprite];
pathStep1.nextPathStep = pathStep2;
```

```
// Connect path steps with a line
CCDrawNode *line1 = [CCDrawNode node];
[line1 drawSegmentFrom:pathStep1.position
to:pathStep2.position radius:1.0f color:[CCColor blueColor]];
[_batchNode addChild:line1];

// Create path step
PathStep *pathStep0 = [[PathStep alloc]
initWithPosition:CGPointMake(-50.0f, _squareSize * 3.5f)];
[_pathSteps addObject:pathStep0];
[_batchNode addChild:pathStep0.pathStepSprite];
pathStep0.nextPathStep = pathStep1;

// Connect path steps with a line
CCDrawNode *line0 = [CCDrawNode node];
[line0 drawSegmentFrom:pathStep0.position
to:pathStep1.position radius:1.0f color:[CCColor blueColor]];
[_batchNode addChild:line0];
```

If you look at the last path step creation, you will realize that we are placing it off the screen, because we want the enemies to start walking out of view so it looks like they are coming from far away.

Time to run the project and look at our brand new path:

Following the path

Now that the path has been created, we just need some enemies to follow it:

1. In the project navigator, right-click the **Classes** group and **select Add Files to "DefenseTheTower"**....

2. Look for the Enemy.h and Enemy.m files in the Resources folder.

3. Be sure that **Copy items into destination group's folder (if needed)** is selected and click on **Add**.

We have just added the class that will support the creation and management of the enemies. If you open Enemy.h, you will see that it derives from CCNode and it declares a property for a sprite, a path step, and life points (to know when they should die).

The enemies' initializer has the peculiarity that it receives PathStep as an input argument corresponding to the initial step. On the other hand, Enemy.m contains the common initialization tasks and the declaration of a constant for the movement speed.

Now we need to provide our enemies with some artificial intelligence, and the best way to do that is to implement the update method so that it allows them to take decisions in every frame.

Add the following lines to Enemy.m:

```
- (void)update:(CCTime)delta {
    // Calculate distance to next step
    float distance = ccpDistance(_enemySprite.position,
    _pathStep.nextPathStep.position);
    // Set the movement speed
    float speed = SPEED;
    // Update speed if needed
    if (distance < speed) {
        speed = distance;
    }

    if (distance > 0.0f) {
        if (self.position.y > _pathStep.nextPathStep.position.y) {
            // Move down
            [self setPosition:CGPointMake(_enemySprite.position.x,
            _enemySprite.position.y - speed)];
        } else if (self.position.y <
        _pathStep.nextPathStep.position.y) {
            // Move up
```

```
            [self setPosition:CGPointMake(_enemySprite.position.x,
            _enemySprite.position.y + speed)];
        } else if (self.position.x >
    _pathStep.nextPathStep.position.x){
            // Move left
            [self setPosition:CGPointMake(_enemySprite.position.x
            - speed, _enemySprite.position.y)];
        } else if (self.position.x <
    _pathStep.nextPathStep.position.x){
            // Move right
            [self setPosition:CGPointMake(_enemySprite.position.x
            + speed, _enemySprite.position.y)];
        }
    } else if (_pathStep.nextPathStep.nextPathStep != NULL){
        // Look for next step
        _pathStep = _pathStep.nextPathStep;
    }
}
```

The enemy will move toward the next path step, which will be reached when the distance is equal to `0.0f`. That's why we need to calculate the distance from the enemy to the next step for each frame.

Then we set the speed of movement, which will be adapted to the current distance in case it's lower than our predefined speed (the number of points the enemy will move in each frame).

If the distance is far enough to the next step, the enemy will move in that direction depending on its position with respect to the step and when it reaches that position, it will look for the next step in the path.

Now we just need to add our enemy to the scene, so include the following import in `GameScene.h`:

```
#import "Enemy.h"
```

Call the following method at the end of `init` in `GameScene.m`:

```
// Load enemy
[self loadEnemy];
```

And implement it with the next lines:

```
- (void)loadEnemy {
    // Initialize enemy
    Enemy *enemy = [[Enemy alloc]
    initEnemyWithPathStep:[_pathSteps
    objectAtIndex:_pathSteps.count - 1]];
```

```
    // Add the enemy to the scene
    [_batchNode addChild:enemy];
    [_batchNode addChild:enemy.enemySprite];
}
```

This method initializes one enemy and places it in the first path step; the rest of the magic happens thanks to the update method in Enemy.m.

Run the project and you will see one robot moving along the path:

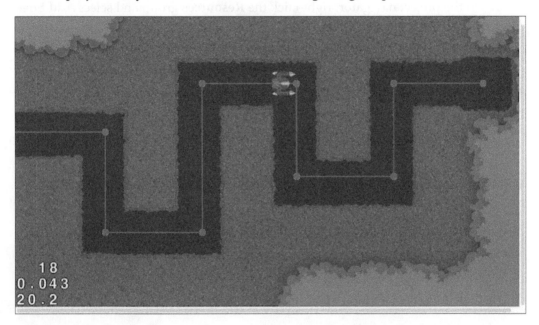

Before proceeding, remove the lines created in loadPathSteps and add the following lines at the end of the method to hide the path, as we don't need to see it anymore:

```
    // Hide path steps
    for (PathStep *pathStep in _pathSteps) {
        pathStep.pathStepSprite.visible = FALSE;
    }
```

Predefining defensive positions

To defend our tower from the attack of the robots, we will be able to set some defenses, which will be placed in predefined positions, as we want the scenario to look neat.

These positions have been defined in a `.plist` file that we need to load, so follow these steps:

1. In the project navigator, right-click the **Resources** group and select **Add Files to "DefenseTheTower"....**
2. Look for the `DefensePositions.plist` files in the `Resources` folder.
3. Be sure that **Copy items into destination group's folder (if needed)** is selected and click on **Add**.

In `GameScene.m`, add the following constant definition:

```
// Number of defenses
const int kNUM_DEFENSES = 30;
```

This is the maximum number of defenses and hence the maximum number of predefined positions.

Declare the following array that will contain the list of predefined positions:

```
// Declare array of defense positions
NSMutableArray *_defensePositions;
```

And call the following method at the end of `init` just before return self:

```
// Load defense positions
[self loadDefensePositions];
```

We need to implement this new method with the following lines:

```
- (void)loadDefensePositions {
    // Retrieve plist
    NSString *defensesPlist = [[NSBundle mainBundle]
    pathForResource:@"DefensePositions" ofType:@"plist"];
    // Retrieve array of positions
    NSArray *defensePositions = [NSArray
    arrayWithContentsOfFile:defensesPlist];

    // Initialize array of defense positions
    _defensePositions = [[NSMutableArray alloc]
    initWithCapacity:kNUM_DEFENSES];
```

```
    // Declare defense position sprite
    CCSprite *defensePositionSprite;
    // Declare auxiliary sprite
    CCSprite *defenseAux = [CCSprite
    spriteWithImageNamed:@"DefenseTheTower/defense_level_1.png"];

    // Declare gap between defensive positions
    float gap = 19.0f;
    // Declare sprite's width variable
    float spriteWidth = defenseAux.contentSize.width;
    float multiplierX, multiplierY;
}
```

In this method, we are retrieving the data included in the `.plist` file into an array. We also initialize the array of defense positions and a `CCSprite` instance to represent these positions. In addition, we declare an auxiliary sprite that we will use to get the size of a defense.

Next, we declare a float for the gap that exists on both sides of the screen and three more floats that will be used to place the positions in an equidistant and organized manner.

The last step consists of loading all the information included in the `.plist` file, so add the following block of code at the end of `loadDefensePositions`:

```
for(NSDictionary *defensePosition in defensePositions) {
    // Initialize defense position sprite
    defensePositionSprite = [CCSprite
    spriteWithImageNamed:@"DefenseTheTower/defense_position.png"];

    // Retrieve x and y position multipliers
    multiplierX = [[defensePosition objectForKey:@"x"]
    floatValue];
    multiplierY = [[defensePosition objectForKey:@"y"]
    floatValue];

    // Set position
    [defensePositionSprite setPosition:CGPointMake(spriteWidth *
    multiplierX + gap, spriteWidth * multiplierY)];
    // Add position to array of defense positions
     [_defensePositions addObject:defensePositionSprite];

    // Add defense position to scene
    [_batchNode addChild:defensePositionSprite];
}
```

In this loop, we retrieve each predefined x and y position and we initialize a new sprite. Note how we set the multipliers with the values in the file and we use them to place the sprites in relative positions.

Run the game now and you will see a number of black dots representing the places where we can raise our defenses:

Placing defenses

Once the predefined positions have been loaded, let's add the defenses.

This will happen when the player touches the screen at one of the available positions, so add the following import at the top of `GameScene.h`:

```
#import "Defense.h"
```

Then in `GameScene.m`, declare an array of defenses:

```
// Declare array of defenses
NSMutableArray *_defenses;
```

Initialize it by adding the following lines at the end of the `init` method:

```
// Initialize array of defenses
_defenses = [[NSMutableArray alloc]
initWithCapacity:kNUM_DEFENSES];

// Enable touches management
self.userInteractionEnabled = TRUE;
```

We are also enabling touch handling, so we can detect when the player is touching the screen.

Finally, let's implement the `touchBegan` method by adding the following lines:

```
- (void)touchBegan:(UITouch *)touch withEvent:(UIEvent *)event {
    // Get touch position
    CGPoint touchLocation = [touch locationInNode:self];

    // Iterate defense positions
    for (CCSprite *defensePosition in _defensePositions) {
        if (CGRectContainsPoint(defensePosition.boundingBox,
        touchLocation)) {
            // Initialize defense
            Defense *defense = [[Defense alloc]
            initDefenseWithLevel:(DefenseLevel)levelOne
            andPosition:defensePosition.position];
            [_defenses addObject:defense];
            // Add defense to the scene
            [_batchNode addChild:defense.defenseSprite z:1];
        }
    }
}
```

We get the location of the touch and then we iterate all the defensive positions, looking for one of them that matches the touch. Then, we create a new defense in this place and we add it to the scene and the array of defenses.

Giving AI to the defenses

Now that we have a way to place the defenses, we should provide them with some intelligence so they know when they have to shoot.

For that reason, we will define an area of influence for each defense so they can attack enemies that move into this area.

First let's represent it visually by adding a new property to Defense.h:

```
// Property for the covered area
@property (readwrite, nonatomic) CCDrawNode *coveredArea;
```

We have defined a draw node, as the area covered will be a circle around the defense.

In Defense.m, initialize it by adding the following lines at the end of the initDefenseWithLevel:

```
// Initialize covered area
_coveredArea = [CCDrawNode node];
_coveredArea.opacity = 0.15f;
```

```
_coveredArea.anchorPoint = CGPointMake(0.0f, 0.0f);
[_coveredArea drawDot:_position
radius:1.5f*self.contentSize.width color:[CCColor
colorWithRed:0.0f green:1.0f blue:0.0f alpha:0.25f]];
```

This will create a green circle with 1.5 times the defense size of the radius and decreased opacity.

Finally, link it to the scene by adding the following lines to `touchBegan`, at the end of the `if` statement:

```
// Add covered area
[_batchNode addChild:defense.coveredArea];
```

If you run the project now, you will see a brilliant circle area around each created defense:

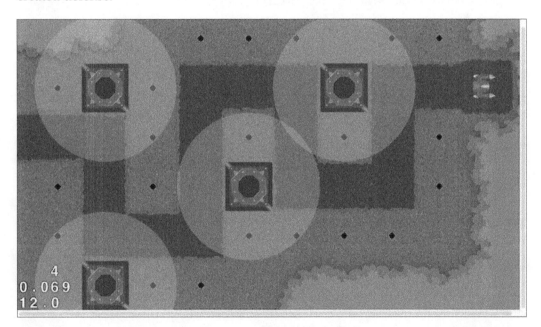

Now that we know the area covered by each defense, let's make them detect enemies inside that area.

For this purpose, we will need to make some changes, so in `Defense.h` add the following properties:

```
// Property for the enemy in range
@property (readwrite, nonatomic) Enemy *enemyInRange;
// Property for the scene
@property (readwrite, nonatomic) GameScene *gameScene;
```

We will need to know which robot has entered the defense area, and for that we will need to get the enemies' info from the scene, which is why we have declared both the Enemy and GameScene properties.

To make the Defense class know that there are classes called Enemy and GameScene, we won't import their header files, as it will create a dependency cycle. To avoid compiler errors, add the following lines after the imports section:

```
@class Enemy;
@class GameScene;
```

Also in Defense.h, replace the initializer declaration with the following one which provides the scene as an input argument:

```
-(Defense *) initDefenseWithLevel:(DefenseLevel)level
scene:(GameScene *)scene andPosition:(CGPoint)position;
```

In Defense.m, replace the method with the following one:

```
-(Defense *) initDefenseWithLevel:(DefenseLevel)level
scene:(GameScene *)scene andPosition:(CGPoint)position {
```

Initialize the scene property by adding the following line at the end of the method:

```
// Initialize game scene
_gameScene = scene;
```

As we will need to get information from the scene, add the following import:

```
#import "GameScene.h"
```

We need to implement the way we make our defenses vigilant, which is why we need to implement the update method:

```
-(void) update:(CCTime)delta {
    if (_enemyInRange == NULL) {
        for (Enemy *enemy in [_gameScene enemies]) {
            if ([self detectEnemyWithDefenseAtPosition:
            _defenseSprite.position
            withRadius:1.5*self.contentSize.width
            andEnemy:enemy.enemySprite.position
            withRadius:enemy.enemySprite.contentSize.width]) {
                _enemyInRange = enemy;
                NSLog(@"ENEMY INSIDE RANGE");
                break;
            }
        }
    }
}
```

In this method, we check if the `enemyInRange` property is NULL, and if so, we look for enemies inside the covered area by calling an auxiliary method that we will implement soon.

If the auxiliary method finds enemies, we update the enemy in range property and show a log.

Implement the new method with these lines:

```
- (BOOL) detectEnemyWithDefenseAtPosition: (CGPoint) defensePosition
withRadius: (float) defenseRadius
andEnemy: (CGPoint) enemyPosition
withRadius: (float) enemyRadius {
    // Get distance from defense to enemy
    float distanceX = defensePosition.x - enemyPosition.x;
    float distanceY = defensePosition.y - enemyPosition.y;
    float distance = sqrt(distanceX * distanceX + distanceY *
    distanceY);

    // If enemy inside covered area
    if(distance <= defenseRadius + enemyRadius) {
        return YES;
    }

    return NO;
}
```

This method receives the positions of the defenses and enemies, and the radius covered by them. In this case, the defense radius is equal to its covered area but the enemy's radius corresponds to its width.

We calculate the distances (vectors) in x and y that will help us to calculate the distance of the hypotenuse of the angle formed by the x and y vectors.

Now, let's make some changes in the scene. Add a new property for an array of enemies in `GameScene.h`:

```
// Property for array of enemies
@property (readwrite, nonatomic) NSMutableArray *enemies;
```

Define the following constant in `GameScene.m`:

```
// Number of enemies
const int kNUM_ENEMIES = 10;
```

Add the following lines to `loadEnemy`, just after the initialization of the enemy:

```
// Initialize array of enemies
_enemies = [[NSMutableArray alloc]
initWithCapacity:kNUM_ENEMIES];
// Add enemy to the array
[_enemies addObject:enemy];
```

We are initializing the array of enemies and adding our robot to it so it can be accessed from the update method in `Defense.m`.

Replace the initialization of the defenses in `touchBegan` with the new way:

```
Defense *defense = [[Defense alloc]
initDefenseWithLevel:(DefenseLevel)levelOne scene:self
andPosition:defensePosition.position];
```

Add the defense to the scene so the `update` method can be scheduled. Add the following lines at the end of the `if` statement in `touchBegan`:

```
// Add defense for update availability
[_batchNode addChild:defense];
```

Come on, run the game, place some defenses and take a look at the logs, you will see something like this:

```
2014-11-01 14:20:39.522 DefenseTheTower[14031:695431] ENEMY INSIDE
RANGE
2014-11-01 14:20:40.838 DefenseTheTower[14031:695431] ENEMY INSIDE
RANGE
2014-11-01 14:20:41.905 DefenseTheTower[14031:695431] ENEMY INSIDE
RANGE
```

Once we know that a robot is near a defense, it should begin shooting the enemy. To achieve this, let's change the batch node to be a property instead of a private variable so it can be accessed from the `Defense` class.

Delete the previous `batchNode` creation and add these lines to `GameScene.h`:

```
// Property for batch node
@property (readwrite, nonatomic) CCSpriteBatchNode *batchNode;
```

Then, in `Defense.m`, add the following lines into the `update` method just before `break;`:

```
// Attack enemy
[self schedule:@selector(attackEnemy) interval:0.5f];
```

It schedules the following method:

```
- (void) attackEnemy {
    if (_enemyInRange != NULL) {
        // Create bullet
        CCSprite *bullet = [CCSprite
        spriteWithImageNamed:@"DefenseTheTower/bullet.png"];
        bullet.position = CGPointMake(_defenseSprite.position.x,
        _defenseSprite.position.y);

        // Add bullet to the scene
        [[_gameScene batchNode] addChild:bullet z:2];
    }
}
```

If there is an enemy in range, this method creates a bullet placed in the center of the defense and adds it to the scene (that's why we created a property for the batch node).

To fire this bullet, add the following block of code at the end of the previous method, inside the `if` statement:

```
// Shoot bullet
CCActionMoveTo *actionMoveBullet = [CCActionMoveTo
actionWithDuration:0.2
position:_enemyInRange.enemySprite.position];

// Hurt enemy
CCActionCallBlock *callHurtEnemy = [CCActionCallBlock
actionWithBlock:^{
    _enemyInRange.lifePoints -= _attackPoints;
}];

// Remove bullet from the scene
CCActionCallBlock *callRemoveBullet = [CCActionCallBlock
actionWithBlock:^{
    [bullet.parent removeChild:bullet cleanup:YES];
}];

// Execute the whole sequence
CCActionSequence *sequence = [CCActionSequence
actionWithArray:@[actionMoveBullet, callHurtEnemy,
callRemoveBullet]];
[bullet runAction:sequence];
```

We create an action movement to move the bullet to the enemy's position. Once this movement ends, we will decrease the enemy's life points, as the bullet is always fast enough to hit the robot.

Once these actions have concluded, we need to remove the bullet from the scene and clean all of its running and scheduled actions.

We create a sequence with these actions and we run it. Execute the game again and now look at how our defenses attack the robots:

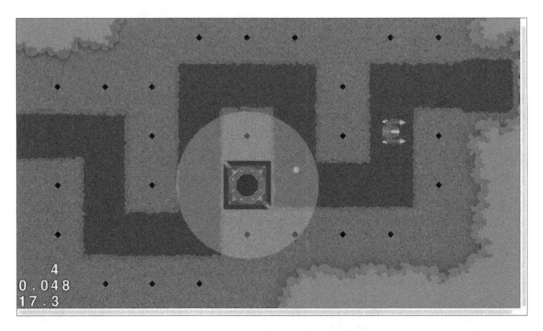

However, we need a way to stop shooting the robots when they are out of range or destroyed.

Sharing information between nodes

As defenses have no way to know when enemies are destroyed, or if they have arrived at the tower by themselves, we are going to develop a solution to share this information between all the nodes.

We will give the Enemy class the responsibility of informing the defenses of their situation, so in Enemy.h, declare the following property:

```
// Property for the attacking defenses
@property (readwrite, nonatomic) NSMutableArray
*attackingDefenses;
```

This is an array of defenses that are attacking the enemy and that should be updated with any modification of its status.

Also, let's declare two new methods:

```
// Declare add attacker method
- (void) addAttackingDefense:(Defense *)attackingDefense;
// Declare out of range method
- (void) outOfRangeFromDefense:(Defense *)attacker;
```

To avoid compilation errors, add the following import:

```
#import "Defense.h"
```

Then in `Enemy.m`, declare the following constant:

```
// Number of defenses
const int kNUMDEFENSES = 30;
```

We will use this constant to initialize the array of defenses by adding the following lines at the end of the `initEnemyWithPathStep` method:

```
// Initialize array of defenses
_attackingDefenses = [[NSMutableArray alloc]
initWithCapacity:kNUMDEFENSES];
```

We need to implement both methods:

```
- (void) addAttackingDefense:(Defense *)attackingDefense {
    [_attackingDefenses addObject:attackingDefense];
}

- (void) outOfRangeFromDefense:(Defense *)attacker {
    [_attackingDefenses removeObject:attacker];
}
```

These methods update the array of defenses by adding or removing each defense.

Go back to `Defense.m` and replace the following line:

```
NSLog(@"ENEMY INSIDE RANGE");
```

Replace it with the following one:

```
// Add defense to array of attackers
[enemy addAttackingDefense:self];
```

We are updating the array of attackers for the enemies in range.

Inside the same `update` method, add the following `else` clause in case there is an enemy in range:

```
else if (![self
detectEnemyWithDefenseAtPosition:_defenseSprite.position
withRadius:1.5f*self.contentSize.width
andEnemy:_enemyInRange.enemySprite.position
withRadius:_enemyInRange.enemySprite.contentSize.width]) {
        // Stop shooting
        [self enemyOutOfRange];
}
```

If the enemy is out of range, we call the following method:

```
- (void) enemyOutOfRange {
    [_enemyInRange outOfRangeFromDefense:self];
    if(_enemyInRange) {
        _enemyInRange = nil;
    }
    [self unschedule:@selector(attackEnemy)];
}
```

In this method, we update the enemy's array of attackers and the `enemyInRange` variable, and we also stop shooting the enemy.

Run the project now and you will see how the defenses stop shooting when there are no enemies in range:

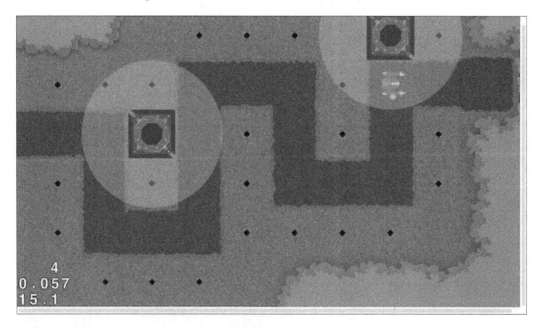

Now we need to implement what happens when an enemy arrives at the tower or its life points are reduced to 0.

In `Enemy.m`, add the following lines at the end of the `update` method:

```
else {
        NSLog(@"TOWER REACHED");
        // Enemy reached tower
        [self removeEnemyFromScene];
}

if (_lifePoints <= 0) {
        [self removeEnemyFromScene];
}
```

The first block covers what happens when an enemy reaches the tower, and the second covers what happens when the enemy is destroyed. In both cases, we need to remove the robot from the scene with the following method:

```
- (void) removeEnemyFromScene {
    NSMutableArray *enumirationArray = [NSMutableArray
    arrayWithArray:_attackingDefenses];
    for (Defense *defense in enumirationArray) {
        [defense enemyKilled];
    }
    [enumirationArray removeAllObjects];
    enumirationArray = nil;
    [_enemySprite removeFromParentAndCleanup:TRUE];
    [self removeFromParentAndCleanup:TRUE];
}
```

This method iterates the array of attackers of the enemy and informs them of the enemy's new status. We also remove the enemy from the scene and stop all the running and scheduled actions relating to it.

In `Defense.h`, add the following method declaration:

```
- (void) enemyKilled;
```

Implement it in `Defense.m` with the following block of code:

```
- (void) enemyKilled {
    [_gameScene.enemies removeObject:_enemyInRange];
    [self enemyOutOfRange];
}
```

This removes the enemy from the array in the scene and updates the status of the defenses to stop them from shooting.

Run the project and check out what happens when the robot reaches the last path step or is killed.

Before proceeding, let's remove the covered area as we don't need it anymore by deleting every appearance of `coveredArea` in `Defense.h`, `Defense.m`, and `GameScene.m`.

Loading waves of enemies

Waves are groups of enemies that try to reach the tower to attack it at the same time and this game consists of holding off as many waves as possible.

Add the following constants to `GameScene.m`, which will be helpful in this stage of development:

```
// Base number of enemies for each wave
const int kWAVES_NUM_ENEMIES = 10;
// Number of waves
const int kNUM_WAVES = 10;
// Waves interval
const int kWAVES_INTERVAL = 24;
```

We are declaring constants for the number of enemies each wave will contain, the number of waves, and the time each wave will take.

Declare also the following variables:

```
// Declare number of wave
int _waveNumber;
// Label to show the wave
CCLabelTTF *_waveLabel;
// Declare count of enemies
int _countEnemies;
```

We keep the wave number, which is shown in a label, and we also declare a counter to know how many enemies we have loaded so far.

In the `init` method, remove this method call:

```
[self loadEnemy];
```

Add the following lines at the end:

```
// Initialize wave number
_waveNumber = 1;

// Initialize and place wave label
_waveLabel = [CCLabelTTF labelWithString:[NSString
stringWithFormat:@"Wave %i", _waveNumber + 1]
fontName:@"Arial" fontSize:15];
_waveLabel.position = CGPointMake(40.0f, _screenSize.height -
25.0f);
_waveLabel.anchorPoint = CGPointMake(0.5f, 0.5f);
_waveLabel.color = [CCColor blackColor];
// Add score label to scene
[self addChild:_waveLabel];

// Schedule waves
[self schedule:@selector(loadWave) interval:kWAVES_INTERVAL
repeat:kNUM_WAVES delay:0.0f];
```

We initialize the wave number and the label, and we schedule a method that will load the waves. As you can see, we are using the `schedule: interval: repeat: delay` method that allows us to schedule a method, kNUM_WAVES multiplied by each kWAVES_INTERVAL seconds, and this details a delay.

Implement this new scheduled method with the following lines:

```
- (void) loadWave {
    // Initialize count and array of enemies
    _countEnemies = 0;
    _enemies = [[NSMutableArray alloc]
    initWithCapacity:kWAVES_NUM_ENEMIES];

    // Update label
    [_waveLabel setString:[NSString stringWithFormat:@"Wave %i",
    _waveNumber]];

    // Load enemies
    [self schedule:@selector(loadEnemy) interval:1.0f];

    // Increase wave number
    _waveNumber++;
}
```

This method initializes the counter and array of enemies and then updates the wave label with the current number value.

Then we schedule our already-familiar `loadEnemy` method, which will load one enemy each second, and we update the wave number.

Next, let's make a couple of changes to `loadEnemy`. Add the following line at the end of the method:

```
_countEnemies++;
```

This way we update the enemy counter each time we create a new one.

Delete the initialization of the array of enemies and wrap all the code with these `if` and `else` clauses:

```
if (_countEnemies < kWAVES_NUM_ENEMIES) {
.

.

.

} else {
    [self unschedule:@selector(loadEnemy)];
}
```

This way we will continue to load enemies until the counter reaches the maximum value for the wave.

Come on, run the code and look at how the waves of enemies load:

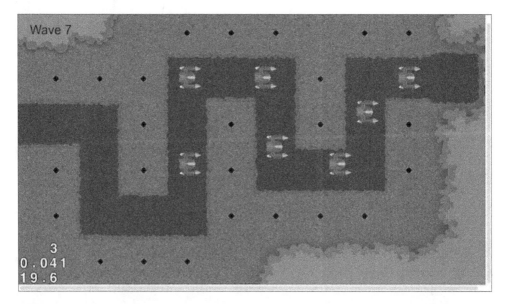

There are a few things to do to finish off our game, for example, aren't we missing the tower? Let's add it: in `GameScene.m` add the following lines at the end of the `init` method:

```
// Add tower
CCSprite *tower = [CCSprite
spriteWithImageNamed:@"DefenseTheTower/tower.png"];
tower.position = ((CCSprite *)[_pathSteps
objectAtIndex:0]).position;
[_batchNode addChild:tower z:2];
```

We are just adding a new sprite to the scene so there is nothing to highlight.

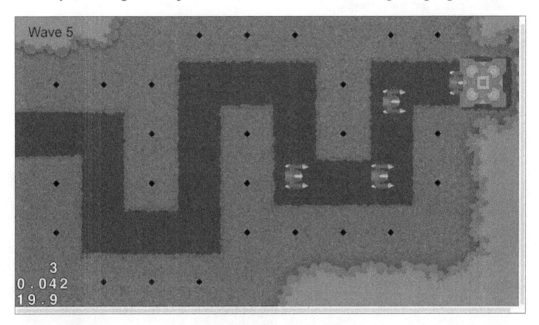

At this moment, there are no consequences when a robot reaches our tower, so let's make them hurt our fortress a little each time. For this purpose, we need to make a few changes in `Enemy.h`, so replace the initializer method declaration with the following one:

```
- (Enemy *) initEnemyWithPathStep:(PathStep *)step
andScene:(GameScene *)scene;
```

Add a property for the scene:

```
// Property for the scene
@property (readwrite, nonatomic) GameScene *gameScene;
```

In `Enemy.m`, add the following import:

```
#import "GameScene.h"
```

Replace the initializer header with this one:

```
- (Enemy *) initEnemyWithPathStep:(PathStep *)step
andScene:(GameScene *)scene {
```

Then, in the same method, add the following line at the end:

```
_gameScene = scene;
```

Finally, replace the following log:

```
NSLog(@"TOWER REACHED");
```

Replace it with this method call:

```
[_gameScene enemyReachedTower];
```

When an enemy reaches the tower, it will call a method from the `GameScene` class that we will implement right now.

In `GameScene.h`, add the following method declaration:

```
- (void)enemyReachedTower;
```

We want to show a label with the tower's life points, which will be updated when an enemy avoids the defenses, so let's declare a pair of properties:

```
// Declare life points
int _lifePoints;
// Label to show the life points
CCLabelTTF *_lifePointsLabel;
```

Initialize them by adding the following lines at the end of the `init` method:

```
// Initialize life points
_lifePoints = 10;
_lifePointsLabel = [CCLabelTTF labelWithString:[NSString
stringWithFormat:@"Life: %i", _lifePoints] fontName:@"Arial"
fontSize:15];
_lifePointsLabel.position = CGPointMake(_screenSize.width -
50.0f , 20.0f);
_lifePointsLabel.anchorPoint = CGPointMake(0.5f, 0.5f);
_lifePointsLabel.color = [CCColor blackColor];
// Add score label to scene
[self addChild:_lifePointsLabel];
```

We are creating an integer counter and a label that will show its value, and we need to update it by implementing the `enemyReachedTower` method:

```
- (void)enemyReachedTower {
    _lifePoints--;
    // Update label
    [_lifePointsLabel setString:[NSString stringWithFormat:@"Life:
    %i", _lifePoints]];
}
```

This method decreases the counter and updates the label. Finally, let's modify the way we initialize the enemies by replacing the old way with the new initializer:

```
Enemy *enemy = [[Enemy alloc] initEnemyWithPathStep:[_pathSteps
objectAtIndex:_pathSteps.count - 1] andScene:self];
```

Come on, run the game now and look at the results!

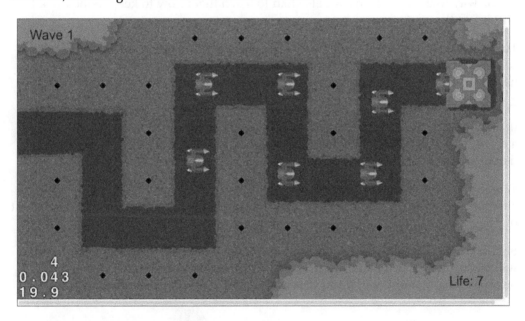

2-star challenge – adding explosions

When the robots reach the tower they explode, which is why we lose one life point, but we need some visual explanation to make it more realistic.

I'm sure you are able to add some explosions when it happens so why don't you take advantage of the code files of *Chapter 2, Explosions and UFOs,* and make the enemies explode when arriving at the final path step?

3-star challenge – upgrading defenses

As you may have realized, the defense initializer method takes into account the level of the defenses in order to give them some skills and characteristics.

In this challenge, I want you to upgrade the `levelOne` defense to `levelTwo` when the player touches it. You don't need to worry about the resources as they are already added to the atlas.

Summary

This chapter has covered how to develop a typical "defend the tower" game, which consists of waves of enemies that try to reach a fortress.

As the robots are idiots, we had to develop a pathfinder algorithm for them to follow on the way to the tower, and we also had to teach them how to keep to the track by moving to the next step.

To defend ourselves from these robot enemies, we raised some watchtowers which we wanted to be placed near the road and kept to neat positions, which is why we have learned how to predefine positions to place nodes.

Our defenses are also idiots, and we had to teach them to recognize enemies that are near to them, so they can start shooting. For this purpose, we created a covered area for each of the defenses, so when an enemy enters this area the defenses start attacking.

To give support to all the checks in the game, we had to share information between enemies and defenses so the defenses know when an enemy they are attacking is out of range or destroyed.

Finally, we learned how to schedule a method that will load waves of enemies that will try to attack our tower. This method will be called with a time interval and will be repeated any number of times that we want until we kill all the robots.

Index

match, finishing 187-191
match status, viewing 191-194
turn, passing 170-173
turn, receiving 174-183

P

parallax effect
  about 67, 78
  CCParallaxNode class 78-86
  implementing 78
Particle Designer
  about 96
  Color Settings 97
  Emitter Settings 97
  Particle Settings 97
  Texture Settings 97
  URL 96, 97
particle systems
  about 87
  CCParticleSystem class, using 87-90
  Particle Designer 96, 97
pathfinding algorithm
  developing 386-392
  enemies, following path 393-395
physics
  CCPhysicsShape class, creating 302, 303
  creating 296-302
  sprites, creating 303-305
Physics Body Editor
  URL 306
PhysicsEditor
  shapes, loading in Xcode 310-312
  URL 306
  used, for defining shapes 306-310
physics engines
  about 292, 293
  Box2D 293
  Chipmunk 293
platform game
  background, scrolling 361-364
  blocks, scrolling 361-364
  custom physics, coding 364-366
  initializing 350-357
  menu, adding 370-376
  pinecones, adding to scene 376-379

score label, adding 379-381
varied scene, configuring 357-361
protocol methods
  initializeNewGame 167
  matchOver 167
  receiveTurn 167

R

R.U.B.E
  URL 306
RunYetiRun
  about 24
  accurate collision detection,
    implementing 62, 63
  actions, controlling 38, 39
  anchor point, setting 29-31
  background image, adding 31-34
  CCScene class, creating 24-27
  CCSprite class, adding 27-29
  collisions, managing 48-50
  finishing 60-62
  labels, adding 51
  lives, implementing 63-65
  noise, creating 55
  snowballs, adding 39-41
  snowballs, initializing 41-48
  touch detection, enabling 34-38

S

scene graph 22
scene, platform game
  configuring 357-361
  pinecones, adding 376-379
score label, platform game
  adding 379-381
shapes
  defining 306
  defining, PhysicsEditor used 306-310
  loading, in Xcode 310-312
shoot 'em up game
  CCSprite class, extending 98-105
  explosions, creating 111
  life bar, drawing 121-123
  UFO – Dr. Fringe collisions, detecting 124

Thank you for buying
Cocos2d Game Development Blueprints

About Packt Publishing

Packt, pronounced 'packed', published its first book, *Mastering phpMyAdmin for Effective MySQL Management*, in April 2004, and subsequently continued to specialize in publishing highly focused books on specific technologies and solutions.

Our books and publications share the experiences of your fellow IT professionals in adapting and customizing today's systems, applications, and frameworks. Our solution-based books give you the knowledge and power to customize the software and technologies you're using to get the job done. Packt books are more specific and less general than the IT books you have seen in the past. Our unique business model allows us to bring you more focused information, giving you more of what you need to know, and less of what you don't.

Packt is a modern yet unique publishing company that focuses on producing quality, cutting-edge books for communities of developers, administrators, and newbies alike. For more information, please visit our website at www.packtpub.com.

About Packt Open Source

In 2010, Packt launched two new brands, Packt Open Source and Packt Enterprise, in order to continue its focus on specialization. This book is part of the Packt Open Source brand, home to books published on software built around open source licenses, and offering information to anybody from advanced developers to budding web designers. The Open Source brand also runs Packt's Open Source Royalty Scheme, by which Packt gives a royalty to each open source project about whose software a book is sold.

Writing for Packt

We welcome all inquiries from people who are interested in authoring. Book proposals should be sent to author@packtpub.com. If your book idea is still at an early stage and you would like to discuss it first before writing a formal book proposal, then please contact us; one of our commissioning editors will get in touch with you.

We're not just looking for published authors; if you have strong technical skills but no writing experience, our experienced editors can help you develop a writing career, or simply get some additional reward for your expertise.

Learning iPhone Game Development with Cocos2D 3.0

ISBN: 978-1-78216-014-4   Paperback: 434 pages

Harness the power of Cocos2D to create your own stunning and engaging games for iOS

1. Find practical solutions to many real-world game development problems.

2. Create games from start to finish by writing code and following detailed step-by-step instructions.

3. Full of illustrations and diagrams, practical examples, and tips for deeper understanding of game development in Cocos2d for iPhone.

Cocos2d-x Game Development Essentials

ISBN: 978-1-78398-786-3   Paperback: 136 pages

Create iOS and Android games from scratch using Cocos2d-x

1. Create and run Cocos2d-x projects on iOS and Android platforms.

2. Find practical solutions to many real-world game development problems.

3. Learn the essentials of Cocos2d-x by writing code and following step-by-step instructions.

Please check **www.PacktPub.com** for information on our titles

Cocos2d-X by Example Beginner's Guide

ISBN: 978-1-78216-734-1   Paperback: 246 pages

Make fun games for any platform using C++, combined with one of the most popular open source frameworks in the world

1. Learn to build multi-device games in simple, easy steps, letting the framework do all the heavy lifting.

2. Spice things up in your games with easy to apply animations, particle effects, and physics simulation.

3. Quickly implement and test your own gameplay ideas, with an eye for optimization and portability.

Learning Cocos2d-x Game Development

ISBN: 978-1-78398-826-6   Paperback: 266 pages

Learn cross-platform game development with Cocos2d-x

1. Create a Windows Store account and upload your game for distribution.

2. Develop a game using Cocos2d-x by going through each stage of game development process step by step.

Please check **www.PacktPub.com** for information on our titles

www.ingramcontent.com/pod-product-compliance
Lightning Source LLC
Chambersburg PA
CBHW081500050326
40690CB00015B/2863